North Woods

Wildflowers

A FIELD GUIDE TO WILDFLOWERS
OF THE NORTHEASTERN UNITED STATES
AND SOUTHEASTERN CANADA

By Doug Ladd

FALCON®

HELENA, MONTANA

A FALCON GUIDE ®

Falcon® is continually expanding its list of recreational guidebooks. All books include detailed descriptions, accurate maps, and all the information necessary for enjoyable trips. You can order extra copies of this book and get information and prices for other Falcon® guidebooks by writing Falcon, P.O. Box 1718, Helena, MT 59624, or calling toll-free 1-800-582-2665. Please ask for a free copy of our current catalog. Visit our website at www.falcon.com or contact us by e-mail at falcon@falcon.com.

Cover photo of Showy Lady's Slippers by Jessie M. Harris.
Cover and interior drawings by DD Dowden.

Project Editor: Gayle Shirley
Copyeditor: Barbara Johnson
Page Compositor: Jeff Wincapaw
Book design by Falcon Publishing, Inc.

Cataloging-in-Publication Data

Ladd, Doug M.
    North Woods wildflowers: a field guide to wildflowers of the
northeastern United States and southeastern Canada / by Doug Ladd.
       p. cm -- (A Falcon guide)
    ISBN 1-56044-979-9
       1. Wild flowers--Northeastern States--Identification. 2. Wild
flowers--Canada, Eastern--Identification. 3. Wild flowers--Northeastern
States--Pictorial works. 4. Wild flowers--Canada, Eastern--Pictorial works.
I. Title. II. Series.
    QK117.L33 2000
    582.13'0974--dc21   00-049091

CAUTION

All participants in the recreational activities suggested by this book must assume responsibility for their own actions and safety. The information contained in this guidebook cannot replace sound judgment and good decision-making skills, which help reduce risk exposure; nor does the scope of this book allow for disclosure of all the potential hazards and risks involved in such activities.

Learn as much as possible about the recreational activities in which you participate, prepare for the unexpected, and be cautious. The reward will be a safer and more enjoyable experience.

Ingesting plant or plant parts poses a potentially extreme health hazard and could result in sickness or even death. No one should attempt to use any wild plant for food or medicine without adequate training by a fully qualified professional.

CONTENTS

CKNOWLEDGMENTS

Creating a field guide is humbling, for it reveals both the extent of one's ignorance and the degree to which one depends on knowledgeable people. Literally dozens of people provided diverse assistance during the past four years as this guide was developing. Their contributions ranged from technical guidance to field assistance, providing local ecological information, reviewing manuscript material, or cheerfully extricating a botanist's stuck vehicle. Among those to whom I am deeply grateful for assistance, information, and suggestions are Dave Barrington, Nancy Braker, William Buck, Stephen Clayden, Irene Edwards, Stephanie Gifford, Blane Heumann, Megan Hiller, Mike Homoya, Barbara Johnson, Mike Nolan, Mike Penskar, Robert Popp, Barbara Pryor, Anton Reznicek, Gayle Shirley, Nancy Slack, Paul Somers, Nancy Totland, Edward Voss, Gerould Wilhelm, Henry Woolsey, George Yatskievych, Steve Young, and Bob Zaremba.

The photographers whose work appears in this book were patient and helpful, and I am grateful for their contributions, which often entailed responding on short notice. For all their help I thank Allison Bell, Keith Board, Lee Casebere, William Chapman, Stephen Clayden, Kenneth Dritz, Casey Galvin, Carol Gracie, Jessie Harris, Don Kurz, Bruce Schuette, Perry Scott, Welby Smith, Kay Yatskievych, and the New England Wildflower Society. Robert Tatina has worked specifically to obtain photos for this project for the past two years, and his dedication, botanical expertise, and field companionship were a pleasure. Edward Voss graciously and generously responded to several last minute requests for images and advice.

Many people who were essential in my early work in northern New England have slipped from memory, but a few bear mention, for their assistance more than two decades ago laid the foundation for this guide. Of particular help were Harry Ahles, William Countryman, Ray Schulenberg, Frank Seymour, and my adviser for my graduate work on the Vermont flora, Robert Mohlenbrock.

As with all my past efforts, my spouse, Deborah Bowen Ladd, has been a constant adviser and contributor. For many years, she and our daughter Melica have accompanied me in fieldwork throughout the region, serving as field assistants and text critics, providing moral support, and assisting with myriad technical and clerical details. Deborah's parents, Pat and Bud Bowen, generously shared their house and provided work space whenever I worked in northern Wisconsin. My father, Douglas Mackay Ladd, as he has since my wedding, continues to be my best man, and fieldwork in New England is always doubly pleasurable because of his decades of experience with the region and its lore. My sister, Heidi Ladd, was as always supportive, understanding, and inspirational. My heartfelt thanks to all of you. I am profoundly grateful.

THE NORTH WOODS

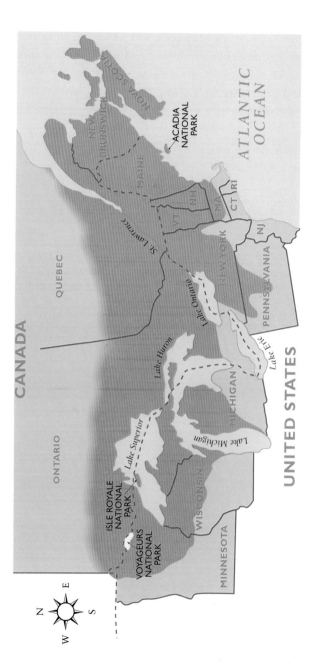

This map shows the North Woods region covered in this wildflower guide. South of the shaded region, in colder or more exposed sites (especially at higher altitudes), are scattered small areas with North Woods vegetation. North of the shaded area is an expanse of boreal forest that extends to the limit of tree growth in the Arctic. Many characteristic wildflowers of this boreal forest are included in this book.

THE LEGENDARY NORTH WOODS

The North Woods country has fascinated people for centuries. Ranging from western Minnesota and Ontario east through New England and the Canadian Maritimes, this vast region shaped much of early American and Canadian history, culture, and lore.

These are the deep, legendary forests that spawned Paul Bunyan and a thousand other north-country myths of heroic deeds and epic struggles. The region's natural resources sustained a vibrant native culture for thousands of years, and later the area's timber helped to build two modern nations, while the many fast-flowing streams and rivers provided power for the beginnings of the industrial age in North America.

Lakes, mountains, and coastal influences contribute to the region's diversity, yet there are compelling similarities in climate, geology, and plant and animal life that make the area a distinct and cohesive cultural and natural region. Stately evergreen forests, frigid, crystalline brooks, sun-dappled lakes and ponds, and dark, impenetrable conifer swamps are common features across the North Woods. This is the home of the porcupine, marten, fisher, moose, and ermine—creatures whose ranges extend much farther north but have their southern limits in the North Woods.

Even to the casual visitor, this is obviously a region shaped by trees and water. The landscape is a mosaic of dense forests and more open woodlands, with a rich mixture of broad-leaved deciduous hardwoods and needle-bearing, mostly evergreen conifers. To the north lie the vast conifer forests that eventually dwindle and grade into arctic tundra. To the south lie the mixed deciduous woodlands that flourish in warmer climates with longer growing seasons. In the North Woods, needle-bearing conifers like balsam fir, hemlock, tamarack, white cedar, spruces, and pines combine with cold-tolerant northern hardwoods such as beech, aspens, birches, and maples.

Because rainfall is plentiful throughout the region and the bedrock is mostly impermeable, water and wetlands are ever-present features of the landscape. An abundance of seeps, springs, streams, brooks, lakes, ponds, and vegetated wetlands characterizes the North Woods. These contribute to a diversity of wetlands and related habitats that greatly enhance the diversity of plant and animal life in the region.

This is a relatively new land. Vast sheets of ice buried virtually all of the North Woods during the last glacial period. About 18,000 years ago, this ice began to melt and the glaciers gradually began receding northward. The melting process took more than 10,000 years, proceeding by fits and starts as the climate fluctuated. The legacy of the ice is evident throughout the landscape: potholes and lakes, scoured valleys, scraped bedrock uplands, and a wealth of deposits of glacially milled rocks and till in kames, eskers, and other unique landforms.

As the ice melted and exposed barren ground devoid of soil, plants and animals gradually colonized in a sequence determined by their habitat needs and dispersal patterns. These plants and animals in turn modified the habitat and rendered it suitable for other plants and animals in a gradual, uneven pattern of biological succession.

Today the climate of the region shapes much of its character. The North Woods has long, cold winters, mild summers, and a relatively short frost-free growing season—less than 90 days long in some places. Prolonged cold spells when the temperature drops below zero degrees F (-18 degrees C) can occur anywhere. Snowfall is moderate to high throughout the North Woods, exceeding 200 inches (500 centimeters) per season in some areas.

Although the landscape of the North Woods is diverse, the vegetation cloaking it is compellingly similar. This vegetation occurs in a fascinating complex of predictable patterns dictated by moisture, soil, altitude, exposure, and other factors. Many characteristic North Woods wildflowers or their close relatives occur not only in repeatable patterns across the region, but also around the world in parts of northern Europe, northern Asia, and western North America. This is a direct result of glacial, geological, and biological history in conjunction with modern climate.

Boreal and Transition Forests

Two kinds of forest shape the vegetation of the region; each has many other natural communities embedded within it. **Boreal forest** (Fig. 1) is the most cold-tolerant type with the strongest northern affinities. Named after Boreas, the god of the north wind in Greek mythology, this forest type occurs on exposed uplands and shorelines, in cold, wet valleys, and at higher elevations in the region. Boreal forest becomes more continuous and extensive northward into the Arctic to the limit of tree growth. Extensive areas of boreal forest occur in the North Woods around and north of Lake Superior and at higher

ALLISON W. BELL

Figure 1. Cold-tolerant conifers such as balsam fir and spruce predominate in the boreal forest.

elevations in the Adirondacks and New England. Smaller pockets are scattered elsewhere throughout the region. This forest type is sometimes called northern coniferous forest. Cold-tolerant conifers such as balsam fir and black and white spruce predominate. Here in the North Woods region, near the southern limits of boreal forest, hemlock and jack, red, and white pines are also present. Hardwood trees are less prominent but include quaking aspen, balsam poplar, and paper birch. Soils in boreal forests are typically wet, acidic, and nutrient-poor.

Much of the North Woods can be broadly classified as **transition forest** (Fig. 2), also called northern hardwoods or northern mixed hardwoods. Essentially confined to the North Woods and a small area of the Appalachian Highlands, this type of forest is intermediate between the conifer-dominated boreal forest and the diverse hardwoods of the eastern deciduous formation to the south. Transition forests occur on a variety of sites and are characterized by an abundance of cold-tolerant hardwoods, usually mixed with conifers. Typical trees in the transition forest include sugar maple, yellow birch, basswood, beech, white ash, hemlock, white pine, and balsam fir. Transition forests generally occur at sites with longer, warmer growing seasons and less

ALLISON W. BELL

Figure 2. Transition forest is characterized by cold-tolerant hardwoods, such as ash, maple, birch, and beech.

severe winter conditions than in boreal forests. Soils tend to be better drained, less acidic, and more nutrient-rich. Toward the southern edge of the region, transition forest grades into the mixed hardwoods of the eastern deciduous formation. In this area, conifers become less prominent and other hardwoods such as oaks, hickories, and elms become more common.

These forest types are generalities, and it is difficult to draw precise boundaries between them. Both boreal and transition forests are variable and diverse. Many species of wildflowers occur regularly in both forests, although some may be more abundant in one than the other. A few characteristic wildflowers of the boreal forest include bluebead lily, goldthread, bunchberry, creeping snowberry, twinflower, and starflower. Typical wildflowers of the transition forest include big-leaved aster, wild sarsaparilla, Indian cucumber root, and feathery false Solomon's seal.

Wetland Habitats

A diversity of other natural communities occupies the North Woods landscape, adding to the region's rich natural heritage. Much of the region has abundant rainfall, shallow soil, impermeable bedrock, and poor drainage. These give rise to numerous habitats with permanent water or wet conditions for much of the year. Relatively few wildflowers grow in the open waters of **ponds and lakes** (Fig. 3), although placid, shallow, open waters harbor such characteristic wildflowers as pickerel weed, water lily, and yellow pond lily. The open, flowing waters of **brooks and rivers** also support few wildflowers, although there may be rich wildflower associations along their shores (Fig. 4). Shorelines and stream banks range from open mud and sand to cobble flats and thicket-covered embankments. Their exposures range from full sun

Figure 3. A few wildflowers, such as pickerel weed and pond lilies, grow in the placid waters of ponds and lakes.

Figure 4. Many wildflowers, including monkey flower and cardinal flower, flourish along riverbanks.

to deep shade. A few of the many wildflowers in these habitats are virgin's bower, Canada lily, cardinal flower, northern bugle weed, and monkey flower.

Other wetlands in the North Woods are more vegetated. **Marshes** (Fig. 5) occur where there is shallow water for much or all of the growing season, usually on mineral soils. Some marshes occur in shallow areas bordering open water, while others occur on flats in valleys and lowlands. Depending on their history, water dynamics, and site conditions, marshy habitats can range from open expanses of grasses or sedges to dense thickets dominated by alders and willows. Individual marshes range in size from less than an acre to hundreds of acres. Typical marsh wildflowers in the North Woods include swamp milkweed, nodding bur marigold, spotted Joe Pye weed, and northern blue

DON KURZ

Figure 5. Marshy habitats can range from open expanses of grass to dense thickets dominated by alders and willows.

flag. Dams constructed by beavers sometimes create beaver marshes, or beaver meadows. These sites often consist of marshy, tangled thickets with a mixture of vines, shrubs, sedges, and marsh wildflowers.

The wetland most evocative of the North Woods is the **bog** (Fig. 6), an undrained or poorly drained permanent wetland fed by surface runoff. Bogs contain nutrient-poor, acidic waters. These sites often have an abundant growth of sphagnum moss, which, along with other plant remains, cannot decompose completely in the cold, oxygen-poor, acidic water. This partially decomposed plant material, called peat, is one of the characteristics of the bog environment. Peat reinforces the bog habitat through its acidifying and water-holding capacity. Bogs typically develop floating mats of mosses and shrubs such as leatherleaf. Well-developed bog mats can support the weight of a person, although they quake and subside when walked on, giving rise to the term "quaking bog." The unique conditions of the bog environment support a distinct group of plants, including several members of the heath family, such as bog rosemary, Labrador tea, and large cranberry. The acidic conditions limit nutrient availability and therefore favor carnivorous plants such as round-leaved sundew

LEE A. CASEBERE

Figure 6. Peat, which is partially decomposed plant material, is characteristic of the bog environment.

and pitcher plant, which can obtain extra nutrients from the insects they trap. Other wildflowers found in bogs include bog candles, bog laurel, and false mayflower. Older bogs may become filled in and wooded, with a canopy of black spruce and tamarack. Sometimes bog plants also grow in wet, acidic sand flats and acidic seepages.

Another type of specialized wetland is the **fen** (Fig. 7), found where a constant supply of mineralized groundwater discharges into a vegetated habitat. In the North Woods, fens are typically alkaline or neutral and occur where the bedrock is rich in calcium or magnesium, such as over limestone. As with bogs, the cold, oxygen-poor water prevents the complete decay of plant materials, and fen soils are usually mucky or peaty, although the peat is mostly formed from sedges and other flowering plants instead of sphagnum moss. Typical fen wildflowers include swamp thistle, bog lobelia, and shrubby cinquefoil. In some cases, fens may be colonized by sphagnum moss, creating locally acidic conditions and a complex patchwork of acid- and alkaline-loving plants growing side by side. Wooded fens are often dominated by white cedar.

Swamps (Fig. 8) are forested wetlands that occur in basins, depressions,

Figure 7. Fens occur where a constant supply of groundwater discharges into a vegetated habitat.

backwater sloughs, and broad, flat river valleys. Soils are flooded or saturated for most or all of the growing season. Generally there is some water movement and little peat development, and conditions tend to be somewhat acidic, although less acidic than in bogs. Black ash and red maple trees are typical of swamps, as are a variety of shrubs such as alders, willows, and wild raisin. Common wildflowers in North Woods swamps include marsh marigold, swamp rose, and white hellebore. Conifer swamps, dominated by black spruce, tamarack, and sometimes white cedar, tend to be more boglike.

Figure 8. The soils of swamps are saturated for most or all of the growing season.

Open Upland Habitats

Embedded within the forested landscape of the North Woods are a variety of drier, unforested habitats. These include extensive barrens, cliffs, dunes, and exposed bedrock and headlands. Exposed **rock outcrops and cliffs** (Fig. 9) support a distinct collection of wildflowers, depending on the site conditions and rock type. Although the geology of the region is diverse, most of the exposed rock is siliceous and acidic. This provides habitat for wildflowers such as black crowberry, three-toothed cinquefoil, and early saxifrage. Exposed limestone or other alkaline rock often harbors unusual plants such as stiff sandwort.

Extensive areas of leached, well-drained, sterile sands and rock flats occur throughout the North Woods. Typically, these are sparsely covered with stunted trees such as jack pine, along with numerous shrubs, especially blueberries. The harshest parts of these **barrens** (Fig. 10) may be open, with only mosses, lichens, and a few wildflowers, such as bearberry, cow wheat, and jointweed.

Figure 9. Exposed rock outcrops and cliffs support a distinct collection of wildflowers.

ALLISON W. BELL

Figure 10. Extensive barrens are among a variety of dry, unforested habitats that may be found in the North Woods.

DOUG LADD

Nonflowering Plants

Along with trees and shrubs, the wildflowers featured in this book are a conspicuous part of the North Woods, but some other plants deserve mention as well. While wildflowers, grasses, sedges, and many trees and shrubs are flowering plants, not all of the region's plants produce flowers. Nonflowering, spore-producing plants are also prominent in the North Woods and are found in all habitats.

The most conspicuous of these are ferns and their relatives. There are more than 50 kinds of ferns in the region (Fig. 11). They have diverse growth forms but are usually easy to recognize as ferns. Club mosses (Fig. 12), which are related to ferns, usually have many small, narrow leaves that resemble miniature conifer needles. Hence, another common name: ground pines. Approximately 15 species of club moss grow in the North Woods, and many are abundant in wooded habitats. Another group of fern relatives, the horsetails (Fig. 13), are typically found in wet sites. Horsetails have no apparent leaves but have unmistakable stiff, jointed, green stems, sometimes with similar side branches. There are about 10 species of horsetail in the North Woods.

Figure 11. More than 50 species of ferns grow throughout the North Woods.

Figure 12. Club mosses, which are related to ferns, have leaves that resemble tiny conifer needles.

The Human Factor

Shortly after the glaciers retreated, humans became a factor in the development of the North Woods. North American Indians influenced the landscape

ROBERT TATINA

Figure 13. Horsetails may be easily identified by their lack of leaves and their stiff, jointed stems.

through hunting, harvesting plants, collecting wood for fuel, and igniting wildland fires. The arrival of European colonists a scant 400 years ago imposed a totally different set of impacts on the land. These included large-scale agriculture and timber removal along with the introduction, accidentally and deliberately, of hundreds of plants and animals alien to the region. These introduced, or exotic, species ranged from cows, chickens, and apples to crab grass, cockroaches, and rats. Many of these plants and animals have adapted to the kinds of impacts modern society has imposed on the landscape. They are now well established throughout the region.

Lumbering and timber clearing in the 1800s vastly altered the North Woods. Even in areas that have since been reclaimed by forest, the repeated harvesting of softwoods has resulted in a proliferation of hardwoods in many stands that were formerly dominated by conifers or mixed trees. Drainage, dams, and other wetland and stream alterations have changed the dynamics of water, with resulting effects on wetland habitats. Although the North Woods region shows fewer post-settlement impacts than many areas of North America, nearly all of the region shows some effects. Remaining examples of diverse, high-quality North Woods systems deserve respect and conservation-based management.

Many North Woods wildflowers occur throughout the region, even in moderately disturbed habitats. One of the best ways to explore the area's wildflower heritage is to visit protected areas, such as nature preserves and national, provincial, and state parks. These encompass some of the most spectacular examples of the North Woods landscape, often including the rarer wildflowers.

Anyone venturing into the North Woods should be prepared for the region's challenges, including sudden changes of weather, fierce storms, cold spells, and onslaughts of black flies, mosquitoes, and deer flies. Exercise caution around deep, mucky pools and swift, cold water. Be aware of how easily you can become disoriented in the vast forests if you do not carry a compass.

USING THIS GUIDE

This book is a field guide to the characteristic native wildflowers of the North Woods. It contains photos and information about most of the wildflowers—including many conspicuous flowering shrubs—that you are likely to encounter in natural habitats throughout the region. Some rare wildflowers are also featured to showcase the diversity of the North Woods. Wildflowers restricted to specialized habitats on the alpine summits of the northeastern mountains or the Atlantic or Great Lakes shores are not included here.

All the wildflowers featured in the main sections of this book are native to the North Woods, although numerous exotic weeds now inhabit the area. Many of these weeds have attractive flowers and flourish in disturbed areas, such as along roadsides and in farm fields, so they are well known to everyone. It is beyond the scope of this book to cover all weeds, but a few common and conspicuous ones that occur regularly in native habitats and may be mistaken for native wildflowers are included in a separate section at the end of the book. Anyone interested in observing wildflowers can use this guide without specialized training. Technical terms have been kept to a minimum, and those that are used are clearly explained in this section and in the glossary.

Organization of Species

The more than 300 wildflowers featured in this book are grouped according to flower color in the following five categories: blue/purple, pink/red, yellow/orange, white, and green/brown/inconspicuous. Weeds are included in a separate section at the end of the main entries.

Flower color is a convenient way to group plants, but a word of caution is needed. Like all living things, wildflowers are variable; no two individuals are exactly alike. These differences result from a combination of heredity (what were the parents like?) and environment (what are the conditions where the plant grows?). Just as different people may have blond, black, or red hair, a single species of plant may have a range of flower colors. Most plants with purple or pink flowers, for instance, also have white-flowered forms. This guide lists wildflowers under the color you are most likely to encounter in the North Woods. For highly variable flowers, a range of colors is provided in the description.

A second challenge in grouping plants by color is the difficulty in distinguishing between colors, such as pink and purple. When you are in doubt about a flower color, check more than one color section. Plants with multicolored flowers are included in the section for the color that is most prominent.

Within each color section, plants are grouped alphabetically by scientific family name and, within families, alphabetically by scientific name. This groups similar wildflowers close together in the guide to facilitate accurate identification. In a few cases, space limitations require that entries are not in exact alphabetical order.

Plant Descriptions

The text accompanying each wildflower photograph includes the common and scientific name of the plant and the family to which it belongs. Most plants have several common names, and a common name applied in one area may elsewhere apply to a totally different plant. The common names used here were selected as the most widely used in the North Woods. Sometimes the **Comments** section gives additional common names for a plant.

Because of the confusion surrounding common names, scientific names of the wildflowers are also provided. These names, rendered in Latin, are a more stable and universal method of referring to a particular plant. Everywhere in the world, each plant should have a single accepted scientific name (although the system is not always that perfect!). The scientific name usually consists of two words. The first word indicates the plant's **genus**, a group of closely related plants with similar characteristics. Goldenrods, for example, are in the genus *Solidago*. Occasionally the scientific and common names for a genus are the same, such as the genus *Aster*.

The second part of the scientific name is the **specific epithet**, which identifies the particular species of plant. Thus, while there are many goldenrods in the genus *Solidago*, the name *Solidago uliginosa* can only refer to the bog goldenrod. Besides being consistent and unique to each plant, scientific names can show relationships by identifying members of the same genus, even if their common names are totally unrelated. Most of the scientific names used in this guide are from Gleason and Cronquist's manual of the plants of the northeastern United States and adjacent parts of Canada. This book is listed with other helpful references at the end of this guide.

In a few cases in this guide, the scientific name for a plant will have a third word, preceded by **var.**, which is an abbreviation for the word **variety**. This indicates that the plant differs slightly but consistently from other plants of the same species. Often such plants have a distinct habitat or range.

Scientists group plants into **families** according to similarities in their structure and biology. The scientific name of a family always ends with the suffix "aceae," as in Asteraceae for the Aster Family. With surprisingly little experience, you can identify many common plant families at first sight. Most people are already familiar with the unmistakable flowers of the Bean Family (Fabaceae), a group that includes beans, peas, clover, and lupine (Fig. 19). Knowing the family of an unknown plant is a big help in identification.

The description for each plant in this guide includes general growth characteristics, identifying features, and a brief summary of leaves, flowers, and other important parts necessary for field identification. Approximate sizes are usually given in feet or inches for plant height, leaves, and flowers. Leaf sizes are for the leafy part only and do not include leaf stalks. Approximate sizes are given for typical plants. One can always find the odd stunted dwarf or overgrown giant, but the measurements provided here apply to the vast majority of plants in North Woods environments. It might help to mentally insert the word "about" before the dimensions in the descriptions. Some species ranging beyond the North Woods have different dimensions in other regions; hence the differences between some sizes provided here and the sizes provided for the same plant in field manuals for other regions.

To identify wildflowers in the field, take a minute to study the plant and its features. Note the general growth form, leaves, flowers, habitat, and any other distinguishing features. Look around for other plants of the same species, and maybe you will discover better-developed individuals or see additional features not present on the first plant. A small magnifying glass or hand lens of about 10X magnification helps for telltale hairs and small flower parts.

The descriptions and photographs in this book are intended to be used together to identify a plant. There may be occasions when a plant does not exactly match the book but is clearly a close relative. In many cases this will be because the plant in question is a different species in the same genus as the book entry. The **Comments** section for many species contains discussions of related species and how to identify them.

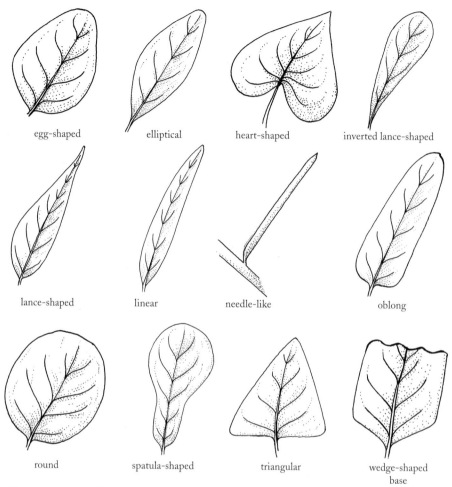

egg-shaped   elliptical   heart-shaped   inverted lance-shaped

lance-shaped   linear   needle-like   oblong

round   spatula-shaped   triangular   wedge-shaped
                                                                    base

Figure 14. Leaf shapes

Plant Terminology and Identification

This guide keeps technical terms to a minimum, but knowledge of a few special terms is necessary. These terms are easy to learn and useful for all plant identifications. A glossary at the back of the book includes the following and other terms.

Most North Woods plants are **perennials**; that is, parts of the plant live from a few years to more than a century. Familiar examples of perennial plants include tulips, raspberries, and oak trees. Perennial plants can be divided into **woody** plants, such as trees and shrubs, and **herbaceous** plants that die back

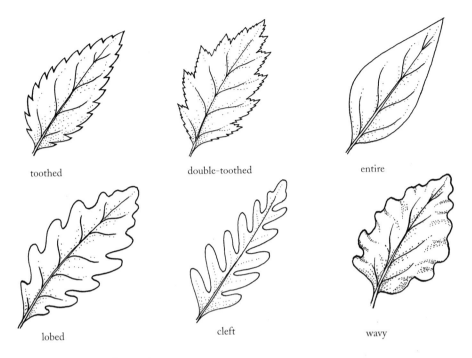

toothed   double-toothed   entire

lobed   cleft   wavy

Figure 15. Leaf margins

to ground level each year; only the underground parts live through the winter. In addition to herbaceous perennials, other herbaceous plants can be classified as **annuals**, which germinate, flower, produce seeds, and die within a year, and **biennials**, which take two seasons to produce seeds and then die.

It is often easy to determine whether a plant is perennial, since parts of the previous year's growth, such as old dead stems, may be visible. Perennials usually have well-developed underground parts, such as bulbs or large tuberous roots, while annuals typically have a small system of fibrous roots. All plants featured in this guide are herbaceous perennials unless stated otherwise in the description.

The descriptions provide the diagnostic features needed for identification, including discussion of overall appearance, leaves, flowers, and occasionally fruits. Features such as fragrant leaves or colored or milky sap are mentioned. These can be determined by gently squeezing and then smelling a leaf or by slightly tearing the tip of a leaf and noting the sap color. Some plants have **winged** parts. These are strips of leaflike tissue attached lengthwise along a stem, stalk, or other parts.

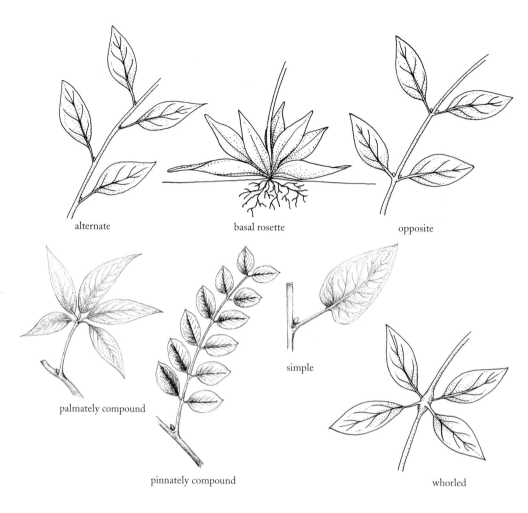

alternate

basal rosette

opposite

palmately compound

pinnately compound

simple

whorled

Figure 16. Leaf arrangements

Another feature useful in plant identification is the presence of hairs on leaves, stems, or flower parts. Some plants are always smooth and hairless, some are always hairy, and some are variable. The size, abundance, and type of hairs are useful for identification. In this guide, the description for each plant mentions whether the plant is hairy or smooth if this is a useful feature for identification. If hairiness is not mentioned, it means that the plant can be smooth or hairy or that the hairs are small, sparse, and easily overlooked.

Leaves are critically important identifying features of wildflowers (Figs. 14 and 15). To describe small differences precisely, scientists use dozens of technical terms for shapes, textures, surfaces, margins, parts, and attachments of leaves. In this guide, these terms are avoided and leaf shapes are described using common language, such as "long and narrow" or "egg shaped."

Important leaf features to note include the arrangement of the leaves on the stems (Fig.16). Are they **opposite** each other, **alternating** along the stem, or **whorled**, with several leaves originating from a common point? Is the leaf tip pointed or blunt? Is the base of the leaf tapering, rounded, heart-shaped, or clasping the stem? Is the leaf texture thick, leathery, waxy, thin, or brittle? Are the leaves evergreen? Are the edges of the leaves smooth, toothed, or lobed? Are the leaves on stalks or stalkless? Many plants produce **basal leaves**, which originate directly from the underground parts of the plant and are not attached to the stems. The shape and features of these basal leaves may be different from the main stem leaves. Sometimes only basal leaves are present.

A distinction crucial to plant identification is whether the leaves are **simple** or **compound**. Simple leaves have a single leaflike blade above each bud. Compound leaves are divided into two or more distinct segments called **leaflets**, with each segment often looking like a separate leaf. The sure way to tell if a leaf is compound is to look for buds. If there are several leaflike segments above a single bud, then the leaf is compound. This can be tricky, but it is important to master since many plant groups can be quickly determined by this feature. Leaflets of a compound leaf can be arranged like feathers along a

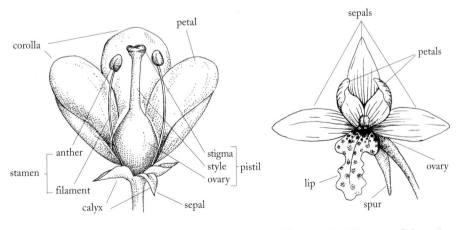

Figure 17. Typical flower in cross section

Figure 18. Flower of the Orchid Family (Orchidaceae)

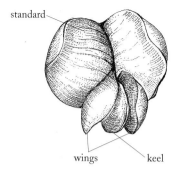

Figure 19.
Flower of the Bean Family (Fabaceae)

standard

wings   keel

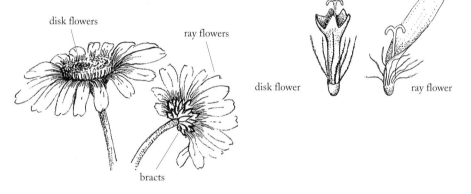

disk flowers

ray flowers

disk flower   ray flower

bracts

Figure 20. Flowers of the Aster Family (Asteraceae)

stalk (pinnate), originate from a common point like fingers on a hand (palmate), or even be doubly or triply compound, with each segment itself divided into one or more further series of leaflike segments. In all cases in the North Woods, the leaflets of compound leaves are arranged in the same plane.

Bracts are reduced scalelike or leaflike structures related to leaves and are often associated with flowers. Bracts may be miniature versions of a plant's leaves, or tiny pointed or rounded scales, or occasionally totally different in size and shape from the leaves. Bracts range from green and leaflike to thin and papery. Sometimes they are even brightly colored like flower petals. Some plants have two specialized bracts, called **stipules**, at the base of the leaf stalks. These may be large and showy or tiny and scalelike, or they may fall off soon after the leaf emerges from the bud.

Flowers are the most complicated parts of a plant, and they come in an array of shapes, sizes, and colors. Flower descriptions in this guide are intended as identification aids, so only prominent or distinctive characteristics are discussed. If a flower part is not mentioned in a discussion, it does not necessarily mean that the part is not present, but only that it is not a useful or conspicuous character for identification.

Flowers have one main function: to facilitate pollination of the female flower parts so that seeds or fruits may develop. Flowers that are pollinated by insects typically have fragrant or showy parts to attract suitable pollinators. On the other hand, plants pollinated by the wind, such as trees and grasses, have reduced flowers suited to launching and capturing windblown pollen; they have no need for showy or fragrant advertising. Flowers of plants such as

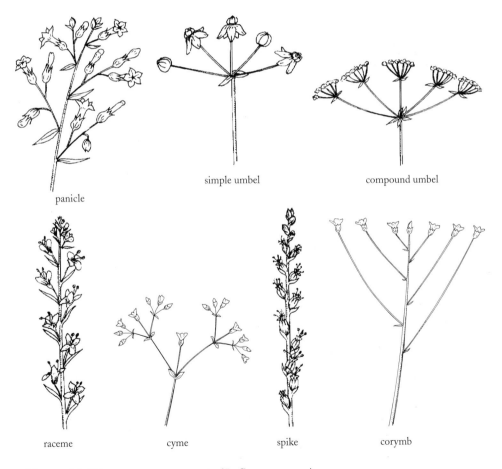

panicle

simple umbel

compound umbel

raceme

cyme

spike

corymb

Figure 21. Flower arrangements (Inflorescences)

grasses are small and highly modified and not discussed in this book.

A diagram of a generalized flower is shown in Figure 17. Most flowers have an outer series of flower parts, called **sepals**, surrounding the base of the flower. Sepals are typically green and can be inconspicuous, but in some species they are showy and brightly colored. The sepals together form the **calyx**, which may consist of separate sepals or sepals joined and fused into a tube or cuplike structure. If the sepals are fused, they are often represented by teeth or points around the top of the calyx. In this guide, sepals are green unless described otherwise.

Inside the calyx of most flowers is a series of showy flower parts called **petals**. These are what we usually see when viewing the average flower. Petals come in a variety of shapes, sizes, and colors. Depending on the kind of plant, there may be no petals or one, three, four, five, six, or more per flower. Petals may be separate from each other or partially or wholly fused together into a cuplike, tubular, or irregular shape. The petals, whether fused or separate, together form the **corolla**. Some flowers have no corolla, and in some plants the sepals and petals are identical.

Within the flower, pollen is produced by the **stamens**. There may be one to more than a hundred stamens per flower—or no stamens at all in female flowers. Stamens are typically thin filaments with clublike appendages (anthers) at the tips. The seed-producing part of the flower is called the **pistil**. It consists of the usually swollen **ovary** where the seeds develop, above which is a usually tubelike **style**. At the tip of the style is a blunt, divided or elongate **stigma** that serves as a pollen receptor and often appears fuzzy. In some flowers the style is absent. While most flowers have both male (stamen) and female (pistil) parts, some plants have separate male and female flowers, and in some species male and female flowers occur on separate plants.

The arrangement of flowers on a plant is also useful for identification purposes (Fig. 21). Again, botanists use many specialized terms for this. To avoid confusion, flower arrangements are described in this guide in general terms such as "open clusters" or "narrow elongate spikes."

Two families of flowers, both well represented in the North Woods, have specialized flower structures that deserve comment here. Asters, goldenrods, daisies, dandelions, and other plants in the Aster Family (Asteraceae) have an unusual flower arrangement (Fig. 20). What at first glance appears to be a single flower is actually a head composed of a few to several hundred modified small flowers. This head of flowers is usually surrounded at the base by a series of sepal-like bracts. The calyx of each flower is absent or reduced to bristles, scales, or hairs. There are two kinds of flowers produced, **disk flowers** and **ray flowers**, or **rays**. The corollas of ray flowers have a single, usually brightly colored strap that looks like the petal of a conventional flower. Disk flowers have small tubular corollas, usually with five tiny lobes. Depending on the species, each flower head may be all disk flowers, all ray flowers, or a combination of the two. When both types are present, there is usually a central circle or cone of disk flowers surrounded by one or more series of ray flowers, the whole creating the appearance of a single typical flower, although there may be more than a hundred flowers present.

A feature of the region's flora is the large number of orchids. Twenty-eight native North Woods orchids are featured in this guide. Plants in the Orchid Family (Orchidaceae) have a unique flower structure (Fig. 18). The ovary is below the other flower parts and often appears as a stalklike tube. There are three sepals, which are often large, colored, and petal-like. In some orchids, such as the lady's slippers, two of the sepals are fused and appear to be a single sepal. Inside the sepals are three petals. One of the petals, called the lip, typically serves as a target and landing platform for pollinating insects. It is larger and often colored and shaped differently from the other petals. There may be a dangling, hollow, tubular spur at the base of the lip. The lip forms at the top of the flower, but in most orchids the flower naturally turns half a revolution so that the lip is positioned at the bottom of the open flower. The stamens, stigmas, and styles are fused into a column that is prominent in some species and not readily apparent in others.

Following the description for each plant is a **Habitat/Range** section that provides a general summary of the plant's distribution, habitats, and abundance in the North Woods. Abundance is described in general terms such as "common," "occasional," and "rare." These terms are by necessity based on generalizations, since species described as common throughout the North Woods may be rare or absent at a particular site. In the same vein, species described as rare may be locally abundant in certain areas. The statements in this section apply only to the North Woods. Many of the plants featured in this guide range beyond the North Woods and in other areas may occupy very different habitats and grow in greater or lesser numbers.

Some entries also have a **Comments** section. This provides information such as discussions of similar species, historical uses for the plant, and other notes of interest. Several plants in this guide are listed as having been used for food or medicine. This information is intended for historical purposes only and in many cases is based on literature reports. Because of the uncertainties of plant identification and the lack of information about the accuracy of early reports, these plants should not be eaten or used medicinally, since many have poisonous counterparts.

Wildflower Stewardship

Many of the most spectacular wildflowers of the North Woods have declined in recent decades. Illegal digging, habitat destruction, and poor land management have all contributed to this. Never dig up North Woods wildflowers except from areas facing immediate destruction and only after obtaining permission to salvage plants. Many North Woods plants are commercially available from reputable nurseries that guarantee that the plants were commercially propagated and not collected in the wild. Potential buyers should deal only with establishments that provide such guarantees. Native landscaping and gardening provides a means of enjoying some of the best wildflowers of the North Woods. It also offers the advantages of locally adapted species that do not require constant fixes of fertilizers and pesticides to flourish. Using North Woods wildflowers in home and corporate landscaping, right-of-way plantings, and other utilitarian roles can provide benefits to people and the environment.

We must ensure good stewardship and conservation of our irreplaceable North Woods heritage. This can be accomplished through a combination of actions, including employing sustainable forestry and watershed management practices, identifying and protecting the most unique and highest quality habitats, ensuring that existing wildflower populations are not dug up, and encouraging habitat restoration. By responsibly integrating conservation with patterns of human activity, future generations can share the marvels of spectacular wildflower displays in the cool, crisp North Woods, where the air is tinged with the scent of balsam fir, hemlock, and spruce and where the calls of ravens and loons echo in the distance.

Blue and Purple Flowers

Northern Blue Flag

*This section includes wildflowers ranging from blue
and lavender to maroon and various shades of
purple and brownish purple. Flower colors are
variable, and pink and purple are often difficult to
separate, so you should consult the pink and red
color section of this guide when in doubt. Some
common weeds with blue and purple flowers are
included on pages 251–255.*

Wild Ginger

WILD GINGER
Asarum canadense
Birthwort Family (Aristolochiaceae)

Description: Low, stemless, hairy plant usually growing in large colonies, with a pair of stalked, broadly rounded, bluntly heart-shaped leaves, between which is a short-stalked flower that nods or lies on the ground. The leaves are up to 5" wide and long at flowering and later enlarge. Each flower is 1–1½" long and has a stout, hairy, urn-shaped calyx with 3 long, pointed, petal-like sepals that are widely spreading or curve back toward the flower stalk; the sepals are brownish purple on the inside.

Bloom Season: Spring–early summer.

Habitat/Range: Locally common in moist woods, shaded ravines, and shaded floodplains, often in beech-maple forests; throughout the region east to New Brunswick and Maine, but absent north of Lakes Superior and Huron.

Comments: The flower is under the leaves and often difficult to detect; it is reportedly pollinated by flies, gnats, and beetles. The roots have the fragrance and flavor of ginger and were formerly used as flavoring and to treat colds and fevers.

Rush Aster

RUSH ASTER
Aster borealis
Aster Family (Asteraceae)

Description: Slender plant to 2½' tall, usually with lines of small hairs below the leaves on the upper stems. The leaves are alternate, long, and narrow, ranging up to 6" long but only about ¼" wide. They have rough and sometimes sparsely toothed edges and narrow bases that slightly clasp the stem. Individually stalked, flowerlike heads arise at the bases of the small upper leaves. Each head is 1" wide, with a series of narrow sepal-like bracts and many blue, lavender, or rarely white petal-like rays surrounding a cluster of tiny, yellow, 5-lobed tubular flowers.

Bloom Season: Midsummer–early fall.

Habitat/Range: Local in cold wet sites in bogs, fens, conifer swamps, springy meadows, gravelly seeps, and along brooks; throughout most of the region, especially northward, but rare in New England.

Comments: Three similar but rarer species occur in parts of the region. Newfoundland Aster (*A. crenifolius*) also has clasping leaves, but these are usually more than ½" wide, and some of the bracts in the flower heads are expanded and leafy. It occurs in moist exposed sites in New England and eastern Canada. Bog Aster (*A. nemoralis*) has evenly hairy stems and stalkless but not clasping leaves up to 2" long. It occurs in bogs, fens, and on damp exposed shores ranging westward to Michigan. Rough-leaved Aster (*A. radula*) is a small plant typically less than 5" tall, with sharply toothed leaves up to 1" wide. It occurs in bogs and wet seepy woods from the Maritime Provinces to New England.

Northern Heart-leaved Aster

NORTHERN HEART-LEAVED ASTER

Aster ciliolatus
Aster Family (Asteraceae)

Description: Plant typically 2–3' tall, with basal and lower leaves pointed, long stalked, sharply toothed along their edges, and broadly squarish to heart shaped at the bases. The leaf stalks are usually wide and flattened. Upper leaves are smaller and narrower, with shorter or no stalks and tapering bases. Flower heads are single or on branched stalks on the upper half of the plant and are accompanied by small leafy bracts. Each lavender-blue head is ⅞" wide and has narrow sepal-like bracts and up to 25 petal-like rays surrounding a cluster of tiny, 5-lobed tubular flowers.

Bloom Season: Midsummer–early fall.

Habitat/Range: Frequent in moist to dry woods, particularly in openings, clearings, and along edges; throughout the region.

Comments: Two similar species occur in parts of the region. Common Heart-leaved Aster (*A. cordifolius*) has flower heads about ¾" wide, broadly heart-shaped main leaf bases, and narrow leaf stalks. It occurs mostly in open hardwood forests throughout the eastern and southern parts of the region, ranging to central Michigan and Minnesota. Sky Blue Aster (*A. oolentangiensis*) has rough sandpapery leaves with few or no teeth along the edges. It occurs in sparse, well-drained woods and openings scattered in the western part of the region, particularly southward, east to Ontario and New York.

Big-leaved Aster

ROBERT TATINA

BIG-LEAVED ASTER
Aster macrophyllus
Aster Family (Asteraceae)

Description: This low plant often forms exten-sive patches of basal leaves which may or may not flower in a given year. The leaf stalks are up to 7" long, and the leaves are heart shaped, grow up to 7" long and 5" wide, with coarsely toothed edges and long pointed tips. Flowering stems are typically less than 2' tall, with leaves that resemble smaller versions of the basal leaves and become smaller upward along the stem. Flower heads are in branched, leafy-bracted clusters at the top of the plant. These branches are covered with short, gland-tipped hairs. Each head is up to 1½" wide and has a series of narrow, pointed, overlapping, sepal-like bracts and 10–20 lavender petal-like rays surrounding a cluster of tiny, 5-lobed, pale yellow tubular flowers.

Bloom Season: Late summer–fall.

Habitat/Range: Abundant in dry to moist woods, woodland edges, and clearings, particu-larly on lightly shaded slopes in sandy soils; throughout the region.

Comments: Algonquin and Ojibway people used the roots and leaves for food. Smooth Forked Aster (*A. schreberi*) is a similar plant that occu-pies the same habitats in the eastern half of the region; it lacks glands on the flower branches and usually has white rays.

LEE A. CASEBERE

Flax-leaved Aster

FLAX-LEAVED ASTER

Aster linariifolius
Aster Family (Asteraceae)

Description: Plant to 2' tall with stiff, often red-dish stems and abundant alternate, stiff, narrowly tapered leaves up to 1½" long and ⅛" wide. The leaves taper to sharp points and break rather than bend when folded. Numerous stalked flower heads occur at the tops of the stems. Each head is 1" wide, with a series of overlapping sepal-like bracts and 10–15 purple, petal-like rays surrounding a cluster of tiny, 5-lobed tubular yellow flowers.

Bloom Season: Late summer–fall.

Habitat/Range: Local and uncommon in open or lightly shaded sterile soils in dry sandy woods and on sand barrens and rocky slopes; mostly in the southern part of the region from Wisconsin to New England and Quebec.

NEW ENGLAND ASTER

Aster novae-angliae
Aster Family (Asteraceae)

Description: Showy plant to 6' tall, with abundant short, stiff hairs on the stems and leaves. The leaves are alternate and up to 4" long and 1" wide. They have rough, untoothed edges, pointed tips, and broad bases that clasp the stems. The individually stalked flower heads are in a branched, rounded cluster at the tops of the main stem branches. The flower stalks and spreading pointed bracts at the base of each head are covered with gland-tipped hairs. Each head is up to 1½" wide and has narrow sepal-like bracts and 40 or more bright purple petal-like rays surrounding a cluster of tiny, yellow, 5-lobed tubular flowers. The rays can also be pink or white.

Bloom Season: Midsummer–fall.

Habitat/Range: Frequent in fields, meadows, marsh edges, stream banks, thickets, and other open, often moist, sites, sometimes becoming weedy; throughout the region but rare northward. Some populations, such as in Nova Scotia, have escaped from cultivation.

Comments: Similar species, such as Swamp Aster (see facing page), have smooth bracts below the flower heads.

DON KURZ

New England Aster

Swamp Aster

SWAMP ASTER

Aster puniceus
Aster Family (Asteraceae)

Description: Stout, hairy, usually purplish stemmed plant to 6' tall with alternate stalkless leaves that clasp the stems at their bases. The leaves are sometimes toothed, up to 6" long and 1½" wide, and widest near or below the middle. They gradually taper to pointed tips. Individually stalked flower heads are in an open leafy cluster on the upper stems. Each head is 1½" wide and has a series of smooth, pointed, sepal-like bracts and 30 or more pale bluish lavender petal-like rays surrounding a cluster of tiny, yellow, 5-lobed tubular flowers.

Bloom Season: Midsummer–fall.

Habitat/Range: Frequent in open or shaded wet sites in swamps, beaver meadows, seeps, stream banks, marshes, wet thickets, bogs, fens, sedge meadows, wet pastures, and along roadsides and wet ditches; throughout the region.

Comments: The stems may be evenly hairy or mostly smooth with distinct lines of hairs along the upper stems. The form of the plant with the lines of hairs is sometimes considered a distinct species, *A. lucidulus*. Two similar species occur in parts of the region. Smooth Blue Aster (*A. laevis*) occurs mostly in dry sites from southern Maine to Minnesota. It has thick smooth leaves with a pale waxy coating and few or no teeth along the edges; it also has up to 25 rays per head. New York Aster (*A. novi-belgii*) occurs in marshes and coastal wetlands in the eastern parts of the region and sporadically west to Wisconsin; it has blunt or short-pointed bracts at the base of the flower heads and broad, strongly clasping leaf bases. New England Aster (see facing page) lacks teeth on the leaf edges and has gland-tipped hairs on the bracts of the flower heads.

CAROL GRACIE

Tall Blue Lettuce

TALL BLUE LETTUCE
Lactuca biennis
Aster Family (Asteraceae)

Description: Smooth-stemmed biennial to 7' or rarely taller, with milky white sap and stalked alternate leaves. The main leaves are up to 14" long and 7" wide and are divided into several lobes on either side of the broad central axis, with the end lobe often large and shaped like an arrowhead. The leaves are progressively smaller upward along the stem; the upper leaves are usually unlobed. The leaves have teeth, as if small bites had been taken along the edges. Flower heads are in an elongate branching cluster on the upper part of the plant. Each head is ⅜" wide and has a series of sepal-like bracts surrounding up to 50 pale blue, petal-like flowers.

Bloom Season: Midsummer–early fall.

Habitat/Range: Frequent in shaded, often moist areas in thickets, open woods, and floodplains, and occasional in open disturbed areas; throughout the region

WILD COMFREY
Cynoglossum virginianum var. *boreale*
Borage Family (Boraginaceae)

Description: Unbranched hairy plant to 2½' tall, with most of the leaves near the base. The basal and lower stem leaves are up to 8" long and 4" wide and gradually taper to stalked bases. The upper leaves are much smaller and sometimes stalkless, often with bases that clasp the stem. Flowers are in a small branched cluster at the top of the stem. Each flower is ¼–⅜" wide and has 5 small, narrowly triangular sepals and a pale blue corolla with 5 spreading lobes.

Bloom Season: Late spring–midsummer.

Habitat/Range: Occasional in dry, open, often rocky woods; throughout most of the region, but rare north of Lakes Superior and Huron.

EDWARD G. VOSS

Wild Comfrey

Northern Blazing Star

NORTHERN BLAZING STAR
Liatris scariosa
Aster Family (Asteraceae)

Description: Mostly unbranched plant to 3' tall, with stalked alternate leaves that are smaller upward along the stem. The largest leaves are up to 9" long and 2" wide. They have smooth edges, pointed tips, and tapering bases. Numerous individually stalked flower heads occur along the upper stem. Each head is 1" wide, although sometimes the topmost head is larger. An overlapping series of blunt, dark-rimmed, sepal-like bracts cups each head of small, pinkish purple, 5-lobed tubular flowers. Each flower has protruding, paired, threadlike style branches.

Bloom Season: Midsummer–early fall.

Habitat/Range: Uncommon in dry or moist sandy or peaty areas, often in burned sites; scattered throughout the region from Maine to Lake Michigan.

Comments: Plants in the eastern part of the region have narrow leaves, usually less than 1" wide. Several other blazing stars occur in the region, including Rough Blazing Star (*L. aspera*), which has broad, puckered, papery edges on the bracts of the flower heads and occurs in the western half of the region north and east to southern Ontario; Prairie Blazing Star (*L. pycnostachya*), which also occurs in the western half of the region and has abundant short, grasslike leaves on the stem and a spike of small flower heads, each about ¼" wide, with spreading bracts; Marsh Blazing Star (*L. spicata*), another narrow-leaved species but with all the bracts pressed against the flower heads, which occurs in the south-central part of the region; and Cylindrical Blazing Star (*L. cylindracea*), which has narrow, long, grasslike leaves and relatively few flower heads, each up to ½" wide, and occurs from western New York and southern Ontario westward.

EDWARD G. VOSS

Stickseed

STICKSEED
Hackelia deflexa
Borage Family (Boraginaceae)

Description: Hairy plant to 3' tall, usually branched in the upper half, with sandpapery, stalkless alternate leaves up to 4" long that taper to pointed tips and narrow bases. Individually stalked flowers are scattered along small upper branches. Each flower is less than $^1/_{10}$" wide and has a tiny, 5-lobed, pale blue (rarely white) corolla. The fruits are a cluster of 4 small, hard, bristly burs that cling annoyingly to clothing.

Bloom Season: Early summer–midsummer.

Habitat/Range: Occasional in moist woods and thickets, often in disturbed areas; throughout most of the region east to northern New England and Quebec.

Comments: A similar but slightly coarser stickseed, *H. virginiana*, has white flowers and occurs in similar habitats throughout the southern part of the region and occasionally northward. The 4 unseparated fruits of *H. deflexa* form a pyramid, while those of *H. virginiana* are rounded.

NORTHERN BLUEBELLS
Mertensia paniculata
Borage Family (Boraginaceae)

Description: Plant to 2' tall, with finely hairy alternate leaves. These leaves are up to 5" long and are widest below the middle. The leaves have smooth edges, long pointed tips, and taper to rounded, stalked bases. Flowers are in branched nodding clusters at the top of the stem. Each flower is ½" long and has 5 hairy narrow sepals and a gobletlike, pale blue corolla with 5 shallow lobes at the mouth.

Bloom Season: Summer.

Habitat/Range: Occasional in moist woods, conifer swamps, and along shaded shores from upper Michigan north and westward.

Comments: Virginia Bluebells (*M. virginica*) has smooth leaves and sepals and flowers ¾–1" long. It occurs in rich woods at the southern edge of the region from New York to southeastern Minnesota.

ROBERT TATINA

Northern Bluebells

SMALL FORGET-ME-NOT
Myosotis laxa
Borage Family (Boraginaceae)

Description: Weak, round-stemmed, sparsely hairy plant usually less than 1' tall. The stalkless alternate leaves are up to 2" long and have tapering bases and rounded or bluntly pointed tips. Flowers are in elongate clusters at the tops of the branches. Each individually stalked flower is about ⅛" wide and has 5 pointed, hairy sepals and a pale blue, 5-lobed corolla with a yellow center.

Bloom Season: Summer.

Habitat/Range: Occasional in moist springy areas, white cedar swamps, and along brooks and muddy shores, often in shallow, gently flowing water; throughout the region.

Comments: Common Forget-me-not (*M. scorpioides*), a popular garden plant from Europe, is a well-established weed in similar habitats and ditches throughout the region. It is a larger, coarser plant with flowers about ¼" wide and often has slightly angular stems. Another European plant well established in parts of the region, Garden Forget-me-not (*M. sylvatica*), has hook-tipped hairs on the calyx. The other species have straight-tipped calyx hairs.

Small Forget-me-not

KAY YATSKIEVYCH

MARSH BELLFLOWER
Campanula aparinoides
Bellflower Family (Campanulaceae)

Description: Slender weak plant up to 3' long, often sprawling over other vegetation. The stems are angular and rough edged and tend to cling to clothing. The widely spaced, alternate leaves resemble short blades of grass. They are up to 3" long but less than ¼" wide. Sometimes the leaf edges are finely toothed. The plants have milky sap and are typically much branched in the upper part, with single flowers on long threadlike stalks. Each pale blue to whitish flower has a cuplike calyx with 5 small, pointed lobes and a flaring corolla divided less than half its length into 5 triangular lobes. The flowers range from tiny to ⅜" wide.

Bloom Season: Summer.

Habitat/Range: Frequent in marshes, wet thickets, bogs, fens, overgrown wet meadows, and along shores, often in neutral to alkaline water; throughout the region.

Comments: Iroquois people used this plant to induce childbirth.

ROBERT TATINA

Marsh Bellflower

Harebell

JESSIE M. HARRIS

HAREBELL
Campanula rotundifolia
Bellflower Family (Campanulaceae)

Description: Delicate spindly plant to 2' tall, with milky sap and often with several erect branches arising near the base. The basal leaves have long stalks and are generally round with angular edges and heart-shaped bases. These leaves usually wither before flowering time. Stem leaves are alternate, narrow, grasslike, and up to 4" long. They are progressively smaller toward the top of the plant. From 1 to a few flowers nod on delicate individual stalks on the upper stem. Each deep blue flower is ¾" wide and has a tiny calyx with 5 spreading, threadlike lobes and a bell-shaped corolla with 5 spreading, triangular lobes.

Bloom Season: Late spring–midsummer.

Habitat/Range: Locally common in dry woods and on exposed cliffs, sandy or rocky shores, and ledges; throughout the region.

INDIAN TOBACCO
Lobelia inflata
Bellflower Family (Campanulaceae)

Description: Pale green, usually branched annual from 3" to 3' tall, with milky sap and alternate, mostly stalkless leaves. There are long hairs on the lower stem, and sometimes on the leaves, which are narrowly egg shaped and up to 3½" long and 1½" wide. They are progressively smaller upward on the plant and have teeth and small white bumps along the edges. The short-stalked flowers are alternate along the upper stem, with a small bract at the base of each flower stalk. Each flower is ¼" long and has 5 needlelike calyx lobes and a pale blue, tubular corolla with 2 narrow, erect upper lobes and 3 downward-pointing lower lobes. The calyx becomes swollen and round in fruit.

Bloom Season: Midsummer–fall.

Habitat/Range: Common in dry, often disturbed woods and sterile fields; throughout much of the region, but mostly absent north of Lake Superior. A typical habitat is the shaded bed of an old logging road.

Comments: The plant has been used to treat asthma but is poisonous in quantity. Pale Spiked

Indian Tobacco

KEITH BOARD

Lobelia (*L. spicata*) occurs in moist, open to lightly shaded sites throughout much of the region. It is a more delicate unbranched plant with more finely toothed leaves and lower stems that are smooth or have short hairs.

GREAT BLUE LOBELIA
Lobelia siphilitica
Bellflower Family (Campanulaceae)

Description: Plant to 3' tall, with yellowish milky sap and mostly unbranched stems that are sometimes sparsely hairy. The leaves are alternate and up to 6" long and 2" wide. They have irregular, shallowly toothed and scalloped edges with small white spots along them. The leaves are widest near the middle and taper to pointed tips and stalkless bases. Numerous short-stalked flowers, each accompanied by a small leafy bract, are in a crowded, alternately arranged cluster near the top of the main stem. Each flower has 5 small, channeled, green, pointed sepals and a deep blue, tubular corolla ¾–1½" long, with pale stripes on the tube. The end of the corolla is split into 2 lips. The upper lip has 2 upright pointed lobes, and the lower lip is divided into 3 spreading pointed lobes. A spur of 5 hairy, purplish stamens closely surrounding a central green style projects along the upper side of the corolla.

Bloom Season: Midsummer–fall.

Habitat/Range: Common in swamps, fens,

Great Blue Lobelia

seepy areas, moist thickets, wet woods, and along shores; throughout most of the region, becoming rare in New England and eastern Canada.

Comments: The plants were once thought to be a cure for syphilis.

BOG LOBELIA
Lobelia kalmii
Bellflower Family (Campanulaceae)

Description: Delicate, usually branched plant to 15" tall, with milky sap. The leaves are alternate and very narrow, ranging up to 1½" long but seldom much over ⅛" wide. Some of the larger leaves have a few teeth along the edges. The basal leaves are broader and more rounded. Flowers are on threadlike stalks that alternate along the upper stems. Small leaves grow at the base of each stalk. Each flower is ⅜" long and has a small cuplike calyx with 5 pointed lobes and a pale blue, tubular corolla with 3 spreading lower lobes, 2 smaller upright upper lobes, and a white center.

Bloom Season: Summer–fall.

Habitat/Range: Common in wet open sites, often in alkaline or mineralized waters, in shallow marshes, fens, wet meadows, sandy or marly shores, and sometimes in wet conifer woods; throughout the region.

Bog Lobelia

BRUCE SCHUETTE

Early Horse Gentian

EARLY HORSE GENTIAN
Triosteum aurantiacum
Honeysuckle Family (Caprifoliaceae)

Description: Coarse hairy plant to 4' tall, often with several stems in a group. The leaves are opposite, smooth edged, widest near the middle, and up to 9" long and 3½" wide. They have long pointed tips and narrow tapering bases. The leaves are arranged so that adjacent pairs form a cross when viewed from above. Occasionally the leaves in a few of the upper pairs have their bases joined around the stem. The middle and upper leaves have 1–4 stalkless flowers nestled at their bases. Each flower is up to ¾" long and has 5 needlelike sepals surrounding a maroon tubular corolla with 5 small, unequal lobes and a knoblike stigma. The fruits are bright orange, ½"-wide berries topped by the persistent sepals.

Bloom Season: Midspring–early summer.

Habitat/Range: Occasional in dry open woods, often on rocky slopes or along edges, and sometimes in shaded moist areas; throughout the region.

Comments: In Late Horse Gentian (*T. perfoliatum*), the leaves of most of the pairs are joined across the stem. It occurs in similar habi-

Early Horse Gentian

JESSIE M. HARRIS

tats in the southern part of the region. The dried, toasted berries have been used as a coffee substitute.

BLACK CROWBERRY
Empetrum nigrum
Crowberry Family (Empetraceae)

Description: Branched, dwarf evergreen shrub with wiry reddish stems usually less than 8" tall and often forming dense mats. The abundant dark green, shiny, thick needlelike leaves are about ¼" long. Tiny flowers occur at the bases of the middle and upper leaves. There are separate male and female flowers. Each is ⅛" wide and has a few tiny, pale-edged bracts at its base, 3 tiny sepals, and 3 blunt purplish petals. The fruits are black berries about ¼" wide.

Bloom Season: Summer.

Habitat/Range: Local, usually at higher altitudes or in exposed locations along coasts and shores, in rocky areas, peaty areas, sand barrens, and on cliff tops; throughout the Canadian part of the region, south to upper Michigan and the mountains of northern New England.

Comments: North American Indians, particularly in Alaska, have used the berries for food. Broom Crowberry (*Corema conradii*), which occurs in sandy areas mostly near the Atlantic coast, is a similar plant with the flowers at the tips of the branches.

EDWARD G. VOSS

Black Crowberry

HOG PEANUT
Amphicarpaea bracteata
Bean Family (Fabaceae)

Description: This hairy-stemmed, wiry, twining vine usually clambers or sprawls over other vegetation. The well-separated, stalked, alternate compound leaves are each divided into 3 broad, toothless, stalked leaflets with broadly rounded bases and pointed tips. Each leaflet can be up to 4" long but is often 2" or less. Flowers are in stalked clusters at the bases of the leaf stalks. Each pale purple to pink or whitish flower is ½" long and has a short, tubular, shallowly 4-toothed calyx and an upper petal over 2 smaller side petals that flank a keel-like lower petal. The fruits resemble small, flattened string beans.

Bloom Season: Midsummer–late summer.

Habitat/Range: Common in moist thickets, marsh borders, rich soil in low woods, and along stream banks, especially in areas with a history of light disturbance; throughout the region.

Comments: The plants produce peanutlike seeds from underground flowers without petals. These seeds have been a favored food of people and livestock and are said to be particularly popular with hogs—hence the common name.

ROBERT TATINA

Hog Peanut

STEPHEN CLAYDEN/NEW BRUNSWICK MUSEUM

Rhodora

RHODORA
Rhododendron canadense
Heath Family (Ericaceae)

Description: Shrub to 4' tall, with short-stalked alternate leaves mostly clustered near the tips of the branches. The leaves are up to 2¼" long and ¾" wide and finely hairy. They have pointed tips and, usually, a fringe of short hairs along the slightly downturned edges. Flowers emerge before the leaves; they appear in small clusters at the tips of the branches. The rose-purple (rarely white) flowers are ¾" long and have 5 tiny sepals and a spreading corolla that is deeply divided into 2 narrow, dangling lower lobes and a broader upper section with 3 shallow lobes. The 10 stamens and long slender style protrude beyond the corolla.

Bloom Season: Midspring–late spring.

Habitat/Range: Locally frequent in moist woods, bogs, swamps, and seepy shaded mountain slopes; in the eastern part of the region west to Ontario and New York.

Comments: Two other pink-to-purple flowered species occur uncommonly in the eastern part of the region, but both have symmetrical 5-lobed flowers with 5 stamens. Mountain Azalea (*R. prinophyllum*) has fragrant flowers and hairy lower leaf surfaces. Pink Azalea (*R. periclymenoides*) has unscented flowers and lower leaf surfaces that are smooth except along the veins. Both species occur in bogs and acidic woods from New England southward. Mountain Azalea also occurs in Quebec.

ROBERT TATINA

Ground Nut

GROUND NUT
Apios americana
Bean Family (Fabaceae)

Description: Sprawling or climbing vine with milky sap and widely spaced, stalked, alternate compound leaves. Each leaf is divided into 3–7 individually stalked leaflets up to 3" long, with smooth edges, broadly rounded bases, and pointed tips. Flowers are in dense clusters at the ends of short stalks at the bases of the leaves. Each fragrant, brownish purple flower is up to ½" long and has a small cuplike calyx and a rounded, hooded to erect upper petal above 2 smaller side petals and a strongly curved, keel-like lower petal. The fruits are wavy pods 2–4" long.

Bloom Season: Summer.

Habitat/Range: Frequent in moist to wet, open or lightly shaded areas in thickets, marshes, wet woods, and along shores and stream banks; throughout the region.

Comments: The thickened tuberous roots can be eaten like potatoes. The Pilgrims reportedly depended upon this plant during their first year in the New World.

JESSIE M. HARRIS

Marsh Vetchling

ROBERT TATINA

Veiny Pea

MARSH VETCHLING
Lathyrus palustris
Bean Family (Fabaceae)

Description: Vinelike plant with angular or narrowly winged stems to 3' long and widely spaced, stalked, alternate compound leaves ending in branched coiling tendrils. Each leaf has a pair of pointed bractlike stipules about ¼" wide at the base of the leaf stalk, as well as 4–8 smooth-edged, narrowly oval leaflets, each typically about 2" long and paired along the central axis. Sometimes one of the upper leaflets is replaced by a tendril. Long-stalked clusters of 2–8 flowers arise at the base of the upper leaf stalks. Each reddish purple flower is ¾" long and has an unequally 5-toothed calyx, a broad, upright upper petal, and 2 smaller side petals flanking a keel-like lower lip. The fruits are flattened pods about 2" long.

Bloom Season: Late spring–summer.

Habitat/Range: Frequent in marshes, swamps, wet meadows, and other moist open sites, less common in wet woods and swamps; throughout the region.

Comments: Two related species occur in the region. Veiny Pea (*L. venosus*) has 8–14 leaflets per leaf and usually more than 10 flowers per cluster. It occurs in well-drained sandy or rocky woods and meadows from Quebec and Vermont westward and is particularly common in Minnesota. Beach Pea (*L. maritimus*) has leafletlike stipules about ¾" wide. It typically has 5 or 6 flowers per cluster and occurs on sandy or gravelly beaches along the Atlantic coast, the Great Lakes, Lake Champlain, and rarely on the shores of other lakes.

American Vetch

ROBERT TATINA

AMERICAN VETCH

Vicia americana
Bean Family (Fabaceae)

Description: This sprawling vine grows up to 4' long and has a slight bluish green cast. The leaves are alternate, with prominent, sharply toothed, bractlike stipules at the base of the leaf stalk. Each leaf has up to 16 narrow, alternate leaflets arranged featherlike along the axis, which is prolonged beyond the leaflets into a branched, coiling tendril. Each leaflet is narrowly oval and up to 1" long and ⅜" wide, with rounded ends and a minutely pointed tip. Flowers are alternate on long stalks at the base of the leaf stalks, with 2–9 flowers per stalk. Each flower is ¾" long and has a hairy cuplike calyx with 2 short teeth above and 3 longer teeth below. The corolla has a narrow, upright, shallowly lobed, deep purple upper petal above 2 shorter petals that flank a small, keel-like lower petal.

Bloom Season: Midspring–midsummer.

Habitat/Range: Occasional in a variety of habitats ranging from dry rocky slopes to moist thickets and riverbanks; from New York and Ontario westward.

Comments: Several similar, introduced, weedy vetches are common in fields, waste ground, and along roadsides in the region. Most have smooth or single-toothed bractlike stipules at the base of the leaf stalk. Among the most common of these weeds are Hairy Vetch (*V. villosa*), which has spreading hairs on the stems, and Bird Vetch (*V. cracca*), which has smooth stems or hairs flat against the stems.

JESSIE M. HARRIS

Closed Gentian

NARROW-LEAVED GENTIAN
Gentiana linearis
Gentian Family (Gentianaceae)

Description: Smooth, usually reddish stemmed plant to 2½' tall, with well-separated pairs of dark green, narrow, opposite leaves, each up to 2½" long and less than ½" wide. Flowers are in one or more dense stalkless clusters at the top of the plant, above pairs or whorls of leaves. Each flower is up to 1½" long, with 5 pointed calyx lobes and a tubular, deep blue, nearly closed corolla with 5 triangular lobes and smaller ragged projections between each lobe.

Bloom Season: Late summer–early fall.

Habitat/Range: Uncommon in wet seepy areas in meadows, marshes, bogs, and along shores; in the eastern part of the region from Quebec and Maine to Ontario and upper Michigan.

Comments: A related species mostly in the western part of the region, Great Lakes Gentian (*G. rubricaulis*), has pale green, broad leaves more than ½" wide and dull blue flowers with usually pale corolla bases.

CLOSED GENTIAN
Gentiana andrewsii
Gentian Family (Gentianaceae)

Description: Plant to 2½' tall, usually with unbranched stems. The stalkless opposite leaves are typically 3–4" long and up to 1½" wide; the upper leaves are usually the largest. The leaves have pointed tips, tapering bases, and a prominent, raised, central vein on the lower surface. Flowers occur in stalked or stalkless clusters at the bases of the upper leaves, with small leaflike bracts under each cluster. Each flower is up to 1½" long and has 5 small, pointed sepals and a pleated, deep blue tubular corolla that remains closed except for a tiny, minutely fringed opening at the tip. The flowers resemble blue Christmas-tree lights.

Bloom Season: Late summer–fall.

Habitat/Range: Occasional in moist open woods, meadows, fens, and along seepy shores; found in most of the region but rare eastward, ranging to western New England and Quebec.

Comments: Bottle Gentian (*G. clausa*) is similar, but the tips of the flowers are not visibly fringed unless they are pried open. It occurs in similar habitats from Maine and Quebec southward. The roots of these and other gentians have been used medicinally and to flavor beverages.

ALLISON W. BELL

Narrow-leaved Gentian

STIFF GENTIAN
Gentianella quinquefolia
Gentian Family (Gentianaceae)

Description: Smooth annual, usually less than 15" tall, with stalkless opposite leaves and several upright branches. The leaves are up to 2½" long, widest near the broadly rounded bases, and taper to pointed tips. Clusters of several upright flowers grow on the upper half of the plant. Each flower is ¾" long and has 5 narrow calyx lobes and a tubular blue corolla with 5 triangular teeth at the narrow mouth.

Bloom Season: Late summer–fall.

Habitat/Range: Occasional in moist seepy meadows, springy stream banks, and moist woods; throughout the southern half of the region from central Minnesota to Maine.

LEE A. CASEBERE

Stiff Gentian

JESSIE M. HARRIS

Fringed Gentian

FRINGED GENTIAN
Gentianopsis crinita
Gentian Family (Gentianaceae)

Description: Smooth annual or biennial to 2' tall, with stalkless opposite leaves that clasp the stems at their rounded bases. Each leaf is typically 1–2" long and usually more than ⅜" wide, with a pointed tip and prominent central vein along its length. Flowers are at the ends of upright branches near the top of the plant or on long stalks at the base of the upper leaves. Each flower is 1" wide and has a cuplike calyx with 4 pointed, often purple-tinged lobes and a deep blue, tubular corolla with 4 broadly rounded lobes that are delicately fringed along the edges.

Bloom Season: Late summer–fall.

Habitat/Range: Uncommon in moist, often alkaline areas in springy meadows, along shores, and in seepy spots on slopes; scattered throughout most of the region east to Maine.

Comments: Small Fringed Gentian (*G. procera*) has narrow leaves usually less than ⅜" wide and small, almost torn-looking fringes on the corolla lobes. It occurs in similar habitats in the western half of the region and also at a few sites eastward.

JESSIE M. HARRIS

Spurred Gentian

SPURRED GENTIAN
Halenia deflexa
Gentian Family (Gentianaceae)

Description: Annual to 2½' tall, sometimes branched, with stalkless, smooth-edged, opposite leaves up to 2" long. The leaves have pointed tips and rounded bases. Clusters of individually stalked flowers are at the base of the upper leaves. Each flower is ¼" wide, with 4 small, pointed sepals and a cylindrical, 4-lobed, purplish green corolla with 4 downward-pointing spurs at the base. In some flowers the spurs may be absent or reduced to bumps.

Bloom Season: Summer.

Habitat/Range: Local in moist mossy areas of wet woods, bog edges, moist stream banks, and damp rocky slopes; scattered throughout the region.

VIRGINIA WATERLEAF
Hydrophyllum virginianum
Waterleaf Family (Hydrophyllaceae)

Description: Branched plant to 3' tall, with alternate, stalked, deeply lobed leaves. Each leaf is up to 8" long, with 4–8 irregular lobes on either side of the central axis and another lobe at the tip. The lobes are typically narrower at the base than in the middle, with coarse teeth and sometimes small lobes along the edges. The upper leaf surfaces are typically splotched with grayish patterns. Flowers are in branched compact clusters on the ends of mostly upright, branching stalks. Each flower is ¹/₃" wide, with 5 narrow hairy sepals, a 5-lobed corolla that is lavender to nearly whitish, 5 protruding threadlike stamens, and a slender style.

Bloom Season: Midspring–early summer.

Habitat/Range: Frequent in rich or moist woods in ravines and on floodplains; throughout all but the eastern part of the region.

Comments: The greens of young plants are edible. Two other species of waterleaf occur in the region. Canada Waterleaf (*H. canadense*), found from Vermont to Michigan, has mostly smooth

JESSIE M HARRIS

Virginia Waterleaf

stems. Its upper leaves are shallowly lobed from a common point and resemble maple leaves; the flowers are usually white. Great Waterleaf (*H. appendiculatum*), which occurs from southern Ontario westward, has densely hairy stems and similar but more deeply lobed leaves than those of Canada Waterleaf.

ROBERT TATINA

Northern Blue Flag

NORTHERN BLUE FLAG
Iris versicolor
Iris Family (Iridaceae)

Description: Plant to 3' tall, typically forming large colonies of stiff, pale bluish green, flat, swordlike leaves that taper to pointed tips. The slightly zigzagging flowering stems are often taller than the leaves and typically have 1 or 2 branches, with leaflike bracts at their bases. Several flowers occur on short stalks near the tops of the stems. Each flower is up to 4" wide and is deep blue-violet with white and greenish yellow markings. What appear to be 6 petals are actually 3 downward-curving sepals, each with a greenish central line inside near the base, and 3 shorter upright petals with pale streaks along their narrow bases. Within each flower are 3 stamens and 3 petal-like style branches. The fruits are round, 3-angled, 2½"-long capsules.

Bloom Season: Midspring–midsummer.

Habitat/Range: Abundant in marshes, open swamps, wet meadows, bogs, wet ditches, and along shores; throughout the region.

Comments: A similar species, Southern Blue Flag (*I. virginica*), has leaves that are often taller than the flowering stems, as well as bright yellow spots at the base of the sepals. It occurs mostly in the southern part of the region from southern Ontario to southeastern Minnesota. The roots of both plants are poisonous to humans but have been used in small amounts in folk medicines.

Mountain Blue-eyed Grass

BLUE GIANT HYSSOP
Agastache foeniculum
Mint Family (Lamiaceae)

Description: Plant to 4' tall, usually branched in the upper half, with stout square stems and widely separated, triangular, opposite leaves that are up to 4" long and 2" wide. These leaves have saw-toothed edges, pointed tips, and whitish lower surfaces. Flowers are in small whorls along the upright upper stems, with small leaflike bracts under each whorl. Each flower is ⅜" long and has a tubular calyx with 5 small, hairy, pointed, purple lobes, and a tubular lavender-blue corolla with a 2-lobed upper lip and a spreading 3-lobed lower lip. Four slender stamens and a style protrude from the flower.

Bloom Season: Summer.

Habitat/Range: Frequent in dry open woods, clearings, and along forest edges from Wisconsin north and west, and occasionally introduced eastward to Quebec and New Hampshire.

Comments: The crushed leaves smell like licorice and have been used to make tea and a cold remedy. Purple Giant Hyssop (*A. scrophulariaefolia*) occurs in moist open woods and low thickets in the southern part of the region from Vermont westward. It has leaves that

MOUNTAIN BLUE-EYED GRASS
Sisyrinchium montanum
Iris Family (Iridaceae)

Description: Smooth, slender, pale green, grass-like plant seldom over 1' tall, with tufted, upright basal leaves and flattened stems about ⅛" wide that are usually longer than the basal leaves. A pair of leaflike bracts near the top of the stem flanks a few flowers on delicate, individual stalks. Each flower is up to ¾" wide and has 3 deep-violet, sharp-tipped sepals and 3 similar petals. The sepals and petals are yellow at their bases, creating a yellow pattern at the center of the flower. Joined together at the center of the flower are 3 yellow-tipped stamens.

Bloom Season: Midspring–early summer.

Habitat/Range: Common in grassy fields, meadows, and open woods, usually in somewhat moist conditions; throughout the region.

Comments: Several similar species of blue-eyed grass occur in the region.

Blue Giant Hyssop

are green on both sides. The flowers are about ½" long and have hairless pale or green calyx lobes.

WILD MINT
Mentha arvensis var. *canadensis*
Mint Family (Lamiaceae)

Description: Square stemmed and usually un-branched, this plant grows up to 2' tall. It is finely hairy and has a strong minty fragrance. The short-stalked, opposite leaves are up to 2½" long, with curving toothed edges and pointed tips. The upper leaves become progressively smaller. Flowers are in dense clusters surrounding the stem at the base of the upper leaves. Each flower is ¼" long and has a hairy calyx with 5 triangular lobes and a pinkish purple corolla with 4 spreading lobes, one of which is notched at the tip. Four slender stamens and a thin style protrude from the flower.

Bloom Season: Midsummer–late summer.

Habitat/Range: Common in moist, exposed sites in muddy marshes, wet depressions, springy seeps, fens, sedge meadows, wet thickets, and along shores; throughout the region.

Comments: Some populations may be European introductions. North American Indians used this plant for more than 100 different medical purposes, as well as to flavor food and make tea.

Wild Mint

SELF-HEAL
Prunella vulgaris
Mint Family (Lamiaceae)

Description: Hairy, square-stemmed, creeping or upright plant to 18" tall, with stalked opposite leaves to 4" long. The leaves have mostly blunt tips and broadly tapering to rounded bases, with wavy or few-toothed edges. Cylindrical heads of flowers occur at the tops of the stems and on short side branches. Under every 3 flowers is a broad pointed bract. Each blue-purple flower is ⅝" long, with a small, hairy, 2-lobed calyx with a square upper lip and a 2-toothed lower lip. The tubular corolla has a hooded upper lip and a spreading, pale, 3-lobed lower lip, with the middle lobe fringed along the edges.

Bloom Season: Late spring–fall.

Habitat/Range: Common in pastures, thickets, disturbed open woods, and in weedy areas in lawns and along roadsides and trails; throughout the region.

Comments: This species is native to Europe, Asia, and North America, and some of our populations are introduced weeds. North American Indians and Europeans used this plant for a variety of folk medicines, especially those used to treat throat and mouth problems.

Self-heal

Marsh Skullcap

MARSH SKULLCAP
Scutellaria galericulata
Mint Family (Lamiaceae)

Description: Square-stemmed plant to 2½' tall, with tiny hairs along the angles of the stem. The leaves are opposite and short stalked to nearly stalkless. They are up to 2" long and about ⅞" wide, with pointed tips, broad bases, and low blunt teeth along the edges. Flowers are single on short stalks at the base of the small upper leaves. Flowers from adjacent leaves face in the same direction and thus appear to be paired. Each flower is ¾" long and covered in fine hairs. It has a cuplike calyx with a ridged bump on the upper side and a blue tubular corolla ending in a lobed, hooded upper lip and a flat, dangling lower lip.

Bloom Season: Late spring–midsummer.

Habitat/Range: Common in wet soil in marshes, bogs, wet thickets, and along shores; throughout the region.

MAD-DOG SKULLCAP
Scutellaria lateriflora
Mint Family (Lamiaceae)

Description: Branching plant to 2½' tall, with square stems and stalked opposite leaves. Each leaf is up to 4" long and has coarse teeth along the edges, a broad base, and a pointed tip. Flowers occur in stalked clusters at the bases of the main leaves on the upper half of the plant. A cluster has several paired flowers facing in the same direction. At the base of each flower pair is a pair of small bracts. Each minutely hairy flower is ⅓" long. It has a small cuplike calyx with a ridged bump on the upper side and a tubular blue corolla ending in a lobed, slightly hooded upper lip and a flat, spreading lower lip.

Bloom Season: Summer.

Habitat/Range: Common in wet sites in marshes, beaver meadows, swamps, thickets, along shores, and sometimes in wet weedy areas; throughout the region.

Mad-dog Skullcap

WOUNDWORT

Stachys palustris
Mint Family (Lamiaceae)

Description: Hairy, square-stemmed, mostly unbranched plant up to 3' tall, with stalkless opposite leaves to 4" long and less than 1" wide. These leaves have toothed edges and pointed tips. Flowers are in a series of usually 6-flowered whorls at the top of the stem, with small leaves at the base of each whorl. Each flower is ½" long and has a small cuplike calyx with 5 needlelike teeth and a pinkish purple tubular corolla with a hooded, 2-lobed upper lip and a broader, spreading, 3-lobed lower lip. The flowers have a slightly unpleasant scent.

Bloom Season: Late spring–midsummer.

Habitat/Range: Frequent in damp areas in marshes, thickets, ditches, and along shores; throughout the region.

Comments: The large middle lobe of the lower lip serves as a landing pad for pollinating insects. Some of our populations are native, and some are European weeds. The plant was formerly used in folk medicine to help heal wounds, and the tubers are said to be edible. Another species, Common Hedge Nettle (*S. tenuifolia*), has stems that are hairy only along the angles. Wild Germander (*Teucrium canadense*) occurs in moist sites throughout the region. It is similar to Woundwort but has a ¾"-long corolla that appears to have only the lower lip present.

ROBERT TATINA

Woundwort

VIOLET BUTTERWORT

Pinguicula vulgaris
Bladderwort Family (Lentibulariaceae)

Description: Small unbranched plant less than 8" tall, with 1 or more leafless stalks rising from a cluster of yellowish green, stalkless basal leaves. These leaves are up to 2" long, with narrowed bases, blunt tips, and upturned edges. The surface of the leaves appears greasy, as if smeared with butter, but is sticky to the touch. A single (rarely 2) cornucopia-shaped flower dangles at the top of the stalk. Each purplish flower is up to ¾" long and has a small 5-lobed calyx and a 2-lipped corolla. The upper corolla lip is divided into 2 lobes, and the lower lip has 3 larger lobes and a tapered spur that points backward.

Bloom Season: Early summer–midsummer.

Habitat/Range: Rare and local on exposed wet rocks, rocky shores, seeping cliffs, and exposed moist sands, usually in limey sites; scattered in the northern half of the region.

Comments: The sticky leaves trap insects, which are digested by the plant.

JESSIE M. HARRIS

Violet Butterwort

Purple Trillium

PURPLE TRILLIUM
Trillium erectum
Lily Family (Liliaceae)

Description: Smooth unbranched plant to 15" tall, with a single whorl of 3 broadly rounded leaves at the top of the stem. These leaves are 2–6" long and about as wide. They taper to stalkless bases and abruptly pointed tips. The single flower is at the top of the stem on a stalk that rises up to 4" above the leaves. Each flower is 2–3" wide and has 3 pointed sepals, 3 maroon petals, and 6 erect stamens surrounding a purplish ovary with 3 narrow stigmas.

Bloom Season: Midspring–late spring.

Habitat/Range: Common in rich, moist to swampy woods; in the eastern part of the region west to Lake Michigan.

Comments: This plant is also called Stinking Benjamin. The flowers have a smell said to resemble that of a wet dog. Rare forms occur with pale or yellow flowers.

FAIRY SLIPPER
Calypso bulbosa
Orchid Family (Orchidaceae)

Description: Delicate single-stemmed plant to 8" tall, with 1 broadly rounded basal leaf up to 2" long that appears in the autumn, overwinters, and dies after flowering. This leaf typically lies along the ground. The delicate purplish stem is nodding at the tip, with a narrow, pointed, upright bract at the base of the single, dangling, purple flower. Each flower is up to 1½" wide and has a slender ovary topped by 2 narrow, pointed, twisting, spreading petals, 3 similar sepals, and a broadly cupped lower lip with purple markings and a prominent zone of yellow or white hairs on the inner surface. A hooded, rounded column extends over part of the lip.

Bloom Season: Midspring–early summer.

Habitat/Range: Rare and local in moist to wet coniferous and mixed forests and in white cedar swamps; scattered throughout the northern two-thirds of the region.

Fairy Slipper

SPOTTED CORAL ROOT

Corallorhiza maculata
Orchid Family (Orchidaceae)

Description: Single-stemmed brown, purplish, or yellow plant seldom more than 1' tall, with no green color. The leaves are reduced to 1 or more yellowish, pointed, alternate, sheathing scales along the stem. Usually 10 or more flowers are alternate along the upper part of the stem. Each flower is 1" long and ½" wide and has a thickened tubular ovary topped by 3 curved, spreading, purplish sepals and 2 similar petals, under which is a pale central column and a prominent pale lower lip with dark purple markings.

Bloom Season: Summer.

Habitat/Range: Occasional in moist to dry, often sandy or loamy forests; throughout the region.

Comments: Unlike green plants, Spotted Coral Root cannot produce food from sunlight and instead takes nutrients from decaying organic matter. Other coral root orchids occur in the region, including Striped Coral Root (*C. striata*), which has purple-striped sepals and petals and a smooth-edged lower lip. Early Coral Root (*C. trifida*) is a smaller and earlier-blooming plant with small flowers and a usually unspotted lower lip. The name comes from the coral-like root mass.

Spotted Coral Root

RAM'S HEAD LADY'S SLIPPER

Cypripedium arietinum
Orchid Family (Orchidaceae)

Description: Delicate plant to 1' tall, with fine hairs and 3–5 pleated alternate leaves near the middle of the stem. Each leaf is up to 4" long and 1" wide, with a pointed tip and a slightly clasping base. A single flower, covered with fine hairs, is at the top of the stem above an upright, green, leaflike bract. The distinctive, unusually shaped "slipper" is ¾" long, hairy around the opening, and white with a network of deep purple lines and a deep purplish pouch below the front. The slipper is under an arching, purplish to greenish sepal and is flanked by 2 narrow, pointed, straplike, slightly twisted petals and 2 similar sepals.

Bloom Season: Late spring–early summer.

Habitat/Range: Rare in white cedar swamps, bogs, moist acidic sand, hillside seeps, and wooded dunes or thin soil over limestone; in all but the southern edge of the region, but sporadic and local.

Ram's Head Lady's Slipper

Purple Fringed Orchid

JESSIE M. HARRIS

PURPLE FRINGED ORCHID
Platanthera psycodes
Orchid Family (Orchidaceae)

Description: Smooth single-stemmed plant to 2½' tall, with several widely spaced alternate leaves up to 7" long. The lower leaves are broadly rounded, have slightly pointed to round tips, and taper to narrow stalkless bases that clasp the stems. The upper leaves are much smaller and narrow and become progressively more bractlike toward the top of the stem. Flowers are alternate in a compact spike along the upper stem. Each flower is up to ⅝" wide and has a small, pointed, green or purplish bract at its base and a short-stalked tubular ovary topped by 3 petal-like, purple sepals. The central sepal is flanked by 2 similar but minutely fringed petals, while the 2 side sepals are strongly bent backward along the ovary. Under this is a lower lip deeply divided into 3 segments with coarsely and irregularly fringed tips and a curving tubular spur underneath.

Bloom Season: Late spring–midsummer.

Habitat/Range: Frequent in wet open sites in marshes, wet meadows, moist thickets, open swamps and woods, stream banks, sandy shores, and wet pastures; throughout the region.

Comments: A large-flowered variety, *P. grandiflora*, is sometimes considered a separate species. It occurs throughout the region.

SHOWY ORCHIS
Orchis spectabilis
Orchid Family (Orchidaceae)

Description: A beautiful, early spring wildflower, typically blooming before trees are fully leafed. Each plant has a single stout stem to 10" tall, with a pair of shiny, fleshy basal leaves that are broadly rounded and up to 7" long. Alternating along the upper part of the stem are up to 10 flowers, each with an upright leafy bract at its base. Each narrow flower is ¾" long and has a distinctly hooded, two-toned appearance. The upper part of the flower, composed of 3 petal-like sepals and 2 smaller petals, is pinkish purple. The lower lip is white with crinkled edges, a blunt tip, and a stout tubular spur projecting downward from the base.

Bloom Season: Midspring–late spring.

Habitat/Range: Occasional in moist to dryish woods, shaded ravines, and along stream banks; in the southern half of the region, but generally not north of the latitude of Lake Superior and rarer eastward.

Showy Orchis

Beech Drops

BEECH DROPS
Epifagus virginiana
Broom Rape Family (Orobanchaceae)

Description: Brownish plant usually less than 15" tall, with several upright branches in the lower half. The plant lacks the green chlorophyll necessary for food production and is parasitic on the roots of beech trees. The leaves are reduced to tiny, pointed, alternate scales up to ⅛" long. Flowers are alternate along the upper part of the plant. Each flower has a small cuplike calyx with 5 triangular lobes. The upper flowers, which are sterile, have a tubular corolla about ⅜" long. It is pale with brownish purple streaks or spots and has 4 shallow lobes at the tip. The lower flowers, which are fertile, have a tiny caplike corolla that falls soon after appearing.

Bloom Season: Late summer–early fall.

Habitat/Range: Common in moist or rich woods where beech trees are present; throughout most of the region west to Wisconsin.

KEITH BOARD

One-flowered Broom Rape

ONE-FLOWERED BROOM RAPE
Orobanche uniflora
Broom Rape Family (Orobanchaceae)

Description: Unbranched, whitish to pale violet plant to 6" tall and covered with fine hairs. This species lacks the green chlorophyll necessary for food production and is parasitic on the roots of other plants. Each leafless stem is topped by a single upright to nodding, curved flower ⅜–1" long. The flower has 5 pointed calyx lobes and a narrowly tubular, pale violet to whitish corolla with a yellow center and 5 spreading lobes at the mouth.

Bloom Season: Late spring–midsummer.

Habitat/Range: Occasional and sporadic from year to year, in thickets, woods, and even grassy areas; throughout the region.

Comments: Asters and goldenrods are said to be the preferred host plants.

BLUE PHLOX
Phlox divaricata
Phlox Family (Polemoniaceae)

Description: Plant to 1½' tall, with finely hairy stems often horizontal at their bases. The dark green opposite leaves are smooth edged, stalkless, and up to 2" long and ¾" wide at flowering. They have pointed tips and rounded to slightly clasping bases. Flowers occur in rounded, branched clusters at the tops of the stems. Each flower is 1" wide and has 5 long, narrow, pointed calyx lobes and a narrow, tubular, blue corolla flaring at the mouth into 5 spreading, narrow-based, broadly rounded to slightly notched lobes.

Bloom Season: Midspring–late spring.

Habitat/Range: Frequent in moist hardwood forests in the southern third of the region from southwestern Quebec to central Minnesota.

DON KURZ

Blue Phlox

FLOWERING WINTERGREEN
Polygala paucifolia
Milkwort Family (Polygalaceae)

Description: Unbranched plant to 6" tall, with stalked, alternate, smooth-edged, pointed leaves clustered near the top of the stem. Each leaf is 1" long and ½" wide. The lower part of the stem has widely scattered, alternate, scalelike leaves. Typically, 1–3 stalked flowers arise singly at the bases of the upper leaves. Each vivid pink-purple flower is ¾" long and has 3 small pointed sepals and 2 spreading winglike sepals that appear petal-like. There is a tubular central corolla of 3 petals, the lower of which is elaborately fringed at its mouth. This is one of the region's most attractive wildflowers. The plant also produces small underground flowers that never open.

Bloom Season: Midspring–early summer.

Habitat/Range: Occasional in open woods, especially in sandy or loamy soils; throughout most of the region east to New Brunswick.

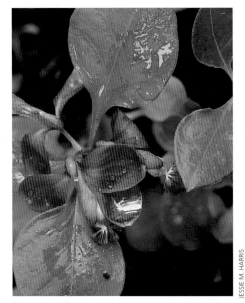

Flowering Wintergreen

JESSIE M. HARRIS

PURPLE MILKWORT
Polygala polygama
Milkwort Family (Polygalaceae)

Description: Small, smooth biennial to 1' tall, with several usually unbranched stems. The leaves are evenly distributed along the stem. They are narrow, alternate, and up to 1¼" long but less than ¼" wide, with tapering bases and pointed to blunt tips. The short-stalked flowers are alternate in a cluster at the top of the stem. Each flower is ⅛" long and has 3 tiny outer sepals, 2 winglike purple sepals that appear petal-like, and a small, 3-petaled, tubular corolla with a fringed tip. There are also underground branches with clusters of pale flowers that never open.

Bloom Season: Late spring–midsummer.

Habitat/Range: Locally common in dry sandy soil in fields, open hardwood stands, and sandy or rocky thickets; mostly in the southern half of the region from Maine to Minnesota.

KENNETH DRITZ

Purple Milkwort

DON KURZ

Pickerel Weed

PICKEREL WEED
Pontederia cordata
Water Hyacinth Family (Pontederiaceae)

Description: Plant to 3' tall, with long, thick-stalked basal leaves and a single similar leaf on the stem. The leaves are variable but typically narrowly triangular and up to 8" long and 3½" wide, with broadly heart-shaped to tapering bases, smooth edges, and blunt tips. Below the dense cylindrical cluster of flowers at the top of the stem is a clasping sheath. Each hairy blue flower is ½" long and has 3 narrow, petal-like lower lobes and an upper 3-lobed segment with 2 bright yellow spots on the middle lobe. There are 3 slender, curved, protruding stamens.

Bloom Season: Summer–early fall.

Habitat/Range: Common in stable shallow water over mud or muck in ponds, lakes, and placid streams; throughout the region.

Comments: The seeds and leaf stalks have been used for food.

BIRD'S-EYE PRIMROSE
Primula mistassinica
Primrose Family (Primulaceae)

Description: Plant typically to 6" tall in flower, or rarely taller, with a single bare stem surrounded by a cluster of basal leaves. These are typically 1" long, though they can occasionally reach 2½" long. They are stalked and have blunt tips, tapering bases, and smooth or shallowly toothed edges. There is sometimes a fine powdery coating on the lower surface of the leaf. Several individually stalked flowers occur in a compact cluster at the top of the stem, with narrow bracts at the base of the cluster. Each flower is ⅜" wide and has a 5-lobed calyx and a tubular, lilac to pinkish corolla with 5 spreading, notched lobes and a bright yellow center.

Bloom Season: Late spring–early summer.

Habitat/Range: Uncommon in damp exposed areas and springy places, usually in alkaline sites; scattered throughout the region, especially on rocky shores around the Great Lakes.

ROBERT TATINA

Bird's-eye Primrose

MOUNTAIN CLEMATIS
Clematis occidentalis
Buttercup Family (Ranunculaceae)

Description: Climbing vine to 6' long, with pairs of opposite, long-stalked leaves that are each divided into 3 stalked leaflets about 2" long. These leaves have irregular teeth or small lobes along the edges. The leaflets usually have broadly rounded to indented bases and pointed tips. At the base of the leaf stalks are narrow bractlike stipules; these are sometimes so close together that they appear whorled. Flowers are single on stalks arising at the bases of the main leaves. Each dangling flower is 1½- 2" long and has 4 thin, pointed, softly hairy, bluish purple petal-like sepals. There are no petals.

Bloom Season: Late spring–early summer.

Habitat/Range: Local in rocky woods, especially in limestone areas, also on riverbanks, rocky slopes, and burned areas; scattered throughout most of the region eastward to Maine and Quebec.

ROBERT TATINA

Mountain Clematis

KEITH BOARD

Round-lobed Hepatica

ROUND-LOBED HEPATICA
Hepatica americana
Buttercup Family (Ranunculaceae)

Description: Hairy, somewhat sprawling plant less than 6" tall, with stalked basal leaves up to 3" wide and nearly as long. The leaves have deeply notched bases, are divided into 3 rounded lobes, and are sometimes mottled with brownish purple. Flowers are single on softly fuzzy stalks, usually with several stalks per plant. Each flower is ¾" wide and has 3 hairy sepal-like bracts, 5–12 pale bluish purple petal-like sepals, and numerous pale stamens. There are no petals.

Bloom Season: Spring.

Habitat/Range: Frequent in well-drained, usually acidic woods; throughout the region.

Comments: Sharp-lobed Hepatica (*H. acutiloba*), a similar plant with somewhat pointed leaf lobes, occurs in shaded, mostly alkaline soils in the southern part of the region from Quebec to Minnesota. Both plants are also called Liverleaf because the lobed leaves were thought to resemble the lobed human liver.

LEE A. CASEBERE

Water Avens

MARSH CINQUEFOIL
Potentilla palustris
Rose Family (Rosaceae)

Description: Erect or sprawling, slightly shrubby, hairy plant with reddish stems up to 2' long. The bluish green leaves have evenly toothed, stalkless leaflets up to 2–3" long that are pale beneath and widest near the middle. They taper abruptly to stalkless bases and blunt or pointed tips. The top 3 leaflets arise at the end of the leaf stalk, below which are 1–2 additional pairs of leaflets. The base of the leaf stalk sheaths the stem. Flowers are scattered along a stalk with small leaves that are simple or have 3 leaflets. The individually stalked, reddish purple flowers are just under 1" wide and have 5 erect triangular sepals alternating with 5 small narrow bracts, above which are 5 smaller rounded petals, numerous stamens, and a conical center.

Bloom Season: Late spring–midsummer.

Habitat/Range: Common in saturated open or shaded sites in or adjacent to quiet water, in bogs, floating mats, ponds and lakeshores, and swamps; throughout the region.

WATER AVENS
Geum rivale
Rose Family (Rosaceae)

Description: Plant typically less than 15" tall, with long-stalked basal leaves. Each leaf has 3 or 5 main leaflets near the tip of the leaf stalk and a pair of toothed leafy stipules at the base. These leaflets are toothed and widest above the middle. The end leaflet is often 3-lobed. Usually several pairs of smaller bractlike leaflets are scattered along the leaf stalk. The stem leaves get progressively smaller and their stalks shorter toward the top of the stalk and are sometimes simple and unlobed. Typically, several long-stalked flowers grow at the top of the stem. Each flower is ½–1" wide and has 5 narrow, pointed, purple sepals and 5 slightly shorter, pale yellow petals surrounding numerous stamens and a rounded center that develops into a bristly oval head.

Bloom Season: Late spring–midsummer.

Habitat/Range: Common in a variety of wet, usually open sites in bogs, marshes, fens, wet meadows, shores, and open conifer swamps; throughout the region.

Comments: The purplish, fragrant roots have been used to make a cocoa like beverage, and the plant is also called Chocolate Root. North American Indians used the root medicinally.

ROBERT TATINA

Marsh Cinquefoil

FLOWERING RASPBERRY
Rubus odoratus
Rose Family (Rosaceae)

Description: Elongate, branched, sprawling shrub to 6' tall, with abundant gland-tipped, purple bristles on the upper stems and branches. The leaves are alternate and up to 10" wide, usually with 3–5 broadly triangular lobes that have sharply and irregularly toothed edges. Striking pinkish purple flowers grow in loosely branched, few-flowered clusters at the end of the branches. Each flower is up to 2" wide and has 5 sepals that abruptly taper to long-pointed tips, 5 rounded petals, and numerous pale stamens. The large red raspberry-like fruits are dry and almost tasteless.

Bloom Season: Summer.

Habitat/Range: Common in moist thickets, along woodland edges, and sometimes also cultivated and escaping; in the eastern part of the region west to Michigan.

Flowering Raspberry

BLUETS
Hedyotis caerulea
Bedstraw Family (Rubiaceae)

Description: Smooth delicate plant typically 6" tall or less, often with several slender stems rising from a cluster of basal leaves. These leaves are spoon shaped and less than ½" long. On each stem are a few pairs of small, bractlike, opposite leaves. The stems are usually branched in the upper half, with a single flower at the top of each upright branch. Each flower is ⅜" wide and has 4 tiny pointed sepals and a pale blue tubular corolla with a yellow center and 4 pointed, spreading lobes.

Bloom Season: Midspring–early fall.

Habitat/Range: Occasional in sandy, often moist areas in fields and meadows in the eastern part of the region, particularly southward, and rarely west to Wisconsin.

Comments: Long-leaved Bluets (*H. longifolia*) has leafy stems with evenly narrow main leaves mostly more than ½" long, as well as dense branching clusters of ¼"-wide whitish or pinkish flowers. It occurs in dry acidic woods throughout most of the region.

Bluets

JESSIE M. HARRIS

Pitcher Plant

PITCHER PLANT
Sarracenia purpurea
Pitcher Plant Family (Sarraceniaceae)

Description: A sprawling cluster of unusual tubular basal leaves and bare, stout flowering stems up to 2' tall, with a single nodding flower atop each stem. The leaves are up to 8" long and usually strongly marked with purple; they are inflated, fluid-filled tubes with an irregular wing along the length and a narrow hooded mouth. Each flower is up to 3" wide and has 3 or 4 small bracts flanking 5 broad, thick, purplish green sepals, each about 1½" long. There are 5 deep reddish, papery petals up to 2" long that fall off soon after the flower opens. Inside the flower is a conspicuous stalked, 5-sided disk up to 3" wide surrounded by yellow-tipped stamens.

Bloom Season: Late spring–midsummer.

Habitat/Range: Common in saturated sphagnum mats in bogs, tamarack swamps, and peaty areas, in both acidic and alkaline wetlands; throughout the region.

Comments: The leaves have downward-pointing hairs on the inside. Insects enter the mouth of the plant and are trapped by the hairs, then drown in the watery leaf fluid, releasing nutrients to feed the plant. This is the provincial flower of Newfoundland.

PURPLE FALSE FOXGLOVE
Agalinis purpurea
Snapdragon Family (Scrophulariaceae)

Description: Annual to 3' tall, with horizontal, opposite, almost needlelike leaves. These are up to 1½" long but typically ¹⁄₁₆" wide. Flowers grow singly on short stout stalks above the upper leaf bases, so 2 flowers are associated with a leaf pair. Each spreading, cone-shaped flower is 1" wide and has a tiny cuplike calyx with 5 triangular teeth and a hairy purple corolla with 5 broadly rounded, spreading, hairy lobes.

Bloom Season: Midsummer–late summer.

Habitat/Range: Frequent in moist acidic or alkaline seeps in sandy or peaty areas, bogs, and along shores; throughout the region.

Comments: Several purple-flowered false foxgloves occur in the region. Another common species, Slender False Foxglove (*A. tenuifolia*), has long slender flower stalks and occurs throughout the region except in eastern Canada.

JESSIE M. HARRIS

Purple False Foxglove

Monkey Flower

ROBERT TATINA

MONKEY FLOWER
Mimulus ringens
Snapdragon Family (Scrophulariaceae)

Description: Angular-stemmed plant to 3' tall, with stalkless opposite leaves up to 4" long and 1" wide. The leaves have pointed tips, tapering bases, and small low teeth along the edges. Flowers grow singly on long stalks at the bases of the upper leaves. Each flower is 1" long and has a 5-toothed, tubular calyx and a tubular blue corolla with ruffled edges on the spreading, 3-lobed lower lip and upright, 2-lobed upper lip. The flowers have a yellowish center.

Bloom Season: Summer.

Habitat/Range: Common in wet places in marshes, woods, swamps, and along muddy shores; throughout the region.

American Brooklime

AMERICAN BROOKLIME

Veronica americana

Snapdragon Family (Scrophulariaceae)

Description: Weak, somewhat sprawling, smooth plant with stems up to 2' long and commonly rooting along their length. The leaves are short-stalked, opposite, and up to 3" long but seldom more than 1" wide. They have broad bases, toothed edges, and mostly blunt tips. Slender-stalked flowers are alternate along the upper stems and short side branches. Each flower is ¼" wide and has a 4-lobed calyx and a corolla deeply divided into 4 broad, nearly separate lobes, with a tiny bract under each flower.

Bloom Season: Late spring–summer.

Habitat/Range: Frequent along spring runs, brooks, shores, and in shaded cool swamps and muddy seeps; throughout the region.

Comments: The leaves have reportedly been used in salads. Several other semiaquatic speedwells occur in the region, including Marsh Speedwell (*V. scutellata*), which has narrow stalkless leaves less than ½" wide, and Water Speedwell (*V. anagallis-aquatica*), which has stalkless leaves mostly more than ½" wide.

BLUE VERVAIN

Verbena hastata

Vervain Family (Verbenaceae)

Description: Slender plant to 6' tall, with grooved angular stems and opposite leaves. These leaves are short stalked and up to 7" long and 2" wide, with pointed tips and coarsely toothed edges. The main leaves sometimes have 2 small, toothed lobes near their bases. Many upright spikes of small bluish flowers occur in an open cluster at the top of the plant. Each flower is ³/₁₆" wide and has a tiny, 5-toothed, hairy calyx and a 5-lobed, bluish purple corolla.

Bloom Season: Late spring–early fall.

Habitat/Range: Common in open marshy areas, wet pastures, moist ditches, open wet thickets, and along shores; throughout the region.

Comments: Both North American Indians and early American physicians used the leaves to prepare medicines for internal ailments.

Blue Vervain

Dog Violet

DOG VIOLET
Viola conspersa
Violet Family (Violaceae)

Description: Smooth plant to 8" tall, with several leafy stems and a cluster of basal leaves. The leaves are stalked, nearly round, and up to 1½" long. They have shallow heart-shaped bases, round to bluntly pointed tips, and low teeth along the edges. The stem leaves are alternate and have a pair of coarsely toothed, bractlike stipules at the base of the stalk. There are a few flowers on slender nodding stalks at the bases of the upper leaf stalks. Each flower stalk has a pair of tiny bracts. Each flower is ½" wide and has 5 narrow, pointed sepals and 5 pale bluish purple petals marked with fine dark lines. The 2 side petals are hairy on the inside, and the lower petal is prolonged at the base into a spur up to ¼" long.

Bloom Season: Midspring–early summer.

Habitat/Range: Frequent in moist woods, swamps, and shaded floodplains; throughout the region.

Comments: Two other leafy-stemmed violets with blue flowers occur in the region. Hook-Spurred Violet (*V. adunca*) occurs in dry woods and exposed areas. It has deep bluish purple flowers and finely hairy leaves. The Long-Spurred Violet (*V. rostrata*) has a spur on its lower petal that is nearly ½" long, and its side petals have no hairs. It occurs in dry or moist woods from Wisconsin to New England and Quebec.

KENNETH DRITZ

Marsh Blue Violet

MARSH BLUE VIOLET
Viola cucullata
Violet Family (Violaceae)

Description: Smooth plant to 10" tall, with several basal leaves and a few leafless flower stalks that are typically taller than the leaves. The leaves, which are stalked, are about 1½" long at flowering time, but by summer some leaves may be 4" long and nearly as wide. The leaves have rounded heart-shaped bases, pointed tips, and small teeth along the edges. Each flower stalk has a pair of tiny bracts near the middle and a single nodding flower at the tip. Each flower is ¾" wide and has 5 pointed sepals and 5 blue-purple petals marked with darker lines and pale bases. The 2 side petals are densely covered with knobby hairs on the inside near the base, and the bottom of the lower petal is prolonged into a short spur.

Bloom Season: Midspring–early summer.

Habitat/Range: Common in saturated, typically shaded sites in bogs, fens, marshes, seeps, and along shores; throughout the region.

Comments: Several other blue-flowered violets with leafless flower stems occur in the region. They can be difficult to distinguish from one another. Four of the most common and widely distributed are mentioned here. Arrow-leaved Violet (*V. sagittata*) has narrow elongate leaves with coarse teeth or lobes at the base. It occurs in sandy open areas, mostly in the eastern half of the region. Great-spurred Violet (*V. selkirkii*) has a well-developed spur at the base of the lower petal, no hairs on the insides of the side petals, and lobes at the base of the leaf that often touch or overlap. It occurs in rich, usually deciduous woods. Downy Blue Violet (*V. sororia*) has hairy, blunt-tipped leaves that are mostly broader than they are long. Its flower stalks are not much taller than the leaves. It occurs in woods, thickets, and shaded lawns throughout the region. Northern Bog Violet (*V. nephrophylla*) is similar to Downy Blue Violet, but it has smooth leaves and occurs in mostly alkaline sites in fens, swamps, and along shores.

PINK AND RED FLOWERS

Dragon's Mouth

JESSIE M. HARRIS

Included here are wildflowers ranging from pale pinkish white to vivid magenta or red. Pink is difficult to distinguish from some shades of purple, and many pale pink flowers can have white forms, so check those color sections, too.

ROBERT TATINA

Spreading Dogbane

SPREADING DOGBANE
Apocynum androsaemifolium
Dogbane Family (Apocynaceae)

Description: Bushy plant to 4' tall, without a well-defined main stalk. The plant has milky sap and stalked opposite leaves at well-spaced intervals along the usually reddish stems. The leaves are hairy beneath and up to 4" long and 2½" wide, with smooth edges, rounded bases, and bluntly pointed tips. The individually stalked flowers occur in open clusters at the branch tips. Each nodding or spreading bell-shaped pink flower is ⅜" long and has 5 small triangular calyx lobes and a corolla with 5 spreading triangular lobes. The inside of the corolla often has reddish markings. The fruits are paired dangling pods about 4–5" long and ⅛" wide.

Bloom Season: Summer.

Habitat/Range: Locally abundant in open to lightly shaded, well-drained sites in thickets, old fields, open sandy woods, and along woodland edges, especially common after fire or light disturbance; throughout the region.

Comments: North American Indians used the tough, fibrous stems to make cordage. Dogbane leaves are poisonous, but the roots have been used medicinally.

SWAMP MILKWEED

Asclepias incarnata
Milkweed Family (Asclepiadaceae)

Description: Plant typically 3–6' tall, with stout leafy stems and milky white sap. The opposite leaves are on short stalks, grow up to 6" long but seldom more than 1½" wide, and taper to pointed tips and blunt bases. Stems are branched near the top, with one or more flower clusters at the tips of the branches. Each cluster is a flattened to shallowly rounded head of individually stalked purple to reddish pink flowers; these are often whitish at the center. Each flower is less than ¼" wide and has 5 tiny, pale, backward-pointing sepals hidden by 5 curved petals that angle downward. Each petal flanks an erect pink hood ending in a protruding horn. The paired narrow seed pods are up to 4" long and taper at both ends.

Bloom Season: Summer.

Habitat/Range: Common in both acidic and alkaline water in wet open areas, marshes, beaver meadows, shores, wet thickets, wet pastures, and less commonly shaded swamps; throughout the region.

Comments: The roots were used medicinally by the Chippewa people.

Swamp Milkweed

ROBERT TATINA

SWAMP THISTLE

Cirsium muticum
Aster Family (Asteraceae)

Description: Coarse biennial thistle to 8' tall with alternate leaves up to 1' long. The leaves have numerous pointed lobes and spine-tipped teeth along the edges. The stems have long cobwebby hairs but no spines. Flower heads are on individual stalks at the top of the stem branches. Each head is 1–1½" wide and has an overlapping series of narrow, spineless, hairy, sepal-like bracts cupping a dense cluster of narrow, tubular, purplish pink flowers. Each flower has 5 slender lobes and 2 protruding, threadlike style branches.

Bloom Season: Midsummer–fall.

Habitat/Range: Locally common in swamps, bogs, fens, and wet thickets; throughout the region.

Comments: This native wetland thistle should not be confused with weedy thistles from Eurasia that have spiny heads and/or stems. Another native thistle common in dry upland sites, Pasture Thistle (*C. pumilum,* including *C. hillii*), has pinkish purple flower heads that are 1–3" wide, as well as spine-tipped, sepal-like bracts and spineless stems.

LEE A. CASEBERE

Swamp Thistle

ROBERT TATINA

Marsh Fleabane

MARSH FLEABANE
Erigeron philadelphicus
Aster Family (Asteraceae)

Description: This hairy short-lived perennial sometimes grows as an annual or biennial. It has stems up to 3' tall that are unbranched below the middle. The stem leaves are alternate, up to 3" long and 1" wide, and they clasp the stem at their bases. The basal leaves are usually larger and are often toothed or have small lobes along the edges. Flower heads are in branched leafy clusters on the upper part of the stems. Each head is up to 1" wide and has a series of sepal-like bracts and at least 120 pink to whitish, bristle-shaped rays that look like narrow petals. These surround a central disk of tiny, yellow, 5-lobed, tubular flowers.

Bloom Season: Midspring–summer.

Habitat/Range: Frequent in moist, open or shaded areas, in meadows and low woods and along stream banks, springy slopes, and road-sides; throughout the region, but sporadic in the extreme north and east.

Comments: A stout, more compact relative with mostly basal leaves, Robin's Plantain (*E. pulchellus*), occurs in similar habitats mostly in the southern half of the region. Its flower heads are mostly more than 1" wide, with 50–100 rays.

SPOTTED JOE PYE WEED
Eupatorium maculatum
Aster Family (Asteraceae)

Description: Plant to 6' tall, with purple or purple-spotted stems that are unbranched below the flowers and finely hairy in the upper half. Along the stem are widely spaced whorls of 4–6 coarsely toothed leaves, each up to 9" long and 3" wide, with pointed tips and narrow bases. The abundant flower heads are in a nearly flat, branched cluster at the top of the plant. Each narrow head is $^{1}/_{3}$" tall and has small sepal-like bracts and 8–22 small, pinkish purple, 5-lobed tubular flowers that have protruding, threadlike, purple styles.

Bloom Season: Midsummer–early fall.

Habitat/Range: Common in wet open sites, including swamps, marshes, fens, bogs, beaver meadows, wet pastures, and along streams and shores; throughout the region.

DON KURZ

Spotted Joe Pye Weed

Purple Rock Cress

PURPLE ROCK CRESS

Arabis divaricarpa
Mustard Family (Brassicaceae)

Description: Slender, unbranched stems to 4' tall and mostly smooth except for some hairs near the base. Stalkless, alternate, gray-green leaves clasp the stems at their bases and have scalloped, slightly downturned edges. The leaves are smooth and ¾–2" long, with 2 small backward-pointing lobes at their bases. The basal leaves, which usually wither before flowering, are wider and have small star-shaped hairs on both surfaces. The alternate, individually stalked flowers are closely clustered at the top of the stems but become more separated in fruit as the stem elongates. Each flower is ¼" long and has 4 sepals and 4 pinkish or rarely white petals. The widely spreading, podlike fruits are up to 3" long and ¹⁄₁₆" thick.

Bloom Season: Late spring–midsummer.

Habitat/Range: Locally common in sandy or rocky well-drained soil in open woods, clearings, along woodland edges, ledges, bluffs, and dry rocky shorelines; scattered from Quebec and Vermont westward.

Cardinal Flower

JESSIE M. HARRIS

CARDINAL FLOWER
Lobelia cardinalis
Bellflower Family (Campanulaceae)

Description: Stout, usually unbranched plant to 4' tall, with milky sap and short-stalked alternate leaves. The leaves are up to 7" long and 2" wide and taper evenly from the middle to both ends. They have teeth and tiny white bumps along their edges. The upper leaves are smaller and often stalkless. At the top of the stem is a dense, alternately arranged cluster of individually stalked flowers, each with a narrow bract at the base. Each vivid scarlet flower is 1–1½" long and has a small cuplike calyx with 5 needlelike tips, as well as a tubular corolla with 2 drooping upper lobes, a prominent, spreading 3-lobed lower lip, and a protruding, red central column of stamens and a style.

Bloom Season: Midsummer–early fall.

Habitat/Range: Occasional in moist, often shaded sites in swamps, wet woods, thickets, and along streams and shores; in most of the region from New Brunswick and Maine to southeastern Minnesota, but more common southward.

Comments: The plants are pollinated by ruby-throated hummingbirds.

TWINFLOWER
Linnaea borealis
Honeysuckle Family (Caprifoliaceae)

Description: This delicate, miniature evergreen shrub has creeping main stems and widely spaced, upright, leafy branches up to 4" tall. The shiny opposite leaves have a few low teeth in the upper half and are typically ¾" long and nearly as wide; they taper to short stalks. A slender hairy stalk at the top of the branch has a pair of small bracts, above which are a pair of nodding flowers on slender individual stalks. Each pink flower is ½" long and has 2 tiny bracts and a small green ovary at the base, topped by a minute calyx with 5 threadlike lobes and a funnel-shaped corolla with 5 shallow, pale-tipped lobes. The inside of the flower is hairy, with 4 short stamens and a slender protruding style.

Bloom Season: Late spring–midsummer.

Habitat/Range: Common in woods, boggy swamps, open moist heaths, and on mountain slopes, often under conifers and in moss mats or needle litter; throughout the region.

Twinflower

ROBERT TATINA

MARSH ST. JOHN'S WORT
Triadenum fraseri
St. John's Wort Family (Clusiaceae)

Description: Slender, few-branched plant to 1½' tall, with thin, opposite, pale green leaves up to 2" long and ¾" wide. These leaves are covered with tiny translucent dots that are visible when the leaf is held up to strong light. Each leaf has a tapering to rounded or slightly clasping base with a very short stalk; the leaf tip is blunt. Short branches with small leaves often grow at the base of the main leaves. Flowers occur in small clusters at the branch tips. Each short-stalked flower has 5 blunt sepals, often marked with red, and 5 salmon to pinkish petals, each less than ¼" long. The flowers usually appear to be in bud and seldom open fully.

Bloom Season: Summer.

Habitat/Range: Frequent in bogs, marshes, swamps, wet thickets, and along shores; throughout the region.

Marsh St. John's Wort

Comments: A closely related species occurring mostly in the southern part of the region, *T. virginicum* has larger pointed sepals and larger petals.

BOG ROSEMARY
Andromeda glaucophylla
Heath Family (Ericaceae)

Description: Small shrub to 2' tall, with alternate, bluish green, evergreen leaves. The leaves are pointed at the tips and are typically 2" long and ¼" wide, with a dense layer of small white hairs and a single prominent raised vein on the lower side. The smooth edges of the leaves are rolled downward along their entire length. The individually stalked flowers occur in small clusters at the tops of the stems. Each flower is ¼" long and has a small 5-lobed calyx and an urn-shaped corolla with 5 small, spreading, triangular lobes at the narrowed mouth. The flowers are usually pale pink, or sometimes white.

Bloom Season: Midspring–early summer.

Habitat/Range: Locally common in open to lightly shaded bogs, often growing in floating sphagnum mats, and also reported from fens; throughout the region.

Comments: North American Indians brewed a tea from the leaves, but the plant contains toxins.

Bog Rosemary

KEITH BOARD

Bearberry

BEARBERRY

Arctostaphylos uva-ursi
Heath Family (Ericaceae)

Description: Dwarf evergreen shrub usually less than 6" tall and often forming an extensive mat. There are abundant leafy branches along the creeping main stems. The leaves are thick, leathery, alternate, and shiny; they average 1" long and ¼" wide and have smooth edges that curve to short stalks and pointed or rounded tips. Compact clusters of a few individually stalked flowers occur at the tips of the branches, with small bracts at the bases of the stalks. Each pink to whitish flower is ¼" long and has 5 small blunt sepals and a vase-shaped corolla with 5 small rounded lobes at its narrowed mouth. The fruits are round, bright red berries that are ¼–⅜" wide.

Bloom Season: Spring.

Habitat/Range: Locally frequent in open well-drained sandy or rocky areas, often in harsh conditions or exposed sites on dunes, open ridges, bluffs, open woods, barrens, and along shores; throughout the region.

Comments: North American Indians used the leaves like tobacco and to prepare medicines. The berries are edible but tasteless. This plant is also called Kinnikinnick.

Sheep Laurel

JESSIE M. HARRIS

SHEEP LAUREL
Kalmia angustifolia
Heath Family (Ericaceae)

Description: Upright-branched shrub to 3' tall, with narrow, smooth-edged, stalked evergreen leaves that are opposite or in whorls of 3 or 4. These leaves are up to 2" long and ¾" wide, but usually narrower, with a prominent, raised central vein on the lower side. Flowers are in compact clusters on the sides of the main branches. Each stalked, reddish pink flower is up to ½" wide and has 5 narrowly triangular sepals and a round, shallowly 5-lobed corolla with 10 small saclike pouches on the inside, as well as 10 spreading central stamens and a protruding erect style.

Bloom Season: Late spring–midsummer.

Habitat/Range: Frequent in moist, acidic, sandy soil in open to lightly shaded areas in sand flats, open woods, and along bog margins; through the region west to Lake Michigan.

Comments: The leaves are poisonous but were used medicinally in small doses by North American Indians. A related species, Mountain Laurel (*K. latifolia*), occurs in the southern part of the region from New York and Ontario eastward, particularly in mountainous areas. It is a large shrub more than 3' tall with alternate leaves mostly more than 2" long and pale lavender flowers at the tops of the branches.

BOG LAUREL
Kalmia polifolia
Heath Family (Ericaceae)

Description: Low shrub usually less than 2' tall, with few branches and narrow, pointed, opposite, stalkless leaves up to 1½" long and ⅜" wide. The leathery leaves have smooth edges that turn downward, forming a raised rim around the pale whitish lower surface, which has a prominent raised central vein. Flowers are on slender upright stalks in compact flattened clusters at the tops of the stems. At the base of each flower stalk are small leafy bracts. Each flower is ⅝" wide and has 5 small pointed sepals and a round, pinkish purple corolla with 5 broadly triangular lobes. There are 10 small saclike pouches on the inside of the corolla, 10 slender spreading stamens, and a slender upright style.

Bloom Season: Midspring–late spring.

Habitat/Range: Common in sunny, saturated sphagnum mats in bogs and open tamarack swamps; throughout the region.

ROBERT TATINA

Bog Laurel

JESSIE M. HARRIS

Wild Azalea

WILD AZALEA
Rhododendron maximum
Heath Family (Ericaceae)

Description: Shrub up to 4' tall, with alternate, stout-stalked, thick evergreen leaves up to 8" long. The leaves are often clustered near the ends of the branches, and they have pointed tips, smooth edges, and tapering bases. Flowers are in dense heads at the end of the branches; the flower stalks are covered with tiny sticky hairs. Each flower is 1¾" wide, with 5 small sepals; a pink or white corolla deeply divided into 5 rounded, somewhat cupped, petal-like lobes; 10 slender stamens of unequal length; and a slender style. The inside of the corolla is usually spotted with yellow on the upper lobes.

Bloom Season: Early summer–midsummer.

Habitat/Range: Rare in moist woods from New England and southern Ontario southward, and formerly in Nova Scotia.

Comments: The plant is toxic if eaten, but it has been used in poultices to relieve pain.

Lowbush Blueberry

ROBERT TATINA

LOWBUSH BLUEBERRY
Vaccinium angustifolium
Heath Family (Ericaceae)

Description: Branched shrub to about 1' tall, with pointed, stalkless, alternate, finely toothed leaves, each up to about 1" long and ⅜" wide. Individually stalked flowers occur in clusters of 2–8 on short side branches. Each flower is ¼" long and has a small cuplike calyx with 5 triangular lobes and a cylindrical white or pinkish corolla with 5 small, curving, triangular lobes at the mouth. The fruits are deep blue berries about ¼" wide.

Bloom Season: Spring–summer.

Habitat/Range: Common in well-drained, acidic, sandy or rocky sites in woods and barrens; throughout the region.

Comments: This is one of the most commonly cultivated blueberries in the region; both wild and cultivated plants are highly variable. Several other species of blueberry occur in the region. Among the more common and widespread

Lowbush Blueberry

JESSIE M. HARRIS

are Velvetleaf Blueberry (*V. myrtilloides*), which has dense velvety hairs on its stems and leaves and mostly smooth leaf edges, and Highbush Blueberry (*V. corymbosum*), a much taller plant with leaves more than 1½" long.

JESSIE M. HARRIS

Large Cranberry

LARGE CRANBERRY

Vaccinium macrocarpon
Heath Family (Ericaceae)

Description: This dwarf, creeping evergreen shrub has slender stems and upright branches up to 6" tall. The small, smooth, alternate, leathery leaves are almost stalkless and seldom more than ½" long, with mostly rounded tips. The smooth edges of the leaves turn slightly downward, forming a rim around the pale lower surface. Near the middle of the stem branches are zones of 2–6 smaller leaves with longer, thread-like, arching flower stalks at their bases. Each stalk has a pair of small green bracts above the middle and a single flower at the tip. Each flower is ⅜" wide and resembles a shooting star, with 4 tiny sepals, a pink corolla deeply divided into 4 narrow, widely spreading to backward-pointing lobes, and 8 erect stamens. The fruits are slightly oval, red to dark maroon berries up to ¾" long.

Bloom Season: Late spring–midsummer.

Habitat/Range: Common in wet acidic sites in bogs, mossy or sandy depressions, and along mossy shores, and sometimes in dry acidic sands; throughout the region.

Comments: This is the commonly cultivated, commercial cranberry; the wild fruits are equally tasty. A similar species, Small Cranberry (*V. oxycoccos*), occurs in wet acidic sites in the region. It has smaller fruits, pointed leaves that are strongly downturned at the edges and whitened beneath, and flowers at the tops of the stems. The pair of bracts on the flower stalk of Small Cranberry is usually reddish and often attached below the middle of the stalk.

BARE-STEMMED TICK TREFOIL
Desmodium nudiflorum
Bean Family (Fabaceae)

Description: Plant to 2' tall, with the stems branched at or just below ground level. One branch has a whorl of stalked compound leaves at the tip, and the other stem is taller and leafless, with alternate, short-stalked flowers along the upper half. The leaves are divided into 3 smooth-edged leaflets, each up to 3½" long, with broadly rounded bases. Each pink flower is ¼–¹/₃" long and has a small cuplike calyx with 4 shallow unequal teeth, a broadly rounded and spreading upper petal, and 2 smaller side petals flanking a keel-like lower lip. The fruits are segmented flattened pods that detach and cling to clothing.

Bloom Season: Summer.

Habitat/Range: Occasional in rich or rocky woods in light shade, usually under hardwoods; in the southern part of the region from Maine to southeastern Minnesota.

Comments: Several other tick trefoils occur in the region. All have stalked alternate leaves along the stem; each leaf is divided into 3 leaflets. Among the more common species are Pointed Tick Trefoil (*D. glutinosum*), which has pointed, broadly rounded leaflets, and Showy Tick Trefoil (*D. canadense*), which has showy flowers more than ¹/₃" long.

Bare-stemmed Tick Trefoil

ALLEGHENY VINE
Adlumia fungosa
Fumitory Family (Fumariaceae)

Description: This unusual biennial vine has stalked compound leaves divided by threes into many segments, each typically up to ¾" long and toothed or lobed. During the first year, the plant produces a cluster of leaves. In the second year, a vining leafy stem up to 10' long, with twining leaf stalks, climbs on other plants. There are branched clusters of dangling, individually stalked flowers. Each pinkish purple flower is ⅝" long and has 2 small sepals that fall off early. Two large outer petals and 2 small inner petals join to form a spongy tubular flower with an inflated base and a narrowed mouth with 4 expanded lobes.

Bloom Season: Late spring–summer.

Habitat/Range: Uncommon and sporadic in rocky or sandy open woods, clearings, and along bluffs and ledges, often appearing after a fire; scattered from Quebec and Maine westward, and sometimes escaped from cultivation elsewhere.

Allegheny Vine

Pink Corydalis

PINK CORYDALIS
Corydalis sempervirens
Fumitory Family (Fumariaceae)

Description: Smooth, soft biennial to 2½' tall, with alternate, pale bluish green leaves divided into many small leaflets with rounded, feathery lobes. The lower leaves are stalked, while the upper leaves are stalkless or nearly so. Flowers are on slender individual stalks in a leafy-bracted cluster at the ends of the stem branches. Each flower is ⅝" long, and its stalk is attached to the side of the flower above the swollen rounded base. There are two small pointed sepals with irregular edges that are often marked with purple and 4 yellow-tipped, pink petals that appear united except at the spreading, keeled tips. The fruits are narrow, somewhat lumpy pods up to 2" long.

Bloom Season: Midspring–summer.

Habitat/Range: Common in disturbed dry sandy or rocky woods, talus slopes, clearings, and burned areas, often disappearing a few years after disturbance ceases; throughout the region.

Comments: Golden Corydalis (*C. aurea*) is a related species of open sandy or rocky habitats that is uncommon and scattered from New Hampshire and Quebec westward. It is a sprawling plant with bright golden yellow flowers. Both plants are poisonous to livestock.

ROBERT TATINA

Northern Cranesbill

NORTHERN CRANESBILL
Geranium bicknellii
Geranium Family (Geraniaceae)

Description: Branched hairy annual typically to 1' tall, with long-stalked leaves that are opposite or occasionally in whorls of 3. Each leaf is up to 2½" wide and long and deeply divided into usually 5 lobes arranged somewhat like fingers on a hand. The lobes are often further lobed, or they may have coarse blunt teeth. Individually stalked flowers are in pairs at the end of the branches. Each flower is ½" wide and has 5 pointed sepals and 5 lavender-pink, blunt or slightly notched, spreading petals surrounding 10 stamens. The fruits are beaked capsules about ¾" long.

Bloom Season: Midspring–summer.

Habitat/Range: Frequent in well-drained areas in open woods, talus slopes, rocky areas, and disturbed or burned sites; throughout the region.

Comments: Herb Robert (*G. robertianum*) is a related species with leaves that are lobed all the way to their bases, while the leaves of Northern Cranesbill are lobed for about two-thirds of their length. Herb Robert occurs in similar habitats throughout most of the region, westward through Wisconsin. Some experts think some or all local populations of Herb Robert are introduced weeds.

ROBERT TATINA

Wild Geranium

WILD GERANIUM
Geranium maculatum
Geranium Family (Geraniaceae)

Description: Hairy plant to 3' tall, with long-stalked basal leaves up to 5" wide and long. Each leaf is deeply divided like fingers on a hand into 3–7 narrow lobes; the lobes are often further lobed or bluntly toothed. On the upper half of the stem are 1 or 2 pairs of similar but short-stalked opposite leaves. At the top of the stem is a loosely branched cluster of several stalked flowers. Each flower is up to 1½" wide and has 5 hairy pointed sepals; 5 spreading, broadly rounded, purplish pink petals; and 10 stamens.

Bloom Season: Spring–early summer.

Habitat/Range: Locally frequent in rich open woods and thickets, typically under hardwoods; throughout the southern part of the region eastward to Maine and rarely northward.

Comments: North American Indians used the roots to treat skin and mouth ailments.

FALSE DRAGONHEAD
Physostegia virginiana
Mint Family (Lamiaceae)

Description: Square-stemmed plant to 4' tall, with widely separated, stiff, narrow, opposite leaves up to 5" long and 1" wide. The leaves taper to a narrow base and have curving sharp teeth along the edges of the upper half. Short-stalked flowers grow singly at the bases of closely spaced, leaflike bracts along the upper stem. Each flower is ¾–1¼" long and has 5 triangular calyx lobes and a tubular pink corolla that broadens at the tip into a hooded upper lip and a dangling, 3-lobed lower lip often marked with purple spots. The flowers are pliant and can be rotated in different directions around the stem, remaining where they are placed.

Bloom Season: Midsummer–early fall.

Habitat/Range: Occasional in wet sites in marshes, sedge meadows, floodplains, thickets, swamps, and along shores; ranging eastward to Quebec, but sporadic east of the Great Lakes, where many populations may have escaped from cultivation.

JESSIE M. HARRIS

False Dragonhead

DOGMINT
Satureja vulgaris
Mint Family (Lamiaceae)

Description: Hairy, square-stemmed, typically unbranched plants to 2' tall, with stalked opposite leaves. Each leaf is less than 2" long and widest near the base, with pointed tips and sometimes a few low teeth along the edges. Pairs of tiny leaves may form at the bases of the main leaf stalks. Flowers are in compact heads at the tops of the stems and sometimes also at the bases of the upper leaf pairs. Each flower is up to ½" long, with a hairy calyx with 5 needlelike lobes that give the head a bristly appearance, and a pinkish purple 2-lipped tubular corolla with the lower lip divided into 3 lobes.

Bloom Season: Early to midsummer.

Habitat/Range: Common in clearings, open woods, moist shaded areas, and rocky slopes, especially in sandy soil; throughout the region.

Comments: This plant is also native to Europe, and some plants in the southern part of the region may be introduced weeds.

JESSIE M. HARRIS

Dogmint

ROSE MANDARIN
Streptopus roseus
Lily Family (Liliaceae)

Description: Usually branched plant to 2½' tall, with alternate stalkless leaves tapering to bases that slightly clasp the stems. Each leaf is up to 4" long and 1½" wide and has fine parallel veins along its length, a narrow pointed tip, and a line of fine straight hairs along the edges. One or 2 flowers occur on slender dangling stalks at the base of the main leaves. Each pinkish purple flower is ⅜" long and appears tubular, with 6 narrow, pointed, petal-like segments that curve outward at their tips. The fruits are round red berries about ⅜" wide.

Bloom Season: Late spring–early summer.

Habitat/Range: Common in rich, moist sites in woods, white cedar swamps, thickets, and clearings; throughout the region.

Comments: See White Mandarin (p. 194).

ALLISON W. BELL

Rose Mandarin

Painted Trillium

JESSIE M. HARRIS

PAINTED TRILLIUM

Trillium undulatum
Lily Family (Liliaceae)

Description: Smooth unbranched plant to 15" tall, with a single whorl of 3 broad leaves at the top of the stem, under a single stalked flower. The leaves are up to 3½" long and broadly rounded at their short-stalked bases. They taper to long pointed tips and appear more triangular than other trilliums in the region. The elegant flowers are typically 2" wide and have 3 pointed sepals and 3 longer white petals with pink markings in the basal half. Six erect stamens surround a central ovary with 3 narrow stigmas.

Bloom Season: Midspring–early summer.

Habitat/Range: Common in moist woods, often on rich slopes or in ravines; in the eastern half of the region, rarely westward to lower Michigan.

MOUNTAIN WOOD SORREL

Oxalis acetosella
Wood Sorrel Family (Oxalidaceae)

Description: Stalked leaves and longer, single-flowered stalks to 6" tall arise from scaly, root-like, creeping, shallow, underground stems. The leaves are compound, with 3 cloverlike, heart-shaped leaflets at the end of the leaf stalk. Each leaflet is 1" wide. Near the middle of each flower stalk are 2 very tiny bracts. Each flower is 1" wide and has 5 small sepals, 5 white petals marked with fine purplish lines and yellow spots near the base, and 10 pale stamens of alternating lengths. The petals are notched and uneven at the tip. Small flowers are produced on short stalks late in the season, but these do not open.

Bloom Season: Late spring–midsummer.

Habitat/Range: Frequent in cool moist woods, particularly in mossy conifer forests; throughout the region.

Comments: The raw leaves have a pleasantly sour taste and have been used to season salads.

Mountain Wood Sorrel

ALLISON W. BELL

Showy Fireweed

JESSIE M. HARRIS

SHOWY FIREWEED
Epilobium angustifolium
Evening Primrose Family (Onagraceae)

Description: Mostly unbranched plant to 7' tall, with narrow, alternate, smooth-edged or slightly toothed leaves up to 8" long that taper to pointed tips and narrow bases. Individually stalked flowers are alternately arranged in a long cluster along the upper part of the stem. The buds initially are nodding but become spreading or upright when they flower. Each flower is up to 1" wide and has 4 narrow spreading sepals; 4 broadly rounded, narrow-based, magenta petals; 8 protruding pale stamens; and a downward-curving style.

Bloom Season: Summer.

Habitat/Range: Common in moist to dry open or lightly shaded areas, often appearing after disturbance, in burned woods, degraded bogs, thickets, rocky slopes, and along roadsides and woodland edges; throughout the region.

Comments: The greens of young plants have been cooked and eaten. North American Indians used the stem fibers to make thread and fishing nets. Another large-flowered species, Hairy Willow Herb (*E. hirsutum*), is a branched, densely hairy Eurasian weed with mostly opposite leaves and notched petals. It occurs in moist disturbed sites.

Fen Willow Herb

ALBERT BUSSEWITZ/NEW ENGLAND WILDFLOWER SOCIETY

FEN WILLOW HERB
Epilobium leptophyllum
Evening Primrose Family (Onagraceae)

Description: Slender, upright-branched plant to 2½' tall, with short hairs pressed against the stems and leaves. The lower and middle leaves are opposite, while the upper leaves are typically alternate. Each narrow, mostly toothless leaf is up to 2" long and typically ⅛" wide, with a prominent central vein and downturned edges. Many of the main leaves typically have a small leafy branch at their bases. The individually stalked flowers are single at the tops of the stems and at the bases of the main leaves. Each pink to white flower is ¼" wide and has 4 small sepals and 4 spreading notched petals. The fruits are slender upright pods about 2" long; a tuft of tan hairs tops each seed.

Bloom Season: Midsummer–late summer.

Habitat/Range: Locally frequent in bogs, fens, marshes, swamps, springy seeps, and along shores; throughout the region.

Comments: Downy Willow Herb (*E. strictum*) is a similar species with longer spreading hairs and leaves mostly ⅛–¼" wide. It occurs in bogs, marshes, and conifer swamps throughout the region. Marsh Willow Herb (*E. palustre*) also has broader leaves, but with smooth, hairless, upper surfaces; it occurs in bogs mostly in the northern part of the region.

JESSIE M. HARRIS

Dragon's Mouth

DRAGON'S MOUTH
Arethusa bulbosa
Orchid Family (Orchidaceae)

Description: Unbranched, single-flowered plant typically to 1' tall, with a single narrow, upright, pointed, stalkless leaf near the middle of the stem. This leaf is 2–4" long and develops after the plant flowers. A few small, alternate, leafy bracts usually occur along the stem below the leaf. The single showy, pink-purple flower at the top of the stem is up to 2" tall and has 3 erect, petal-like sepals, under which are 2 arching petals above a showy, curved lower lip. This lip is usually mottled with darker purple spots. It has crinkly edges and 3 white or yellow parallel, fringed crests on its inner surface.

Bloom Season: Midspring–early summer.

Habitat/Range: Rare in cool saturated bogs and sphagnum mats and in conifer swamps, often with other orchids; throughout the region.

Comments: This species has become much rarer in recent years and should be protected where it is found.

JESSIE M. HARRIS

Grass Pink Orchid

GRASS PINK ORCHID
Calopogon tuberosus
Orchid Family (Orchidaceae)

Description: Single-stemmed, unbranched plant usually less than 2½' tall, with 1 (rarely 2 or 3) long, grasslike, pointed leaf near the base of the stem. Typically, 3 or more flowers are arranged alternately along the top of the stem. Each vivid magenta-pink flower is 1–1½" wide and has a narrow stalklike ovary at the base. Unlike most orchid flowers, which are twisted so that the prominent lip is at the bottom of the flower, Grass Pink Orchid flowers have the lip at the top. This lip is erect or arching, with narrow sides and a broadly rounded, triangular tip. The inner face of the lip is covered with yellow-tipped, clublike hairs. Below this lip are 3 spreading, petal-like sepals and 2 petals, along with a prominent central column.

Bloom Season: Late spring–midsummer.

Habitat/Range: Occasional in acidic or mineral-rich waters of bogs, swamps, and wet meadows, especially in full sun; throughout the region.

MOCCASIN FLOWER
Cypripedium acaule
Orchid Family (Orchidaceae)

Description: Unbranched plant usually less than 1' tall, often growing in groups, with a pair of basal, pleated, finely hairy, stalkless leaves up to 8" long and 4" wide. At the top of the stem is a single flower with an arching leaflike bract at its base. Each flower has a pink, inflated, slipperlike lip about 2" long that is cleft along the middle. The lip is flanked by a pair of tapering, narrow, twisted petals. Broader, finely hairy, yellowish green to purplish sepals curve above and below the lip.

Bloom Season: Late spring–midsummer.

Habitat/Range: Common in open woods, especially on well-drained sandy or acidic soils, and on mossy hummocks and old stumps in swamps and bogs, often increasing after minor disturbance; throughout the region.

Comments: North American Indians used the roots in a variety of medicines.

ALLISON W. BELL

Moccasin Flower

Showy Lady's Slipper

SHOWY LADY'S SLIPPER
Cypripedium reginae
Orchid Family (Orchidaceae)

Description: Finely hairy plant to 3' tall, with stout, unbranched, leafy stems. Up to 7 alternate, pleated, pale green leaves grow along the stem. Each leaf is up to 10" long and 7" wide, but usually smaller. The leaves are stalkless and taper to rolled, clasping bases that surround the stem. At the top of the stem are 1 to a few spectacular flowers, each with an upright leaflike bract. The strongly inflated, pouchlike slipper is up to 2" long and tinged with deep pink. Two narrow, white, spreading petals flank the slipper, and 2 broader, white, petal-like sepals arch above and below the flower.

Bloom Season: Late spring–early summer.

Habitat/Range: Occasional but locally abundant, in bogs, swampy woods, seepy stream banks, fens, peaty marshes, and tamarack or white-cedar swamps; throughout the region except for parts of the extreme north.

Comments: This, the state flower of Minnesota, is one of the region's most spectacular wildflowers, sometimes occurring in colonies of several hundred. It has suffered from misguided attempts to transplant it—it usually dies, because orchids require a certain type of soil fungus to grow. This plant is sometimes marketed commercially. Insist on proof that the plants have not been dug from the wild before purchasing, and refuse to do business with any nursery that sells plants collected in the wild. Some people experience skin irritation after handling this plant.

One-leaved Orchis

ONE-LEAVED ORCHIS
Orchis rotundifolia
Orchid Family (Orchidaceae)

Description: Single-stemmed, delicate plant usually less than 9" tall, with a single broadly rounded leaf that is typically 2–4" long at the base of the stem. The upper part of the stem has several small alternate flowers, each with a narrow pointed bract at its base. Each flower is ⅝" wide and has a tapering cylindrical ovary topped by 3 pink to whitish petal-like sepals, the lower 2 of which spread widely on either side of the flower. Two smaller, pale pinkish petals lie against the inside of the hooded, arching, upper sepal. Below this is a lower lip with 2 small side lobes and a broad, notched tip. This lip has small, bright purple spots and a short tubular spur arching below.

Bloom Season: Late spring–midsummer.

Habitat/Range: Rare and local in bogs, swamps, and wet conifer forests, often in limey or mineralized waters; throughout the northern parts of the region.

SNAKE-MOUTH ORCHID
Pogonia ophioglossoides
Orchid Family (Orchidaceae)

Description: Single-stemmed plant to 15" tall, with a narrow upright leaf up to 3" long near the middle of the stem and a small upright bract below the single flower at the top of the stem. Both the leaf and the bract are stalkless and clasp the stem at their bases. The vivid pink flower is 1½" wide and has a long narrow ovary topped by 2 petals with somewhat rounded tips, along with 3 longer, narrower, widely spreading, petal-like sepals. At the bottom of the flower is a lip with prominent fringed edges, darker purple mottling, and 3 rows of yellow bristles along the middle of the upper surface.

Bloom Season: Late spring–midsummer.

Habitat/Range: Occasional in bogs, fens, acidic swamps, peaty wetlands, and sometimes in wet open sand; throughout the region.

Comments: Rarely plants will have 2 flowers. The similar Dragon's Mouth (p. 87) has no leaves at flowering time; its flowers are a deeper purple, and they usually bloom earlier.

Snake-mouth Orchid

FIELD MILKWORT
Polygala sanguinea
Milkwort Family (Polygalaceae)

Description: Annual less than 1' tall, with un-branched or few-branched angular stems. The leaves are alternate and up to 1¾" long but only about ⅛" wide, sometimes with nearly micro-scopic teeth along the edges. Flowers grow in short cylindrical clusters at the tops of the stems. Each pinkish purple to whitish flower is ⅛" long and consists of 3 tiny green sepals and 2 larger petal-like sepals flanking a central tube of 3 small petals.

Bloom Season: Late spring–early fall.

Habitat/Range: Occasional in open sandy ar-eas, usually in moist acidic sites but also in dry areas, in fields, meadows, and rocky barrens; throughout the southern half of the region and occasionally northward.

Field Milkwort

HALBERD-LEAVED TEARTHUMB
Polygonum arifolium
Buckwheat Family (Polygonaceae)

Description: Weak sprawling annual to 6' long, with tiny, backward-pointing, prickly bristles on the angular stems. The leaves are alternate, stalked, widely spaced, and strongly arrowhead shaped. The larger leaves have 2 triangular lobes at their broad bases and are up to 6" long and 4" wide, or rarely larger. A bristly, papery sheath surrounds the stem at the base of the leaf stalk. Flowers are in stalked, few-flowered clusters at the bases of the upper leaf stalks. Each flower is $^3/_{16}$" wide and has a pinkish calyx with usually 4 petal-like lobes.

Bloom Season: Midsummer–early fall.

Habitat/Range: Occasional in moist, often shaded sites in wet thickets, swamps, springy areas, and wet depressions; throughout all but the northwestern part of the region.

Halberd-leaved Tearthumb

Water Knotweed

WATER KNOTWEED
Polygonum amphibium
Buckwheat Family (Polygonaceae)

Description: This unbranched, sprawling or floating plant has weak rooting stems and stalked alternate leaves, each with a small papery sheath encircling the stem at the base of the leaf stalk. The leaves are up to 4" long and 1½" wide. They have pale central veins and taper to broadly rounded bases. There are up to 4 stalked, conical clusters of small, densely packed, vivid pink flowers; each cluster is up to 1½" long. Each flower is ⅛" wide and has a pink calyx divided into 5 blunt petal-like lobes. An erect variety of the plant in muddy areas and marshes has thick, fingerlike flower clusters up to 6" long.

Bloom Season: Summer.

Habitat/Range: Common in shallow quiet waters, where the leaves float on the surface; also in bogs, ponds, marshes, lakes, slow streams, and exposed mud flats; throughout the region.

JOINTWEED
Polygonella articulata
Buckwheat Family (Polygonaceae)

Description: This joint-stemmed annual is wiry, often reddish, and usually less than 18" tall. It has upright branches and somewhat rolled, narrow leaves less than ½0" wide and up to ¾" long. The leaves are alternate and widely spaced along the stem. Sometimes smaller leaves arise at the bases of the main stem leaves. The dangling flowers are alternate along the upper part of the stems, and below each flower is a small sheathing bract. Each flower is less than ⅛" wide and has 5 tiny, pinkish or whitish, petal-like sepals and 8 stamens.

Bloom Season: Late summer–fall.

Habitat/Range: Locally frequent in open, sterile, sandy, or rocky areas in barrens, disturbed sites, and open dry woods; from Maine to Minnesota.

KAY YATSKIEVYCH

Jointweed

CAROLINA SPRING BEAUTY
Claytonia caroliniana
Purslane Family (Portulacaceae)

Description: Soft, smooth, single-stemmed plant typically to 6" tall, with a single pair of opposite, usually stalked leaves attached near the middle of the stem. Each leaf is up to 3" long and ¾" wide, with smooth curving edges. Several individually stalked flowers occur along the upper stem. Each flower is typically ¾" wide and has 2 rounded sepals, 5 spreading pink petals marked with darker pink lines, and 5 stamens.

ALLISON W. BELL

Carolina Spring Beauty

Bloom Season: Spring.

Habitat/Range: Common in rich woods, especially under conifers; throughout the region, especially northward.

Comments: A related species, Spring Beauty (*C. virginica*), has narrow stalkless leaves typically more than 2½" long but usually less than ⅓" wide. It occurs mostly in the southern half of the region and often grows in moist areas. Both of these species have small potato-like bulbs that have been used as food by North American Indians and pioneers.

JESSIE M. HARRIS

Pipsissewa

PIPSISSEWA
Chimaphila umbellata
Shinleaf Family (Pyrolaceae)

Description: This somewhat shrubby evergreen plant usually is less than 10" tall. It has a few whorls of 4–6 shiny, thick, dark green, almost succulent leaves. These leaves are up to 2½" long and widest above the middle; they taper to short stalks and have rounded to pointed tips, usually with low teeth along the edges of the upper half. The individually stalked, nodding flowers are clustered near the top of the stem. Each pinkish to white flower is ½" wide and has a small 5-lobed calyx, 5 thick waxy petals, and 10 purple-tipped stamens. The fruits are brown, rounded, 5-lobed capsules.

Bloom Season: Early summer–midsummer.

Habitat/Range: Occasional in well-drained sandy or rocky woods, usually in light shade, and sometimes in wetter sites under conifers; throughout the region.

Comments: Spotted Wintergreen (*C. maculata*) is a similar species in the southeastern part of the region from Lake Michigan eastward. It has leaves with rounded bases and distinctive pale zones along the veins. North American Indians and settlers used both species to treat a variety of ailments.

ROBERT TATINA

Pink Shinleaf

PINK SHINLEAF
Pyrola asarifolia
Shinleaf Family (Pyrolaceae)

Description: Brownish stemmed, unbranched plant to 10" tall, with several long-stalked, shiny evergreen leaves clustered near the base. The broadly rounded leaves are up to 2½" long and nearly as wide. They have rounded to heart-shaped bases and slight indentations along the edges. The leaf stalks are channeled or grooved on the upper side and are often longer than the leaves. A few papery bracts are usually scattered along the stem, while the flowers are alternate along the upper part of the stem. At the base of each nodding or spreading short-stalked flower is a small bract. Each flower is up to ½" wide and has a small, papery, 5-lobed calyx; 5 pale pink to purplish petals with slightly bumpy edges; 10 stamens arching under the cupped 2

upper petals; and an upwardly curved style that protrudes well beyond the petals.

Bloom Season: Late spring–midsummer.

Habitat/Range: Occasional in moist woods, bogs, and white cedar swamps, and on wet mossy banks, said to favor calcium-rich areas, but also in acidic bogs; throughout the region.

Comments: A similar species with white flowers, Round-leaved Shinleaf (*P. rotundifolia*), occurs in similar habitats and drier sites throughout the region. Both of these plants have a combination of curved styles and sepals that are longer than they are broad, distinguishing them from all other shinleafs.

JESSIE M. HARRIS

Wild Columbine

WILD COLUMBINE
Aquilegia canadensis
Buttercup Family (Ranunculaceae)

Description: A smooth, bluish green, branching plant to 2' tall, Wild Columbine has stalked, compound basal leaves, each divided into 3 stalked divisions. Each division is divided into 3 lobed leaflets up to 1½" long. The leaflets are pale beneath and lobed into rounded segments. Stem leaves are similar but stalkless, with the upper stem leaves sometimes merely lobed. Flowers dangle singly from arching stalks along the upper half of the plant. Each flower is 1–1½" long and has 5 red, petal-like sepals and 5 yellow-tipped petals that are prolonged backward into long, hollow, red spurs. A cluster of yellow stamens protrudes from the flower.

Bloom Season: Midspring–early summer.

Habitat/Range: Frequent in dry or moist woods, especially in calcium-rich soils, also on ledges, cliffs, rocky shores, and shaded talus slopes; throughout most of the region eastward to New Brunswick.

Comments: Ruby-throated hummingbirds and long-tongued moths pollinate the flowers. North American Indians prepared a headache remedy from the crushed seeds.

Bristly Rose

BRISTLY ROSE
Rosa acicularis
Rose Family (Rosaceae)

Description: Branching slender shrub to 5' tall, with an abundance of needlelike thorns. The alternate leaves have a conspicuous pair of bractlike stipules along the base of their stalk, and the stipules have a row of small rounded glands along their edges. Each leaf has 3–7 sharply toothed, egg-shaped leaflets up to 2" long with tapering to rounded bases. Flowers usually grow singly at the tip of small branches. Each flower is 1½–2½" wide and consists of 5 slender sepals, 5 broadly rounded, pink petals, and numerous yellow stamens. The fruits are red berrylike "hips" topped by the persistent erect sepals.

Bloom Season: Late spring–early summer.

Habitat/Range: Occasional in dry open woods, open sandy or gravelly sites, and moist thickets, and on stream banks and rocky ridges; from Maine and Quebec westward, but relatively rare in the eastern half of the region.

Comments: Several other roses with needlelike thorns occur in the region. Pasture Rose (*R. carolina*) is usually less than 1½' tall, and the flower stalks and base of the flowers are covered with knobby gland-tipped hairs. It occurs in pastures and fields in the southern part of the region from Nova Scotia and southern Maine westward. Early Wild Rose (*R. blanda*) is larger than Pasture Rose and has thorns only along the lower parts of the plant. It is common in sandy or rocky areas from Maine and Quebec westward. A cultivated European rose, Sweetbriar (*R. eglanteria*), sometimes escapes into pastures and thickets. Its leaflets are usually less than 1" long, and it has tiny knob-tipped hairs on the lower surfaces of the leaves.

DON KURZ

Swamp Rose

SWAMP ROSE
Rosa palustris
Rose Family (Rosaceae)

Description: Sprawling branched shrub to 8' tall, with curved, broad-based thorns; it often clambers on other vegetation. The alternate compound leaves have a pair of narrow bractlike stipules along the base of their stalks. Each leaf has 5–9, typically 7, narrowly egg-shaped, finely toothed leaflets, each 1–2" long. Flowers grow singly or in small branched clusters at the ends of the main stems and on short side branches. Each flower is 1½–2" wide and has 5 slender, pointed, sometimes lobed sepals; 5 broad pink petals; and usually more than 200 yellow stamens.

Bloom Season: Late spring–midsummer.

Habitat/Range: Frequent in bogs, swamps, wet conifer woods, moist thickets, and along shores; throughout most of the region, but less common west of Lake Michigan.

Comments: A similar species with broad-based thorns, Virginia Rose (*R. virginiana*), occurs in woods and thickets and along shores in the eastern part of the region, especially in coastal and maritime areas, westward to southern Ontario. It has coarser teeth on the leaflets—often less than 20 teeth per side—while Swamp Rose usually has more than 24 teeth on the side of the larger leaflets. If one wishes to count, Virginia Rose is said to have fewer than 160 stamens. All roses in the region produce red rounded fruits, called hips, that are rich in vitamin C and have been used for food and medicine.

HARDHACK
Spiraea tomentosa
Rose Family (Rosaceae)

Description: Low shrub to 3' tall, with upright branches and long strands of cobwebby hairs lying against the smaller twigs. The leaves are closely spaced, alternate, and mostly upright or ascending. The lower surface of each leaf is hidden by a dense mat of tangled, pale or tan hairs. Flowers grow in pyramid-shaped, branched clusters at the tips of the branches. At the base of each branch in the cluster is a small, narrow, pointed, tan, hairy bract. Each pink flower is 3/16" wide and has 5 small hairy sepals; 5 small, rounded, papery petals that taper to narrow bases; and numerous pale to pinkish stamens.

Bloom Season: Summer.

Habitat/Range: Common in exposed to lightly shaded, acidic, usually moist sites in bogs, marshes, and thickets, on open sandy soils, and along shores; throughout the region.

CAROL GRACIE

Hardhack

JESSIE M. HARRIS

Lopseed

LOPSEED
Phryma leptostachya
Vervain Family (Verbenaceae)

Description: Plant to 3' tall, typically branched in the upper half, with widely separated, stalked, opposite leaves, the lowest pair of which is smaller than the main leaves. The main leaves are up to 6" long and 3" wide. They have broad or tapering bases, pointed tips, and coarse broad teeth along the edges. Flowers are paired in elongate clusters along the upright upper branches and spread horizontally from the stem. Below every flower are 3 tiny, needlelike bracts. Each flower is ¼" long and has a tiny calyx with 3 long-pointed upper lobes and 2 shorter lower lobes, and a narrow, tubular, pink corolla with a straight upper lip and a longer, spreading, 3-lobed lower lip.

Bloom Season: Summer.

Habitat/Range: Frequent in disturbed woods, usually under hardwoods, from Quebec westward in all but the far northern part of the region.

Comments: This plant has been used in a variety of folk medicines.

JESSIE M. HARRIS

Indian Paintbrush

INDIAN PAINTBRUSH
Castilleja coccinea
Snapdragon Family (Scrophulariaceae)

Description: Unbranched hairy annual to 2' tall but often flowering at 6" tall. The leaves are alternate, yellowish green, and up to 2" long. They are usually divided into 3–5 narrow, spreading lobes. Flowers form at the top of the plant in a dense spike that elongates as the season progresses. The actual flowers are about 1" long and inconspicuous, each with a thin, tubular, 2-lipped calyx and a greenish yellow, tubular corolla. The showy appearance of the plant comes from the brightly colored scarlet or yellow leafy bract that grows under each flower. The plants are partially parasitic, attaching to the roots of several other kinds of plants.

Bloom Season: Midspring–midsummer.

Habitat/Range: Frequent in moist, open, often seepy areas, usually in peat, sand, or gravel, in bogs, marshes, fens, swamps, and along shores; throughout the region eastward to Ontario and southern New England.

Yellow and Orange Flowers

ALLISON W. BELL

Bluebead Lily

*Plants with yellow and orange flowers are usually
easy to distinguish. Some plants with pale, creamy
yellowish flowers may be included in the white
flower section of this book. Some plants with
greenish flowers occasionally produce brighter,
yellowish flowered forms, so you should also check
the green flower section of this guide. A few
common weeds with yellow and orange flowers
are included on pages 251–255.*

JESSIE M. HARRIS

Golden Alexanders

GOLDEN ALEXANDERS

Zizia aurea
Carrot Family (Apiaceae)

Description: Smooth-branched plant to 3' tall, with alternate compound leaves. The basal and lower stem leaves are divided into a branched array of finely toothed and sometimes lobed leaflets, each up to 3" long and 1¼" wide, with pointed tips. The upper leaves are smaller, short stalked, and sometimes less divided. Flowers are in umbrella-like heads at the tops of the stem branches. Each head has 6–20 flower clusters on radiating, spokelike stalks. Each bright yellow flower is less than ⅛" wide and has 5 tiny curved petals and 5 protruding yellow stamens.

Bloom Season: Midspring–midsummer.

Habitat/Range: Common in moist, exposed to lightly shaded sites in meadows, marshy fields, and swampy areas, and along streams; throughout the region.

Comments: Heart-leaved Meadow Parsnip (*Z. aptera*) has undivided basal leaves with heart-shaped bases. It occurs rarely in drier sites in the western half of the region, eastward to New York. Wild Parsnip (*Pastinaca sativa*), a common European weed of roadsides and disturbed areas, also has yellow flowers. It is a larger, coarser plant with furrowed, angular stems and flat flower heads.

JESSIE M. HARRIS

Northern Wormwood

NORTHERN WORMWOOD
Artemisia campestris
Aster Family (Asteraceae)

Description: Bluish green plant to 3' tall, usually with several stems rising from a cluster of compound basal leaves. The leaves are repeatedly divided into narrow segments less than $1/10$" wide. Stem leaves are smaller, less divided, and alternate. Flower heads are upright or nodding in a cluster along the upper stem. Each head is ⅛" wide and has a series of pale-edged, sepal-like bracts and a central disk of tiny, greenish yellow, tubular flowers. The outer flowers lack stamens and produce seeds, while the inner flowers are sterile.

Bloom Season: Midsummer–early fall.

Habitat/Range: Uncommon in open well-drained sites, including exposed talus slopes, outcrops, dry sandy or gravelly areas, and exposed rocky beaches; scattered and rare throughout the eastern half of the region and becoming more frequent from Michigan westward.

Comments: North American Indians used this plant to treat eye, skin, and scalp problems. Yarrow (p. 161) also has aromatic, fernlike alternate leaves, but the flattened flower cluster has flower heads with 4–6 white, petal-like rays.

Grass-leaved Goldenrod

ROBERT TATINA

GRASS-LEAVED GOLDENROD
Euthamia graminifolia
Aster Family (Asteraceae)

Description: Leafy plant to 3½' tall, usually with many branches in the upper half. The leaves are up to 5" long but less than ⅜" wide, and they taper to stalkless bases and pointed tips. They have smooth edges and 3 distinct parallel veins along their length. Flower heads are in a branched, flat-topped cluster at the top of the plant. Many of the heads are typically stalkless. Each head is ¼" wide, with a series of small, yellowish green, sepal-like bracts and 15–25 small, petal-like, yellow rays, usually surrounding 5–10 tubular, 5-lobed flowers.

Bloom Season: Midsummer–fall.

Habitat/Range: Abundant in open areas ranging from dry sandy fields to marshes and sedge meadows, as well as in open swamps and damp thickets and along shores and beaches; throughout the region.

Comments: Ohio Goldenrod (*Solidago ohioensis*) occurs in fens and limey seeps from New York and Ontario to Wisconsin. It is a narrow plant, and most of its leaves are more than ⅜" wide, with a single central vein.

JESSIE M. HARRIS

Bur Marigold

BUR MARIGOLD
Bidens cernua
Aster Family (Asteraceae)

Description: Annual to 3' tall, with widely spaced pairs of smooth opposite leaves that are sometimes joined at their bases, enveloping the stem. The leaves are up to 8" long and 2" wide and are usually toothed along the edges. The upper leaves are much smaller. One to several individually stalked flower heads occur near the top of the plant. Each head is up to 1¼" wide and has 5–8 long narrow bracts surrounding a series of shorter sepal-like bracts and 6–8 petal-like yellow rays. There is a central cluster of tiny, 5-lobed, yellow, tubular flowers. The flattened black fruits are topped with 3 or 4 sharp, barbed prongs that cling to clothing. These annoying prongs have earned the plant the nickname "beggar's tick."

Bloom Season: Summer–early fall.

Habitat/Range: Common in wet, often muddy sites where other vegetation is limited, in swamps, beaver ponds, and wet thickets and along muddy shores; throughout the region.

Comments: Several other species of beggar's ticks occur in moist areas in the region. These include Swamp Beggar's Ticks (*B. connata*), which has stalked, undivided leaves and no apparent petal-like rays, Common Beggar's Ticks (*B. frondosa*), which has compound leaves and no rays, and Tall Swamp Marigold (*B. coronata*), which has compound leaves and 6 or more petal-like rays.

ROBERT TATINA

Sneezeweed

SNEEZEWEED
Helenium autumnale
Aster Family (Asteraceae)

Description: Branching plant to 5' tall, with alternate leaves and narrow leafy strips extending down the stem from the leaf bases. The main leaves are typically 3–5" long and up to ¾" wide, and taper from the middle to pointed tips and narrow bases, usually with small widely spaced teeth along the edges. On the upper stems is an open cluster of individually stalked flower heads. Each head is 1–1¾" wide, with several narrow, pointed, sepal-like bracts and 10–20 broadly fan-shaped, yellow, petal-like rays surrounding a nearly spherical yellow disk up to ¾" wide. The disk flowers are tiny, tubular, and 5-lobed. The rays are cleft at their tips into 3 or 4 narrow lobes.

Bloom Season: Midsummer–early fall.

Habitat/Range: Occasional in swamps, fens, seeps, and wet pastures and along shores; mostly in the southern part of the region from Quebec to Minnesota, and introduced in New England.

Comments: Sneezeweed is poisonous to livestock but is usually not eaten. The dried flower heads were reportedly used as snuff.

Tall Sunflower

DON KURZ

TALL SUNFLOWER
Helianthus giganteus
Aster Family (Asteraceae)

Description: Plant to 6' tall or taller, usually with hairy purplish stems and narrow, sandpapery, short-stalked leaves that are opposite in the lower half of the plant and usually alternate above. The leaves are up to 6" long and 1½" wide, with tapering bases and long pointed tips. The leaf edges may be smooth or shallowly toothed. Individually stalked flower heads occur near the top of the plant. Each head is about 2" wide and has a series of narrow, pointed, sepal-like bracts and 10–20 pointed, yellow, petal-like rays surrounding a yellow disk of tiny, 5-lobed, tubular flowers.

Bloom Season: Midsummer–fall.

Habitat/Range: Occasional in moist, open to lightly shaded sites, in fens, swamps, sedge meadows, and moist woods; throughout much of the region, but populations eastward in New England and the Canadian Maritimes may be escapes from cultivation.

Comments: Two other hairy-stemmed sunflowers occur in the region. Jerusalem Artichoke (*H. tuberosus*) has broader, coarsely toothed leaves usually more than 2" wide. It occurs in thickets and along woodland edges; many North Woods populations are probably introduced. The plant has been cultivated for centuries for its edible tubers, which are still marketed today. Prairie Sunflower (*H. pauciflorus*) has blunt or bluntly pointed bracts in the flower head and stiff, mostly opposite leaves. It occurs in open well-drained sites from New York westward and occasionally escapes from cultivation eastward.

Pale-leaved Sunflower

JESSIE M. HARRIS

PALE-LEAVED SUNFLOWER
Helianthus strumosus
Aster Family (Asteraceae)

Description: Plant to 5' tall or rarely taller, with the stems below the flowers smooth to slightly hairy and often covered with a whitish waxy coating. The leaves are short-stalked, sandpapery, toothed, pale beneath, and up to 8" long and 3½" wide. They have somewhat rounded bases and tapering pointed tips. Most of the leaves are opposite, but the leaves near the top of the plant are typically alternate. Flower heads are on individual stalks on the upper part of the plant. Each head is 1½–2½" wide, with a series of small, pointed, sepal-like bracts and 8–15 pointed, yellow, petal-like rays surrounding a disk of tiny, 5-lobed, tubular flowers.

Bloom Season: Midsummer–fall.

Habitat/Range: Frequent in well-drained woods, especially under hardwoods, and in openings and thickets; throughout the region eastward to Maine.

Comments: Iroquois people used the roots as a treatment for parasitic worms. Two other smooth-stemmed sunflowers occur in parts of the region. Thin-leaved Sunflower (*H. decapetalus*) has thin, broadly rounded leaves and larger, somewhat leafy bracts in the flower head. It occurs in thickets and along woodland edges from Quebec to Wisconsin. Woodland Sunflower (*H. divaricatus*) has leaves that are stalkless or on stalks less than ¼" long. It is common in dry woods from Maine westward through Wisconsin and Ontario.

JESSIE M. HARRIS

Canada Hawkweed

CANADA HAWKWEED
Hieracium kalmii
Aster Family (Asteraceae)

Description: Plant to 4' tall, with milky sap and often with many branches above the middle. The leaves are alternate and up to 6" long and 1½" wide, with long, unevenly spaced teeth along the edges and narrowed bases that often clasp the stem slightly. Flower heads are in an open branched cluster near the top of the plant, with small narrow bracts on the branches. The stalks of the flower heads have tiny branched hairs. Each head is up to 1" wide and resembles a miniature dandelion, with a series of narrow sepal-like bracts and 40 or more small, yellow, petal-like flowers.

Bloom Season: Midsummer–early fall.

Habitat/Range: Common in open sandy woods, fields, and rocky areas and along shores and open stream banks; throughout the region.

Comments: Several leafy-stemmed hawkweeds occur in the region, including Northern Hawkweed (*H. umbellatum*), which has rough sandpapery leaves and ranges from Michigan northward and westward; Rough Hawkweed (*H. scabrum*), which has dark, stalked glands on the bracts and flower stalks and mostly toothless leaves and which ranges throughout the region; and Panicled Hawkweed (*H. paniculatum*), which has delicate slender branches, pale lower leaf surfaces, and fewer than 20 flowers per head. It is found mostly in the eastern half of the region.

Rattlesnake Weed

RATTLESNAKE WEED
Hieracium venosum
Aster Family (Asteraceae)

Description: Slender plant to 2' tall, with milky sap and a basal cluster of hairy, stalkless, purple-veined or purplish leaves. Each leaf is up to 6" long and 2" wide, with a tapering base. The stem is branched in the upper half and has no leaves or only a few small leaves near the base. Flower heads are in an open cluster at the ends of the branches. Each head resembles a miniature dandelion and is up to ¾" wide, with a series of narrow, pointed, sepal-like bracts and typically up to 25 small, yellow, petal-like rays.

Bloom Season: Late spring–midsummer.

Habitat/Range: Occasional in open sandy or rocky woods, often under aspens and pines, and in burned areas; from southern Maine through southern Ontario to Michigan.

Comments: A related plant that appears occasionally at the southern edge of the region, Hairy Hawkweed (*H. gronovii*), also has a cluster of basal leaves, but it has several well-developed leaves on the lower half of the stem and a narrow, elongate cluster of flower heads. Several introduced hawkweeds have only basal leaves, but these are not veined with purple. Among the most common of these lawn and roadside weeds are Yellow King Devil (*H. caespitosum*), which has pale, smooth to sparsely hairy leaves, and Glaucous King Devil (*H. piloselloides*), which has darker, densely hairy leaves.

YELLOW WILD LETTUCE
Lactuca canadensis
Aster Family (Asteraceae)

Description: Smooth-stemmed biennial to 8' tall, with milky, orange-tan sap and alternate leaves. The leaves are up to 12" long and 6" wide and vary from rounded and unlobed to deeply lobed into several segments on each side of the broad central axis, with toothed or smooth edges. Flower heads are usually abundant on spreading or upright branches on the upper part of the plant. Each head is ⅜" wide and resembles a miniature dandelion, with a series of pointed sepal-like bracts of 2 distinct lengths surrounding up to 20 yellow, petal-like flowers.

Bloom Season: Summer–early fall.

Habitat/Range: Common in a variety of habitats, from disturbed ground and open fields to thickets and open woods; throughout the region.

Comments: The leaves have been cooked as greens, but the cooking water must be changed a few times to remove the bitterness. Hairy Wild Lettuce (*L. hirsuta*), which has larger pinkish yellow to salmon flowers, is uncommon in open woods and clearings in the eastern part of the region westward to Wisconsin.

Yellow Wild Lettuce

BLACK-EYED SUSAN
Rudbeckia hirta
Aster Family (Asteraceae)

Description: Coarsely hairy plant typically 1–2' tall, usually unbranched below the middle, with rough alternate leaves. The basal leaves are long-stalked, while the stem leaves may be stalkless or may even clasp the stem at their bases. The main stem leaves are typically about 3" long, widest near the middle, and tapered to pointed tips, sometimes with a few teeth along the edges. The upper leaves are smaller than the middle and lower leaves. The flower heads are single at the top of the stems. Each head is 2–3" wide, with a series of narrow, hairy, sepal-like bracts and up to 20 deep yellow, petal-like rays surrounding a chocolate brown, rounded dome of small 5-lobed disk flowers mixed with pointed hairy bracts.

Bloom Season: Late spring–early fall.

Habitat/Range: Abundant in open, well-drained, often weedy areas in fields, pastures, and open rocky woods; throughout the region.

Black-eyed Susan

Wild Golden Glow

WILD GOLDEN GLOW
Rudbeckia laciniata
Aster Family (Asteraceae)

Description: Smooth, single-stemmed plant to 8' tall, usually branched only in the upper half, and often with a bluish, waxy coating on the pale green stems. The leaves are alternate and widely spaced along the stem. They grow on stalks up to 6" long. Each main leaf is up to 10" long, sharply toothed, and deeply lobed to divided. The uppermost leaves are often undivided and smooth-edged. Several leafy-stalked flower heads usually form near the top of the plant. These heads are extremely variable in size, ranging up to 4" wide. Each head has 8 or more sepal-like bracts, each about ½" long and typically bent downward. These surround 8–10 often drooping, yellow, petal-like rays and a rounded central cluster of many small, yellowish green, tubular flowers.

Bloom Season: Midsummer–fall.

Habitat/Range: Occasional in moist shaded places, especially on wooded floodplains and in streamside thickets and springy places; throughout the region.

Comments: A form of this plant with all or most of the flowers in each head consisting of rays is widely cultivated and occasionally escapes into the wild.

BALSAM RAGWORT
Senecio pauperculus
Aster Family (Asteraceae)

Description: Plant to 1½' tall, usually with at least a few scattered tufts of white cobwebby hairs. Typically, several stems grow from a well-developed cluster of stalked, egg-shaped, basal leaves that are widest near the middle. Each leaf is up to 4" long and less than 1" wide and has toothed edges and tapering bases. At least some of the leaves are 3 or more times as long as they are wide. Scattered stalked or stalkless, alternate, usually lobed leaves occur on the flowering stems. Flower heads form a branched cluster at the top of the plant. Each head is up to 1" wide and has a series of narrow sepal-like bracts and about 10 petal-like yellow rays surrounding a central disk of tiny, tubular, yellow flowers.

Bloom Season: Midspring–midsummer.

Habitat/Range: Common in open, limey, moist places in fens, meadows, pastures, conifer swamps, and along shores; throughout the region.

Comments: Prairie Ragwort (*S. plattensis*) occurs in drier sites from southern Ontario westward. It is usually single-stemmed and woolly/hairy, with basal leaves that are usually less than 3 times as long as they are wide.

Balsam Ragwort

Golden Ragwort

GOLDEN RAGWORT
Senecio aureus
Aster Family (Asteraceae)

Description: Plant typically to 2½' tall, often with several stems rising from a single cluster of basal leaves. The stems branch above the middle into a flat cluster of flower heads at the top of the plant. Young plants have scattered tufts of bright white, cobwebby hairs, but older plants are smooth. The basal leaves are toothed, long stalked, and up to 4" long and often nearly as wide, with mostly heart-shaped bases. The stem leaves are smaller, alternate, stalkless, and often divided featherlike into several narrow segments. Each flower head is ¾" wide, with a series of narrow sepal-like bracts and several petal-like yellow rays surrounding a disk of tiny yellow tubular flowers.

Bloom Season: Midspring–early summer.

Habitat/Range: Common in marshy or springy areas, swamps, bogs, and fens and along shores, often in limey places in both open and shade; throughout the region.

Comments: A nearly identical northern species, *S. indecorus*, extends southward into Minnesota and Michigan. It either has no rays or its rays are less than ⅛" long. Another northern species, Northern Swamp Ragwort (*S. congestus*), is an annual or biennial with many well-developed, coarsely toothed stem leaves. Robbins' Ragwort (*S. schweinitzianus*) has narrowly triangular basal leaves, usually more than twice as long as they are wide, with broadly flattened bases. It occurs in habitats similar to those of Golden Ragwort in the eastern part of the region westward to Quebec and northern New York.

Common Goldenrod

ROBERT TATINA

COMMON GOLDENROD
Solidago canadensis
Aster Family (Asteraceae)

Description: Hairy-stemmed plant to 10' tall, usually unbranched except near the top of the plant. There are abundant stalkless, slightly sandpapery, alternate leaves, the largest of which appear near the middle of the stem and are up to 6" long and 1¼" wide. The leaves usually have a few scattered sharp teeth near the pointed tips, as well as 3 prominent raised veins along the length of their hairy lower surfaces. The tiny flower heads are abundant along the upper sides of a somewhat pyramid-like cluster of branches at the top of the plant. Each head is ¼" wide and has a series of narrow sepal-like bracts and 3–15 narrow, petal-like, yellow rays surrounding a few tiny, yellow, 5-lobed, tubular flowers.

Bloom Season: Midsummer–fall.

Habitat/Range: Abundant in open disturbed areas, including fields, pastures, roadsides, and sometimes in moist areas and thickets; throughout the region.

Comments: This species and some other goldenrods often have galls—globelike swellings along the stem that are caused by insects. In a similar species, Late Goldenrod (*S. gigantea*), the middle and lower parts of the stems are smooth and hairless. It occurs in moist, often shaded sites throughout the region. Rough Goldenrod (*S. rugosa*) has rough, crinkle-surfaced leaves with a single central vein. It occurs in moist thickets in the eastern part of the region westward to Michigan. Swamp Goldenrod (*S. patula*) is a tall spindly plant with stalked, rough basal leaves up to 16" long and a few much smaller stem leaves. It occurs in fens, swamps, and limey seeps from New Hampshire to Wisconsin.

ROBERT TATINA

Zigzag Goldenrod

ZIGZAG GOLDENROD
Solidago flexicaulis
Aster Family (Asteraceae)

Description: Plant to 3' tall and mostly un-branched below the middle, with broad, alternate, coarsely and sharply toothed leaves, most of which are stalked. The leaves in the middle of the stem are the largest, up to 6" long and 4" wide, with rounded or tapering bases. The upper stems zigzag slightly. Small clusters of flower heads form at the bases of the upper leaves and the tips of the stems. Each head is ⅜" wide, with a series of narrow sepal-like bracts and 3 or 4 petal-like yellow rays surrounding a few tiny, yellow, tubular flowers.

Bloom Season: Midsummer–early fall.

Habitat/Range: Common in rich, often limey woods, drier areas of shaded swamps, and on shaded seepy slopes; throughout the region.

Comments: Blue-Stemmed Goldenrod (*S. caesia*) has tapering leaves less than 1" wide and smooth stems with a waxy, bluish coating. It occurs in rich woods, particularly near limestone, through the region westward to Wisconsin. The flower heads of Stout Goldenrod (*S. squarrosa*) have sepal-like bracts whose tips bend strongly outward. It occurs in open and rocky woods from New Brunswick and southern Ontario southward.

JESSIE M. HARRIS

Hairy Goldenrod

OLD-FIELD GOLDENROD

Solidago nemoralis
Aster Family (Asteraceae)

Description: Slender, mostly unbranched plant to 2½' tall, with alternate leaves that grow progressively smaller toward the top of the stem. The lower stem leaves are stalked and up to 3" long and ½" wide, while the upper leaves are stalkless. The larger leaves may be toothed along the edges. The entire plant has short gray hairs, giving it a grayish green appearance. At the top of the stem is a narrow elongate spray of flower heads, along the top side of short, arching side branches. Each head is less than ¼" wide and has a series of narrow sepal-like bracts and up to 9 petal-like, yellow rays surrounding 3–6 tiny, yellow, tubular flowers.

Bloom Season: Midsummer–fall.

Habitat/Range: Abundant in sterile, dry, open or lightly shaded sites in open woods, old fields, sand barrens, and rocky areas; throughout the region.

Comments: Early Goldenrod (*S. juncea*) has smooth stems below the flower branches. It occurs in similar habitats throughout the region, blooming as early as June.

HAIRY GOLDENROD

Solidago hispida
Aster Family (Asteraceae)

Description: Mostly unbranched plant to 2½' tall, with dense long hairs on the stems and leaves. There is usually a cluster of stalked basal leaves, while the stem leaves are alternate, progressively smaller, and frequently stalkless. The leaves are up to 8" long and 2" wide but typically smaller, sometimes with teeth along the edges. Flower heads form a cylindrical cluster at the tops of the stems. Each head is ¼" wide, with a series of narrow sepal-like bracts and 7–15 petal-like yellow rays surrounding a few tiny, yellow, tubular flowers.

Bloom Season: Midsummer–early fall.

Habitat/Range: Occasional in dry open woods, especially in sandy or rocky areas; throughout the region.

Comments: Silverrod (*S. bicolor*) is a nearly identical plant with white flowers. It occurs in similar habitats in the region westward to Wisconsin. Rand's Goldenrod (*S. simplex*) is a less hairy plant that occurs in sandy or rocky areas westward to Michigan and westward in Canada.

KEITH BOARD

Old-field Goldenrod

Bog Goldenrod

JESSIE M. HARRIS

BOG GOLDENROD
Solidago uliginosa
Aster Family (Asteraceae)

Description: Narrow, alternate-leaved plant to 4' tall and unbranched below the middle. The middle and lower stems are smooth and hairless, while the upper stems are usually hairy. The basal and lower leaves are stalked and up to 8" long and 2" wide, with smooth or toothed edges. The stalks of the lower leaves broadly clasp the stems at their bases, while the middle and upper leaves are progressively smaller and often stalkless. Individually stalked flower heads occur on short upright branches in an elongate cluster along the upper stem. Each head is ¼" wide and has narrow sepal-like bracts and up to 8 petal-like yellow rays surrounding a few tiny, yellow, tubular flowers.

Bloom Season: Midsummer–early fall.

Habitat/Range: Common in wet, open sites in bogs, fens, and peaty marshes and along moist shores; throughout the region.

Comments: Showy Goldenrod (*S. speciosa*) has smooth leaves that do not clasp the stems at the bases of the stalks, as well as a narrow, spikelike cylinder of flower heads. It occurs in dry, usually sandy sites from southern New Hampshire to Wisconsin. Mountain Goldenrod (*S. macrophylla*) has broad, coarsely toothed leaves and flower heads about ½" wide. It grows in moist cool woods, often in the mountains, in the eastern part of the region westward to New York. Downy Goldenrod (*S. puberula*) has stems and leaves with soft, fine hairs. It occurs in open sandy or rocky areas in eastern Canada and New England.

ROBERT TATINA

Orange Jewelweed

ORANGE JEWELWEED
Impatiens capensis
Touch-me-not Family (Balsaminaceae)

Description: Smooth, branched plant to 5' tall, with shiny, pale green, translucent stems. The slender-stalked leaves are alternate, with coarse rounded teeth along the edges. The main stem leaves are typically up to 4" long and 2" wide. They are broadest near the middle and taper at both ends. Flowers are on dangling stalks in clusters of 1 to a few flowers associated with small leaves on the upper part of the stems. The flowers are cornucopia shaped and attached to the stalks on the top near the mouth, where there are 2 tiny yellowish sepals. Each orange flower is 1" long and has deep orange to reddish spots. At the base of the corolla is a prominent, forward-curving spur. The cornucopia and spur are actually a third sepal, which is flanked by a broadly rounded, hooded upper petal and 2 dangling, lobed lower petals. The fruits are lumpy, pale green pods, each with a single row of seeds. The ripe pods "explode" at the slightest touch,

as their seams burst and the segments coil rapidly, scattering the seeds. Because of this, the plant is also called Spotted Touch-me-not.

Bloom Season: Summer.

Habitat/Range: Abundant in moist to wet areas in woods, swamps, beaver marshes, floodplains, and along shores; throughout the region.

Comments: North American Indians used the plant for a variety of medicinal purposes and to make a yellow dye. Yellow Jewelweed or Pale Touch-me-not (*I. pallida*) has a larger lemon-yellow flower with fewer and smaller reddish spots and a smaller, sideways-pointing spur. It occurs in moist woods throughout most of the region but is less common. The sap of both species is said to prevent symptoms of poison ivy and to relieve the irritation caused by contact with nettle.

BROAD-LEAVED PUCCOON
Lithospermum latifolium
Borage Family (Boraginaceae)

Description: Hairy, usually branched plant to 2' tall, with alternate, veiny leaves up to 7" long and 1½" wide. These taper to long pointed tips and short-stalked bases. Flowers are single on slender stalks at the base of the upper leaves. Each flower is ¼" wide and has 5 hairy, needle-like sepals and a short tubular corolla ending in 5 yellow to greenish lobes. The fruits are shiny, porcelain-like, pointed globes nearly ⅛" long.

Bloom Season: Midspring–late spring.

Habitat/Range: Uncommon in dry woods, thickets, and on lightly shaded sandy or rocky slopes; in the southern part of the region from New York to southeastern Minnesota, especially south of the Great Lakes.

JESSIE M. HARRIS

Broad-leaved Puccoon

KENNETH DRITZ

Marsh Yellow Cress

MARSH YELLOW CRESS
Rorippa palustris
Mustard Family (Brassicaceae)

Description: Plant typically grows as an annual to 3' tall, with stalked alternate leaves up to 5" long. These leaves are divided into narrow lobes or coarse teeth along either side of the central vein, with the lobes often toothed along the edges. Flowers are usually numerous on short stalks alternating along the upper branches. Each flower is ⅛" wide and has 4 tiny sepals and 4 spreading yellow petals. The fruits are stalked, squat pods about ¼" long that spread at right angles from the stems.

Bloom Season: Summer.

Habitat/Range: Common in wet open ground in depressions, marshes, mud flats, and along shores, usually in areas where other vegetation is sparse; throughout the region.

Comments: This plant is native to North America and Europe, and some populations in the region are introduced weeds.

ROBERT TATINA

Dwarf Honeysuckle

DWARF HONEYSUCKLE
Diervilla lonicera
Honeysuckle Family (Caprifoliaceae)

Description: Compact shrub usually less than 2' tall, with flat or arching upper branches. The leaves are opposite and short stalked, with finely toothed edges, broadly rounded bases, and long pointed tips. The pale yellow flowers emerge from long slender buds in stalked clusters of 3–8 near the branch tips. Each flower is ¾–1" long and densely hairy inside, with 5 narrow sepals, a tubular corolla with 5 curved lobes, and 5 protruding hairy stamens surrounding a blunt style. The flowers turn orange to reddish with age.

Bloom Season: Late spring–summer.

Habitat/Range: Common in dry sandy or rocky woods, especially in burned areas, openings, and on rocky slopes; throughout the region.

Comments: North American Indians used this plant to prepare a variety of medicines.

COMMON ROCKROSE
Helianthemum canadense
Rockrose Family (Cistaceae)

Description: Slender plant to 1½' tall and unbranched below the middle, usually with several stems growing from the same base. The narrow, stalkless, alternate, smooth-edged leaves are about ¾" long and covered with tiny starlike hairs. At the top of the stem is a loose, fewflowered cluster. The first 1 or 2 flowers in the cluster are 1" wide, with 2 narrow, short, outer sepals, 3 larger inner sepals, and 5 broadly rounded petals surrounding numerous stamens. Subsequent flowers are smaller and lack petals.

Bloom Season: Late spring–summer.

Habitat/Range: Occasional in exposed sandy areas or lightly shaded sterile woods; throughout the region.

Comments: The flowers open in bright light and last a single day. A nearly identical species, *H. bicknellii*, has 3 or more petal-bearing flowers with nearly equal sepals. It occurs in similar habitats in the region from Maine westward.

JESSIE M. HARRIS

Common Rockrose

NORTHERN ST. JOHN'S WORT
Hypericum boreale
St. John's Wort Family (Clusiaceae)

Description: Slender, upright-branched plant seldom more than 1' tall, with short, rounded, opposite, stalkless leaves up to 1" long and ½" wide. The individually stalked flowers are in an open cluster on the upper branches and stems and are accompanied by scattered, small, leafy bracts. Each flower is $^3/_{16}$" wide and has 5 blunt sepals, 5 orange-yellow petals, and up to 15 stamens surrounding a flask-shaped ovary.

Bloom Season: Midsummer–early fall.

Habitat/Range: Common in wet mud, sand, or peat, in swamps, marshes, bogs, mud flats, and along shores; throughout the region.

Comments: Two other St. John's worts with tiny flowers occur in the region. Weak St. John's Wort (*H. mutilum*) has pointed sepals and narrow pointed leaves in the flowering branches. It occurs in similar habitats, mostly in the eastern half of the region. Orange Grass (*H. gentianoides*) also has tiny yellow flowers, but all

Northern St. John's Wort

of the leaves are tiny and scalelike. It occurs in sterile, acidic sand and rocky barrens in the southern part of the region from Maine to Wisconsin.

PALE ST. JOHN'S WORT
Hypericum ellipticum
St. John's Wort Family (Clusiaceae)

Description: Plant to about 15" tall and mostly unbranched below the flowers. The leaves are opposite and about 1" long and ⅜" wide, with blunt tips, round or tapering bases, and smooth edges. A few smaller leaves often grow at the base of the main leaves. Flowers are in a branched cluster at the top of the stem. Each flower is ⅝" wide and has 5 small pointed sepals, 5 spreading yellow petals, and numerous stamens surrounding a flask-shaped ovary.

Bloom Season: Summer.

Habitat/Range: Common in moist, often acidic areas in marshes, seeps, bogs, wet thickets, and along shores; throughout the region.

Pale St. John's Wort

Sand St. John's Wort

LAWRENCE NEWCOMB/NEW ENGLAND WILDFLOWER SOCIETY

SAND ST. JOHN'S WORT
Hypericum majus
St. John's Wort Family (Clusiaceae)

Description: Slender plant to 1½' tall and usually unbranched below the flowers, with stalkless, narrow, opposite, smooth-edged leaves up to 1½" long and less than ⅜" wide. The leaves have broadly rounded bases and 5–7 lengthwise nerves. The leaves of a pair often touch at their bases. Flowers are in a compact branched cluster at the top of the stem. Each flower is ¼" wide and has 5 pointed sepals, 5 yellow petals, and numerous stamens surrounding a flask-shaped ovary.

Bloom Season: Midsummer–early fall.

Habitat/Range: Common in moist open areas in wet meadows, muddy depressions, marshes, peaty areas, and along shores; throughout the region.

Comments: Canadian St. John's Wort (*H. canadense*) is similar but has only 1–3 veins along the leaves, which taper to narrowed bases. It occurs in similar habitats from Wisconsin eastward. Spotted St. John's Wort (*H. punctatum*) is a larger plant with leaves and flowers that are spattered with tiny black dots. It occurs in marshy areas and wet thickets, mostly in the southern part of the region from Quebec to southeastern Minnesota. See Common St. John's Wort (p. 253).

GREAT ST. JOHN'S WORT
Hypericum pyramidatum
St. John's Wort Family (Clusiaceae)

Description: Large, shrubby-looking plant to 6' tall, with short branches mostly above the middle. The minutely pale-spotted leaves are stalkless, opposite, smooth edged, up to 5" long and 1½" wide, and horizontally spreading, with bluntly pointed tips and slightly clasping bases. At the top of the plant are a few large showy flowers, each up to 2" wide. Each flower has 5 broadly pointed sepals, 5 large rounded petals, and abundant yellow stamens surrounding a flask-shaped ovary. The fruits are thick, brown, pyramid-like capsules up to 1" long.

Bloom Season: Early summer–midsummer.

Habitat/Range: Frequent in moist thickets, moist open woods, marshy areas, and along shores; in the western half of the region and rare eastward.

Comments: Kalm's St. John's Wort (*H. kalmianum*) is a smaller, more bushy shrub with leaves up to 1½" long and flowers up to 1⅛" wide. It occurs in moist alkaline areas around the Great Lakes from western New York to Wisconsin.

Great St. John's Wort

SCREWSTEM
Bartonia virginica
Gentian Family (Gentianaceae)

Description: Pale, delicate, slender plant to 1' tall that is unbranched below the flowers and sometimes has curving or spiraled stems. The leaves are reduced to small pairs of pointed, mostly opposite scales along the stem. Flowers are in short, opposite-branched clusters along the upper half of the stem. Each flower is ⅛" long and has 4 needlelike sepals and a pale yellowish, urn-shaped corolla with 4 small pointed lobes.

Bloom Season: Midsummer–early fall.

Habitat/Range: Occasional in acidic sites, usually in wet areas of bogs, sandy shores, seeps, and moss mats in conifer swamps; throughout the region.

Comments: Another species, *B. paniculata*, has mostly alternate scales on the stem; in this region it occurs rarely in Michigan and Ontario and along the Atlantic coast.

Screwstem

ROBERT TATINA photos

Bluebead Lily

BLUEBEAD LILY
Clintonia borealis
Lily Family (Liliaceae)

Description: Plant usually less than 10" tall, with 2–5 thick, shiny, broadly rounded basal leaves up to 10" long, each with bluntly pointed tips and tapering, sheathlike bases. There are usually some fine hairs along the leaf edges. The bare flowering stem is topped with a cluster of a few pale yellow flowers. Each slender-stalked flower is ¾" wide, with 6 pointed, petal-like segments surrounding 6 stamens. The fruits are deep blue berries about ⅜" wide.

Bloom Season: Late spring–early summer.

Habitat/Range: Common in and characteristic of a variety of shaded habitats, including dry to moist woods of all types, bogs, swamps, and rocky slopes, especially common in open birch/fir or spruce woods; throughout the region.

YELLOW TROUT LILY
Erythronium americanum
Lily Family (Liliaceae)

Description: Smooth plant to 10" tall, with thick, shiny, narrowly oval basal leaves that taper to pointed tips and narrow sheathlike bases. The leaves are usually mottled with reddish brown. Flowering plants have a pair of basal leaves, while sterile plants have a single leaf. The bare flower stalk arises between the leaves and has a single nodding flower at the top. This flower is up to 3½" wide and has 6 yellow, pointed, petal-like segments that are widely spreading or even curved backward. The segments often are tinged with a copper color on the outside. There are 6 erect, yellow to reddish stamens and a single 3-lobed ovary with a club-shaped style.

Bloom Season: Spring.

Habitat/Range: Common in rich woods, including mountain conifer forests, sometimes forming extensive patches; throughout the region.

Comments: The bulbs and greens are said to be edible. A similar species with white flowers,

JESSIE M. HARRIS

Yellow Trout Lily

White Trout Lily (*E. albidum*), is uncommon from southern Ontario westward, mostly in the southern part of the region.

ALLISON W. BELL

Canada Lily

DON KURZ

Michigan Lily

CANADA LILY
Lilium canadense
Lily Family (Liliaceae)

Description: Smooth, stout plant to 5' tall, with several whorls of narrow pointed leaves along the stem. There are usually also some alternate leaves on parts of the stem. The thick waxy leaves are typically 2½–6" long, with minutely roughened edges and tapering, stalkless bases. Long-stalked flowers dangle in 1 to several clusters near the top of the plant. Each flower is 2–3" wide, with 6 yellow-orange, pointed, widely spreading or slightly curving petal-like segments. The inside of the segments is usually spotted with reddish purple. Within the flower are 6 large, clustered, orange-tipped stamens and a style with a knobby 3-lobed tip.

Bloom Season: Late spring–midsummer.

Habitat/Range: Occasional in moist meadows, low thickets, wet woods, and along seepy banks; in the eastern half of the region westward to Lake Huron.

Comments: The cooked bulbs have been used for food. Michigan Lily (*L. michiganense*) is a close relative found in similar habitats and in fens from Ontario southward and westward. It has strongly arching, petal-like segments that curve upward above the dangling flower, with protruding, spreading stamens.

Wood Lily

DON KURZ

WOOD LILY
Lilium philadelphicum
Lily Family (Liliaceae)

Description: Smooth, usually branched plant to 2½' tall, with a whorl of 3–7 narrow, pointed, stalkless leaves up to 3" long on the upper stems. Below this whorl are alternate leaves, or additional whorls of leaves, or both. The vivid orange-red flowers are upright at the top of the stems. Each plant usually has 1 flower but occasionally more. Each open, cuplike flower is up to 4" wide and has 3 petals and 3 similar petal-like sepals, all tapering to narrow stalklike bases. There are 6 protruding, orange- to brownish tipped stamens and a long style with a knobby 3-lobed tip. The insides of the petals and sepals are usually spotted with dark purple.

Bloom Season: Late spring–midsummer.

Habitat/Range: Uncommon in open woods, thickets, open sandy or rocky areas, moist meadows, and along shores; throughout all but the northernmost part of the region, eastward to Maine.

Comments: North American Indians used the bulbs for food.

Large-flowered Bellwort

JESSIE M. HARRIS

LARGE-FLOWERED BELLWORT
Uvularia grandiflora
Lily Family (Liliaceae)

Description: Unbranched or once-branched plant to 2½' tall. It appears wilted or droopy at flowering and later becomes straighter and taller. The lower part of the stem has several sheathing bracts and sometimes a few leaves, while the upper part of the stem has numerous alternate, smooth-edged leaves that are small at flowering but later expand up to 5" long. Each leaf has a finely hairy lower surface, a pointed tip, and several parallel veins along its length, and each appears to be pierced by the stem, which is completely surrounded by the leaf. On the upper part of the plant are a few dangling, bright yellow flowers. These never open fully. Each flower has 6 narrow, yellow, petal-like segments that are 1–2" long. The fruits are strongly 3-lobed, almost triangular, capsules.

Bloom Season: Early spring–midspring.

Habitat/Range: Occasional in rich moist woods, especially on lower slopes, in ravines, and along streams; throughout the region eastward to New Hampshire and Quebec, but rarer eastward.

Comments: Two other species of bellwort occur in the region. Merrybells (*U. sessilifolia*) has leaves whose bases merely clasp the stem. The lower leaf surfaces are whitened, and the pale yellow flowers are less than 1½" long. It occurs in similar habitats, as well as in drier sites throughout the region. Perfoliate Bellwort (*U. perfoliata*) has leaves like those of Large-Flowered Bellwort, except there are no hairs on their undersides. Its pale yellow flower segments have tiny, orange, wartlike bumps on their insides. It occurs in woods in the eastern half of the region westward to southern Ontario. Bellworts were once thought to cure throat diseases because the dangling flower was thought to signify the uvula at the back of the human throat.

Pinesap

Pine Drops

PINESAP
Monotropa hypopithys
Indian Pipe Family (Monotropaceae)

Description: Yellow to reddish, finely hairy, unbranched, fleshy plant to 1' tall, with scales arranged alternately along the stem and at the bases of the flowers. This plant lacks the green chlorophyll that other plants use to produce food and instead derives nutrients from fungi that feed on roots or decaying plants. At the top of the nodding stem is a dense cluster of yellow to reddish tubular flowers, each up to ½" long. Each flower has 4 or 5 narrow ragged petals, as well as 2 or more pointed sepals that usually fall early. Inside the flower are 8 or 10 stamens. The flower stem becomes upright as the fruits develop into fuzzy round capsules topped by stout styles.

Bloom Season: Late spring–midsummer.

Habitat/Range: Local in a variety of well-drained acidic woods, often in thick leaf litter; throughout the region.

Comments: Early-flowering plants tend to be yellow, while later-flowering plants are reddish. A similar but rare species, Pine Drops (*Pterospora andromedea*), is a reddish plant up to 3' tall with a clammy-sticky hairiness and flowers dangling on individual stalks from the upper stem. The flowers are up to ½" long and have 4 or 5 clammy, hairy, reddish sepals and an urnlike white corolla with 4 or 5 small lobes at the narrowed mouth. Pine Drops occurs under conifers in dry woods. Although often thought to be parasitic on pine roots, it is actually associated with fungi, just like Pinesap.

JESSIE M. HARRIS

Yellow Pond Lily

YELLOW POND LILY
Nuphar variegata
Water Lily Family (Nymphaeaceae)

Description: Aquatic plant with stalked leaves that mostly float on the water, although the leaves can also be completely submerged or emerge above the water. The leaves in bud are curled like a scroll. Each leaf is a broad oval up to 10" long and 7" wide, with a U-shaped notch where the stalk is attached. The leaf stalks are thick, soft, and flattened on the top side. The flowers, which grow to about 2" wide, are deep yellow above and often reddish on the lower parts. They grow above the water on individual stalks. Each flower usually has 6 upright, rounded sepals marked with combinations of red, green, and yellow, along with many small yellow petals and numerous flattened yellow stamens surrounding a yellowish disklike stigma marked with lines like the spokes on a wheel.

Bloom Season: Late spring–summer.

Habitat/Range: Common in quiet, shallow water in ponds, lakes, marshes, and backwaters of rivers and streams, usually rooting in mud or sand; throughout the region.

Comments: A closely related species in similar habitats in the southern half of the region from Wisconsin eastward, Southern Pond Lily (*N. advena*) has round or oval leaf stalks and flowers that are usually yellow without red overtones. A rarer species scattered through the northern and eastern parts of the region, Small Yellow Pond Lily (*N. microphylla*), has 5 sepals and a red stigma disk.

STEPHEN CLAYDEN/NEW BRUNSWICK MUSEUM

Evening Primrose

EVENING PRIMROSE
Oenothera parviflora
Evening Primrose Family (Onagraceae)

Description: Coarse, hairy biennial to 6' tall, often with reddish tinged stems. The leaves are alternate and up to 8" long and 2½" wide. They have prominent, raised veins on the lower surface and smooth to weakly toothed edges. The leaves grow progressively smaller upward along the stem. Stalkless flowers are alternate along the upper stems, with a small leaflike bract at the base of each flower. Each flower is up to 1½" wide and has a long tubular ovary topped by 4 pointed, backward-angled sepals; 4 spreading, rounded, pale yellow petals; 8 yellow stamens; and a style with a cross-shaped tip. At dusk, the flowers open from bud into full bloom within minutes. The flowers produce a creosote-like aroma, which attracts the night-flying sphinx moths that pollinate them.

Bloom Season: Summer–fall.

Habitat/Range: Common in disturbed, mostly open sites, including waste ground, roadsides, thickets, and along woodland edges; throughout the region.

Comments: The roots are edible. There are several closely related species in the region, including Common Evening Primrose (*O. biennis*), a coarser plant with larger flowers. Scientists distinguish between the two plants by minute differences in their sepal tips.

LARGE YELLOW LADY'S SLIPPER

Cypripedium calceolus var. *pubescens*
Orchid Family (Orchidaceae)

Description: Plant to 2½' tall, with finely hairy stems and leaves. The alternate, pleated, parallel-veined leaves are up to 9" long and 5" wide. They have pointed tips and bases that clasp the stem. Typically, 1 or 2 flowers grow at the top of the stem, above an erect, leaflike bract. Each flower has an inflated, pouchlike, yellow slipper up to 2" long, flanked by thin, narrow, pointed, strap-shaped petals up to 2½" long. Two broad sepals arch above and below the slipper. The sepals and side petals are yellowish green to brown, sometimes with purplish brown markings.

Bloom Season: Midspring–early summer.

Habitat/Range: Occasional in woods, bogs, moist meadows, and swampy areas; throughout the region.

Comments: A smaller-flowered variety with dark purple side petals, Small Yellow Lady's Slipper (*C. calceolus* var. *parviflorum*), occurs in similar but often wetter sites in the region. In this variety, the slipper is no more than 1" long.

Large Yellow Lady's Slipper

ROBERT TATINA

Some people experience skin irritation after contact with the hairs of lady's slippers.

SMALL SUNDROPS

Oenothera perennis
Evening Primrose Family (Onagraceae)

Description: Usually unbranched stems to 20" tall, with stalkless, alternate, smooth-edged leaves to 2" long. These leaves have tapering bases, and there are sometimes small bractlike leaves at the bases of the main leaves. Flowers grow singly at the bases of the upper leaves, which become progressively smaller toward the top of the plant. Each flower is ⅝" wide and has a ridged, clublike ovary topped by a slender tube ending in 4 backward-pointing sepals; 4 slightly notched, rounded, yellow petals with narrow bases; 8 stamens; and a central style.

Bloom Season: Late spring–midsummer.

Habitat/Range: Frequent in open sandy areas, often in moist sandy seeps, and along sandy shores; throughout the region.

JESSIE M. HARRIS

Small Sundrops

Cancer Root

JESSIE M. HARRIS

CANCER ROOT
Conopholis americana
Broom Rape Family (Orobanchaceae)

Description: Hard-based, stout, unbranched, yellowish brown stalks to 8" tall. These fleshy stems are densely covered with upright, scalelike leaves, each up to ¾" long, with pointed brown tips. The plant lacks the green chlorophyll most plants use to produce food from sunlight and is parasitic on the roots of oak trees. Half-inch long flowers form a dense cluster along the stem, and below each flower is a pointed bract. At the base of the irregularly toothed, cuplike calyx are 2 narrow, much smaller bracts. The curved, yellowish, tubular corolla ends in a hooded upper lip over 3 spreading lobes and 4 slightly protruding stamens.

Bloom Season: Midspring–early summer.

Habitat/Range: Uncommon in rich or dry woods, typically in sandy oak-pine stands, where it is sometimes locally abundant; in the eastern part of the region westward to Wisconsin.

YELLOW WOOD SORREL
Oxalis stricta
Wood Sorrel Family (Oxalidaceae)

Description: Plant usually less than 10" tall, with spreading hairs on the stems. At the end of each long, spreading leaf stalk are 3 cloverlike, heart-shaped leaflets up to ¾" wide. Flowers are on individual stalks on the upper part of the plant. Each flower is ⅜" wide and has 5 pointed sepals, 5 yellow petals that often have slightly notched tips, and 10 stamens of alternating lengths. The candlelike seed capsules are on upright stalks.

Bloom Season: Midspring–fall.

Habitat/Range: Common and weedy in moist woods, clearings, thickets, and waste ground throughout the region.

Comments: The tart leaves contain oxalic acid and have been used in salads. A similar but less common plant in the region, *O. dillenii*, has small hairs pressed against the stem, and its fruit stalks point downward.

KENNETH DRITZ

Yellow Wood Sorrel

FRINGED LOOSESTRIFE
Lysimachia ciliata
Primrose Family (Primulaceae)

Description: Plant to 3' tall and sometimes branched above the middle, with stalked, opposite leaves up to 5" long and 2" wide. The leaves have rounded bases, pointed tips, and irregular, minutely fringed edges. Bristly hairs project along the sides of the leaf stalks. Flowers grow singly on long, slender, arching or dangling stalks at the bases of the leaf stalks. Each flower is 1" wide and has 5 narrow pointed sepals and 5 protruding yellow stamens. The spreading, 5-lobed corolla is yellow and nearly flat, with ragged, finely pointed tips and a reddish base.

Bloom Season: Early summer–midsummer.

Habitat/Range: Common in moist thickets, marshes, damp meadows, and on shaded floodplains; throughout the region.

Comments: Narrow-leaved Loosestrife (*L. quadriflora*) occurs in fens and alkaline marshes mostly in the south-central part of the region. It has narrow stalkless leaves less than ¼" wide.

JESSIE M. HARRIS

Fringed Loosestrife

SWAMP CANDLES
Lysimachia terrestris
Primrose Family (Primulaceae)

Description: Smooth plant to 2½' tall, often with short, upright side branches. The leaves are opposite and gradually taper to short, broad stalks and pointed tips, with the main leaves typically 3" long and ½" wide. Sometimes pairs of smaller leaves grow at the bases of the main leaf stalks. Each plant usually has a single narrow elongate cluster of alternate, individually stalked flowers at the top of the main stem, with a narrow bract below every flower. Each flower is ⅝" wide, with 5 small pointed sepals, 5 spreading, narrow yellow petals marked with 2 reddish spots at the base and sometimes with fine dark lines, and 5 protruding stamens. In late summer, some plants produce narrow reddish bulblets at the bases of the leaf stalks.

Bloom Season: Early summer–midsummer.

Habitat/Range: Common in open or lightly shaded wet places in swamps, marshes, bogs, wet meadows, and along shores; throughout the region.

KEITH BOARD

Swamp Candles

JESSIE M. HARRIS

Tufted Loosestrife

TUFTED LOOSESTRIFE
Lysimachia thyrsiflora
Primrose Family (Primulaceae)

Description: Plant to 2' tall, with narrow opposite leaves about 3–4" long and ½" wide. The leaves are broadest near the middle and taper to pointed tips and narrow stalkless bases. The upper part of the stem is squarish and often covered with fine hairs. Small yellow flowers are in dense oval clusters about ¾" thick on short stalks. The clusters are usually paired at the base of opposite leaves near the middle of the plant. Each flower has 5 tiny sepals that are united at their bases; 5–6 spreading, narrow, yellow corolla lobes that are often spotted with black; 5 or 6 threadlike yellow stamens; and a slender, upright, green style.

Bloom Season: Late spring–early summer.

Habitat/Range: Common in a variety of open or shaded wet areas, often in shallow quiet water; throughout the region.

SMALL-FLOWERED BUTTERCUP
Ranunculus abortivus
Buttercup Family (Ranunculaceae)

Description: Annual to 1½' tall, with shiny leaves and upright branches. The basal leaves have long stalks and vary from round and merely toothed along the edges to deeply lobed or divided into long narrow segments. The stem leaves are alternate, stalkless, and divided into 3–5 narrow segments that may be toothed or lobed. Individually stalked flowers occur at the bases of the upper leaves and the tips of the branches. Each flower is ¼" wide and typically has 5 pointed sepals, 5 smaller yellow petals, and several yellow stamens.

Bloom Season: Midspring–early summer.

Habitat/Range: Common in moist, often disturbed areas in woods and thickets, and sometimes in drier sites; throughout the region.

KEITH BOARD

Small-flowered Buttercup

ALLISON W. BELL

Marsh Marigold

MARSH MARIGOLD
Caltha palustris
Buttercup Family (Ranunculaceae)

Description: Smooth, often sprawling plant with hollow ridged stems up to 2' long and shiny alternate leaves up to 7" long. These leaves are broadly rounded to kidney shaped, with heart-shaped bases and a network of angular veins. The leaf edges are usually finely toothed. Lower leaves are stalked, while upper leaves are smaller and often stalkless. The bright yellow flowers are up to 2" wide and grow on individual stalks near the top of the plant. Each flower has 5 or 6 (rarely more) shiny petal-like sepals, no petals, and numerous yellow stamens.

Bloom Season: Spring.

Habitat/Range: Common, often forming large stands in open to lightly shaded wet places, typically in or near shallow standing water in marshes, open swamps, wet woodland depressions, seeps, and wet ditches; throughout the region.

Comments: The stems and leaves have been used medicinally and can be boiled and eaten like spinach. Multiple water changes are required to reduce the bitter taste.

Creeping Spearwort

CREEPING SPEARWORT
Ranunculus flammula
Buttercup Family (Ranunculaceae)

Description: Weak creeping stems up to 2' long, with clusters of a few narrow leaves at widely spaced intervals. These leaves are up to 2½" long and less than ⅛" wide. The stems often root at the leaf clusters and send up weak flowering branches that are leafless or have a few alternate leaves. There is usually a single flower at the top of a flowering branch. Each flower is ⅜" wide and has 5 small sepals, 5 larger yellow petals, and several yellow stamens.

Bloom Season: Summer.

Habitat/Range: Occasional in open wet sand or mud along ponds, lakes, and streams; throughout the region.

SWAMP BUTTERCUP
Ranunculus hispidus var. *caricetorum*
Buttercup Family (Ranunculaceae)

Description: Low plant with initially upright stems that eventually arch and root at the tips. The alternate, stalked, compound leaves have 3 parts. Each leaflet is up to 2½" long, toothed, and sometimes lobed. The middle leaflet is always stalked, and the side leaflets are stalked or stalkless. Several individually stalked flowers occur on the upper part of the branches. Each flower is up to 1¼" wide and usually has 5 spreading sepals; 5 larger, rounded, shiny yellow petals; and several stamens.

Bloom Season: Spring–midsummer.

Habitat/Range: Common in moist woods, swamps, wet muddy meadows, along shores, and on shaded floodplains; throughout the region.

Comments: See Tall Buttercup (p. 255).

Swamp Buttercup

JESSIE M. HARRIS

Hooked Buttercup

HOOKED BUTTERCUP
Ranunculus recurvatus
Buttercup Family (Ranunculaceae)

Description: Hairy plant to 2' tall, with deeply lobed, stalked, alternate leaves. The basal and lower stem leaves are deeply divided into 3 toothed or lobed segments. The middle and upper leaves may be stalked or stalkless and lobed or unlobed. Individually stalked flowers occur at the bases of the upper leaves and tops of the branches. Each pale yellow flower is up to ⅜" wide and has 5 sepals, 5 slightly shorter petals, and numerous stamens.

Bloom Season: Midspring–early summer.

Habitat/Range: Frequent in shaded moist areas in fens, springy thickets, and boggy or swampy woods and along shaded stream banks; throughout the region.

Comments: Cursed Crowfoot (*R. sceleratus*) is a similar but smooth, hollow-stemmed plant. It occurs in open muddy places throughout much of the region. Bristly Buttercup (*R. pensylvanicus*) occurs in open wet mud. It is a coarser plant with more bristly hairs, and most of its leaves are deeply lobed. It is most common in the western half of the region.

Early Meadow Rue

ROBERT TATINA

EARLY MEADOW RUE
Thalictrum dioicum
Buttercup Family (Ranunculaceae)

Description: Stems to 2½' tall, with 1–3 stalked, grayish green, main leaves that are pale beneath and repeatedly divided by threes into stalked segments. Each segment is typically up to 1½" long, with a rounded base and 4 or more shallow lobes at the tip. The lobes may have teeth along the edges. The upper leaves are similar but less divided. There are papery bracts at the bases of the upper leaf stalks. Flowers grow abundantly in branched clusters at the top of the plant, with male and female flowers on separate plants. There are no petals, and the 4 small sepals fall soon after the flower opens. The male flower (pictured) consists of a cluster of dangling, greenish yellow stamens. The female flower consists of several fuzzy purple stigmas topping the ovaries.

Bloom Season: Spring–early summer.

Habitat/Range: Common in rich moist woods, shaded rocky areas, streamside thickets, and on forested slopes; throughout most of the region eastward to Maine and Quebec.

Comments: This plant is also called Quicksilver Weed. Two related species have stalkless leaves, so that the stalked leaf segments appear to be a whorl of 3 stalked leaves from a common point on the stem, with 2- to 3-lobed leaflets. Purple Meadow Rue (*T. dasycarpum*) has drooping stamens on the male flowers and occurs in the western half of the region, rarely as far east as Vermont. Tall Meadow Rue (*T. pubescens*) has erect stamens on the male flowers and occurs in the eastern half of the region westward to Ontario. Another species, Northern Meadow Rue (*T. venulosum*), has many teeth and lobes on the leaflets, like Early Meadow Rue, but its leaves are stalkless or nearly so. It occurs on exposed rocky shores and in moist thickets from Lake Michigan westward.

Woodland Agrimony

ROBERT TATINA

WOODLAND AGRIMONY
Agrimonia striata
Rose Family (Rosaceae)

Description: Single-stemmed, unbranched plant to 3' tall, with long, soft, brownish hairs. The short-stalked leaves are alternate and compound, with conspicuous 2- to 3-toothed, pointed, bractlike stipules at the base of each leaf. There are typically 7–11 coarsely toothed main leaflets. The end leaflet is the largest and ranges up to 2" long. Tiny leafy bracts often grow between the main leaflets. The lower surfaces of the leaves have many tiny, clear, dotlike glands. Flowers grow in an elongate cluster along the hairy upper stem. Each flower is ¼" wide and has a tiny, 3-lobed, leafy bract at its base. The base of the flower, which contains the ovary, is topped by hooked green bristles, inside of which are 5 small sepals, 5 rounded, bright yellow petals, and 10 tiny yellow stamens.

Bloom Season: Midsummer–early fall.

Habitat/Range: Occasional in moist to dryish areas in open woods and thickets and along shores; throughout the region, but rare in the southern parts.

Comments: Tall Agrimony (*A. gryposepala*) is a similar plant found in disturbed woods. It has many clear glands along the flower-bearing part of the stem, while Woodland Agrimony lacks glands on the flower stem.

Yellow Avens

YELLOW AVENS
Geum aleppicum
Rose Family (Rosaceae)

Description: Coarse plant to 3' tall, with stiffly spreading hairs on the stem. The leaves are alternate, compound, and variable, but usually the main leaves are stalked, with a broad, sometimes lobed end leaflet that tapers to the base. The end leaflet is larger than the side leaflets, which often alternate with tiny bracts. All of the leaflets are toothed and sometimes also lobed, and the leaf stalk has a pair of toothed, bractlike stipules at its base. The upper leaves are usually stalkless and sometimes unlobed. Flowers occur singly on stout stalks near the top of the plant. Each flower is ⅞" wide and has 5 pointed hairy sepals about as long as the 5 bright yellow petals, and 10 or more stamens surrounding a conical center. The seed head appears bristly, and the sepals turn downward in fruit.

Bloom Season: Late spring–midsummer.

Habitat/Range: Common in moist, open to lightly shaded areas in swamps, moist thickets, and along seepy slopes and shores, as well as occasionally in drier areas and woods; throughout the region.

Comments: Alpine Avens (*G. macrophyllum*) is a similar species scattered throughout the northern half of the region. The end leaflet of its main leaves is large and round, with a broad or heart-shaped base.

JESSIE M. HARRIS

Silverweed

SILVERWEED
Potentilla anserina
Rose Family (Rosaceae)

Description: This low plant has tufts of basal leaves and wiry, reddish, creeping stems to 3' long or longer. Widely spaced clusters of smaller leaves and often roots sprout along the stems. The stalked, compound leaves are bright green above and silvery-white with dense fine hairs on the lower surface. Each leaf is up to 8" long, with a pair of papery stipules at the base of the leaf stalk and up to 15 toothed main leaflets, each up to 1½" long and arranged in opposite pairs along a hairy axis. Several much smaller leaflets are usually scattered among the main leaflets. A single hairy-stalked flower arises from a leaf cluster. Each flower is ¾" wide and has 5 pointed sepals alternating with 5 smaller green bracts, 5 bright yellow petals, and numerous stamens.

Bloom Season: Late spring–early fall.

Habitat/Range: Common in moist, open sand or gravel in sparse vegetation, along shores and beaches, and in open sand flats; throughout the region.

Comments: The boiled roots of this plant are said to taste like parsnips. Silvery Cinquefoil (*P. argentea*) is an introduced weed that sometimes occurs in similar habitats. It is a compact plant without trailing stems, flowers less than ½" wide, and leaflets arranged like fingers on a hand.

ROBERT TATINA

Prairie Cinquefoil

PRAIRIE CINQUEFOIL
Potentilla arguta
Rose Family (Rosaceae)

Description: Hairy, stout-stemmed plant to 3' tall and unbranched below the flowers, with widely spaced, alternate, compound leaves that become progressively smaller toward the top of the plant. Each leaf has a pair of toothed leafy stipules at the base of its stalk and 3–11 toothed, egg-shaped leaflets, as well as often some small bracts. The leaflets near the tip of the leaf stalk are usually the largest, ranging up to 3" long. Flowers appear in compact, branched clusters at the top of the plant. Each individually stalked flower is typically ⅞" wide and has 5 pointed sepals alternating with 5 smaller bracts, 5 creamy to pale yellow, narrow-based petals, and 25 or more stamens surrounding a conical center.

Bloom Season: Late spring–midsummer.

Habitat/Range: Infrequent in open areas in dry woods, fields, and pastures, and on sandy slopes, usually in neutral to alkaline soil; throughout most of the region eastward to Maine and Quebec.

Comments: Sulfur Cinquefoil (*P. recta*), a European weed common throughout the region, also has pale yellow flowers, but its leaflets arise at the end of the leaf stalk like fingers on a hand.

SHRUBBY CINQUEFOIL
Potentilla fruticosa
Rose Family (Rosaceae)

Description: Bushy shrub to 3' tall, with stringy bark and abundant alternate leaves. Each stalked leaf has a pair of papery stipules at the base and 3–7 narrow, pointed, silky-hairy leaflets up to 1½" long clustered near the tip. The individually stalked flowers are about 1" wide and occur singly or in few-flowered clusters at the tip of the branches. Each flower has 5 pointed sepals alternating with 5 equally long but narrower bracts, 5 broadly rounded bright yellow petals, and numerous stamens.

Bloom Season: Late spring–early fall.

Habitat/Range: Local in wet, typically alkaline sites in wet meadows, fens, seepy areas, and along shores, as well as in swamps with white cedar, tamarack, or black spruce; also on dry limestone; throughout the region.

KEITH BOARD

Shrubby Cinquefoil

ROBERT TATINA

Common Cinquefoil

COMMON CINQUEFOIL
Potentilla simplex
Rose Family (Rosaceae)

Description: Arching or trailing, hairy, reddish, wiry stems to 3' long and rooting at the tips, with widely spaced clusters of 1 to a few compound leaves. Each long-stalked leaf has 2 bractlike stipules at its base and 5 narrow leaflets arranged at the tip of the stalk like fingers on a hand. The leaflets are typically 1–2" long and toothed except near the tapering bases. Long-stalked flowers occur singly in the leaf clusters. Each flower is ½" wide and has 5 narrow pointed sepals alternating with 5 narrower bracts, 5 broadly rounded, bright yellow petals, and typically 20 yellow stamens surrounding a conical center.

Bloom Season: Midspring–early summer.

Habitat/Range: Common in dry open woods, fields, pastures, and along stream banks; throughout the region.

Comments: Canada Cinquefoil (*P. canadensis*) is a rarer species occurring in the region from southern Ontario eastward. Its leaflets are usually less than twice as long as they are broad, and some flowers grow at the first cluster of leaves above the roots. The leaflets of Common Cinquefoil are usually more than twice as long as they are broad, and the plant has no flowers at the first leaf cluster. Another cinquefoil with similar flowers, Rough Cinquefoil (*P. norvegica*), is an erect weedy plant with 3 coarsely toothed leaflets per leaf.

Cow Wheat

COW WHEAT
Melampyrum lineare
Snapdragon Family (Scrophulariaceae)

Description: Branched, pale green annual to 15" tall, with opposite, short-stalked leaves. The leaves have smooth edges, pointed tips, and rounded bases. They range up to 2½" long and vary from ⅛–¼" wide. The short-stalked flowers are arranged in pairs along the upper parts of the branches, each above a leaflike bract. These bracts usually have 1 or 2 coarse triangular teeth or small lobes on each side near the base. Each flower is ½" long and has a cuplike calyx with 4 pointed lobes and a tubular white corolla with a prominent yellow tip. The plants are partially parasitic on the roots of other plants.

Bloom Season: Summer.

Habitat/Range: Common in dry open woods, exposed rocky areas, blueberry heaths, and sand barrens; throughout the region.

BARREN STRAWBERRY
Waldsteinia fragarioides
Rose Family (Rosaceae)

Description: Delicate, hairy plant usually less than 6" tall, with a basal cluster of long-stalked compound leaves, each of which has 3 coarsely toothed and sometimes lobed leaflets at the tip of the stalk. The leaflets are widest above the middle and have smooth-edged, wedge-shaped bases. There are from 1 to a few leafless upright stems, each with scattered small bracts and a few individually stalked flowers at the top. Each flower is ½" wide and has 5 pointed sepals that sometimes alternate with tiny bracts, 5 yellow petals with narrow bases, and many slender stamens.

Barren Strawberry

Bloom Season: Midspring–late spring.

Habitat/Range: Uncommon but sometimes locally frequent in well-drained, open woods and thickets; in most of the region eastward to southern Maine and New Brunswick.

YELLOW MONKEY FLOWER
Mimulus glabratus
Snapdragon Family (Scrophulariaceae)

Description: Weak, smooth to minutely hairy, sprawling plant often rooting along its stem. The leaves are round and typically less than 1" across, with irregular teeth along the edges. The lower leaves are on short stalks, but the upper leaves are often stalkless. Stalked flowers arise singly at the bases of stem leaves. Each flower is ⅝" long and has a small tubular calyx with 5 unequal teeth and a bright yellow, 2-lipped, tubular corolla with a 2-lobed upper lip and a flaring 3-lobed lower lip that is hairy on the inside.

Bloom Season: Late spring–early fall.

Habitat/Range: Local in cold, usually alkaline, springy places, often in shallow, clear, flowing water; in the western part of the region eastward to Ontario.

Comments: Muskflower (*M. moschatus*) occurs in muddy or springy places here and there in the region. It is a densely hairy plant with needlelike calyx teeth. Most local populations are escapes from cultivation.

Yellow Monkey Flower

CLAMMY GROUND CHERRY
Physalis heterophylla
Nightshade Family (Solanaceae)

Description: Sprawling, bushy-branched, clammy-hairy plant usually less than 2' tall, with stalked, coarse, few-toothed, alternate leaves that often appear opposite. The leaves are up to 4" long and 3" wide, broadly rounded to indented at the base, and pointed at the tips. The flowers grow singly on slender nodding stalks at the branch junctions and bases of the leaf stalks. Each flower is ¾" wide and has a hairy cuplike calyx with 5 triangular lobes and a 5-angled, pale yellow corolla with a dark purplish center and 5 stamens. The calyx enlarges in fruit to become an inflated papery husk that encloses the berry.

Bloom Season: Late spring–midsummer.

Habitat/Range: Common in open sandy or gravelly areas, fields, open thickets, waste ground, and along woodland edges; throughout the region.

Comments: Several other species of ground cherry occur here and there in the region, but most are smaller and lack sticky hairs.

Clammy Ground Cherry

Lousewort

KEITH BOARD

LOUSEWORT
Pedicularis canadensis
Snapdragon Family (Scrophulariaceae)

Description: Hairy, pale yellowish green plant to 18" tall, often forming mats of fernlike basal leaves up to 6" long. The stems have a few alternate, stalked leaves that are divided along their length into numerous short, toothed lobes. The leaves have a crinkly and often purple-tinged surface. Flowers grow in dense clusters at the tops of the stems. Each flower is 1" long and located directly above a small leaflike bract. The flower has a calyx with a slanted mouth and a pale yellow (rarely purple), arching, 2-lipped corolla. The hooded upper lip is longer and has 2 downward-pointing teeth at the end, while the lower lip is usually wrinkled and lobed.

Bloom Season: Midspring–early summer.

Habitat/Range: Occasional in sandy upland woods, meadows, and well-drained rocky forest openings; mostly in the southern half of the region from Maine and Quebec westward.

Comments: The name Lousewort came from the belief that livestock would get lice if they ate the plant. Lousewort is partially parasitic on the roots of other plants. Swamp Betony (*P. lanceolata*) occurs in wet, often alkaline sites throughout the southern part of the region from Massachusetts westward. It is a taller plant with smooth stems and mostly opposite, shallowly lobed leaves.

YELLOW VIOLET
Viola pubescens
Violet Family (Violaceae)

Description: Smooth to densely hairy plant to 15" tall, with 1 or more basal leaves and 1–4 stems, each with 2–4 leaves clustered in the upper half. All of the leaves are long stalked and up to 4" long, with flat to shallowly heart-shaped bases, pointed tips, and toothed edges. The stem leaves are alternate, with a pair of bractlike stipules at the base of the leaf stalk. Flowers are single on nodding stalks arising at the bases of the upper leaves. Near the middle of each flower stalk is a pair of tiny bracts. Each flower is ¾" wide and has 5 pointed sepals and 5 yellow petals marked near their bases with fine brownish lines. The insides of the 2 side petals are hairy, and the lower petal is prolonged at the base into a short spur.

Bloom Season: Spring.

Habitat/Range: Locally common in rich woods, typically under hardwoods; throughout the region.

Comments: Round-leaved Violet (*V. rotundifolia*), another yellow-flowered species, has leafless flower stems. It occurs in conifer forests from Maine to Ontario.

Yellow Violet

BOG YELLOW-EYED GRASS
Xyris montana
Yellow-eyed Grass Family (Xyridaceae)

Description: Slender plant to 15" tall, with tufts of slightly twisted, grasslike leaves and bare, wiry, somewhat angular stems topped with a single, small, oval flower head. The leaves are up to 4" long and less than ⅛" wide. The head consists of a series of bracts, each containing a flower with 3 scalelike sepals and a short-lived, 3-lobed, yellow corolla that is ⅛" wide.

Bloom Season: Midsummer–early fall.

Habitat/Range: Infrequent in wet sandy or boggy areas; in the northern part of the region southward to the north shore of Lake Michigan and southern New England.

Comments: Twisted Yellow-Eyed Grass (*X. torta*) occurs in the region, particularly east of Lake Michigan. It is a larger plant with strongly spiral-twisted leaves. If the corollas are not present, the stems can resemble common sedges called spike rushes (*Eleocharis* sp.), which lack basal leaves.

Bog Yellow-eyed Grass

WHITE FLOWERS

Large-flowered Trillium

White flowers can encompass a surprising variety of shades, ranging from pale translucent to vivid cotton-white or creamy. Some typically pink-flowered plants also produce white forms, so you should also check the pink section of this guide. A common white-flowered weed is shown on page 255.

JESSIE M. HARRIS

Common Arrowhead

COMMON ARROWHEAD
Sagittaria latifolia
Water Plantain Family (Alismataceae)

Description: Soft plant to 3' tall, with milky sap and several large arrowhead-shaped basal leaves on long thick stalks that have broad papery bases. The leaves are up to 15" long and 1–10" wide, with 2 large, sharply pointed lobes at the base. Well-separated whorls of 3 or more long-stalked flowers occur near the top of the flower stem. At the base of each whorl are 3 papery bracts up to $7/16$" long. Each flower is 1" wide and has 3 small blunt sepals and 3 broad white petals. The upper flowers are male, each with 25 or more yellow stamens, and the lower flowers are female.

Bloom Season: Summer.

Habitat/Range: Common in shallow quiet water in bogs, marshes, and along shores, typically in mud; throughout the region.

Comments: A close relative, Northern Arrowhead (*S. cuneata*), is occasional in similar habitats but has long-pointed bracts longer than $7/16$" and 20 or fewer stamens in the male flower. Both plants are also called Wapato or Duck Potato. Both species can develop odd ribbon-like leaves when growing completely submerged. North American Indians relied upon the starchy potato-like tubers of arrowhead plants as a food source.

GREAT ANGELICA
Angelica atropurpurea
Carrot Family (Apiaceae)

Description: Smooth plant to 6' tall, with thick, hollow, purplish stems and large, alternate, compound leaves. The base of each leaf stalk broadens into a papery sheath surrounding the stem. The basal and lower leaves are the largest, consisting of a branched array of numerous toothed and occasionally lobed segments, each up to 5" long. These are widest near the middle, with pointed tips and tapered bases. The upper leaves are progressively smaller and less compound and have shorter stalks. Flowers are at the tops of the stalks in branched, rounded, umbrella-like heads 5–10" wide. Each head has 20–50 long-stalked clusters of small white to greenish white flowers. Each flower is ⅛" wide and has 5 tiny petals and 5 longer stamens.

Bloom Season: Late spring–summer.

Habitat/Range: Local in seepy or springy areas, wet woods, and along moist shores; scattered throughout most of the region.

Comments: North American Indians used the roots to prepare medicine for colds, fevers, and other ailments.

Great Angelica

FEN WATER PARSNIP
Berula erecta
Carrot Family (Apiaceae)

Description: Low, sparsely branched plant usually less than 15" tall, with alternate compound leaves. Each leaf has 7 or more narrow leaflets up to 2" long that are sharply and irregularly toothed and sometimes narrowly lobed. The flowers are in flat, umbrella-like heads of 5–15 unequally long-stalked clusters of small white flowers. Each flower is less than ⅛" wide and has 5 petals and 5 stamens.

Bloom Season: Summer.

Habitat/Range: Uncommon and local in cool, clear, calcium-rich or alkaline groundwater flows in fens, hillside seeps, and spring outlets; from New York and Ontario westward, mostly in the southern part of the region.

Fen Water Parsnip

BULBLET-BEARING WATER HEMLOCK
Cicuta bulbifera
Carrot Family (Apiaceae)

Description: Spindly plant to 3' tall, usually with a few branches in the upper half. The widely spaced, stalked, alternate compound leaves are progressively smaller toward the top of the stem. The upper leaves are sometimes narrow and stalkless. The main leaves are each divided into a branching array of very narrow leaflets, with a few sharp teeth or lobes along the edges of the larger leaflets, which can be up to 3" long. Small, rounded, green bulblets nestle at the base of the upper leaves. The flowers are less than ⅛" wide and often sparse or poorly developed. They occur in 1–2" wide umbrella-like clusters. Each flower has 5 small white petals and 5 slender stamens.

Bloom Season: Midsummer–late summer.

Habitat/Range: Occasional in swamps, wet meadows, springy seeps, bogs, fens, and along shores, usually in shallow standing water; throughout the region.

Comments: The bulblets can form new plants and may compensate for the poor seed production. The plant is extremely poisonous if eaten.

Bulblet-bearing Water Hemlock

ROBERT TATINA

DON KURZ

Water Hemlock

WATER HEMLOCK
Cicuta maculata
Carrot Family (Apiaceae)

Description: Smooth, branched biennial to 6' tall, with alternate compound leaves that are progressively smaller toward the top of the plant. The lower part of the stem is hollow and often purple. The main leaves have a branched array of sharply toothed and sometimes lobed leaflets. These have pointed tips and are up to 4" long and 1½" wide. The veins of the leaflets end at the notches between the teeth, rather than at the tips of the teeth as in most plants. The tiny white flowers are in rounded umbrella-like clusters up to 5" wide. Each flower is ⅛" wide and has 5 petals and 5 stamens.

Bloom Season: Late spring–early fall.

Habitat/Range: Common along shores and in swamps, marshes, wet woods, and wet areas in fields and pastures; throughout the region.

Comments: This is one of the most poisonous plants in North America. Even a small quantity of the roots is fatal if eaten.

HONEWORT

Cryptotaenia canadensis
Carrot Family (Apiaceae)

Description: Smooth plant to 3'
tall, with alternate, stalked, compound leaves that sheath the stem
at their expanded papery bases.
Each leaf has 3 leaflets arising at
the tip of the leaf stalk. These
leaflets are up to 7" long and 3½"
wide and have abundant irregular teeth along the edges. The
leaflets are often asymmetrical or
sometimes unevenly lobed and
have pointed tips. Flowers are in
small, unequally branched clus-
ters on long stalks toward the top of the plant.
Each flower is less than ⅛" wide and has 5
spreading white petals and 5 tiny stamens.

Honewort

ROBERT TATINA

Bloom Season: Late spring–summer.

Habitat/Range: Common in rich or moist woods
and on shaded floodplains, usually under hardwoods, and often increasing with disturbances
such as light grazing or selective logging; throughout the region eastward to Maine and New
Brunswick, but sporadic northward.

Cow Parsnip

ROBERT TATINA

COW PARSNIP

Heracleum lanatum
Carrot Family (Apiaceae)

Description: Stout, hairy-stemmed plant typically 3–6' tall but occasionally up to 10' tall, with
large, alternate, compound leaves whose stalks
clasp the stems at their expanded papery bases.
Each leaf is divided into 3 or more stalked leaflets that are up to 15" long and about as wide.
The leaflets are sharply toothed, unevenly lobed,
and indented at their bases. Flowers are at the
tops of the stems in flat umbrella-like heads up
to 10" wide, with 15–30 clusters on spokelike
stalks in each head. Each flower is $^3/_{16}$" wide
and has 5 petals (often notched) and 5 stamens.
The outside petals of the outer flowers are often larger and more deeply notched.

Bloom Season: Midspring–midsummer.

Habitat/Range: Common in rich moist soils,
usually in partial shade, in thickets, wet meadows, floodplains, and along woodland edges and
stream banks; throughout the region.

Comments: Contact with the plant can cause
severe skin irritation in some people. North
American Indians used the plant for a variety
of medicines and reportedly used the stalks as a
food source, although the foliage is poisonous
to livestock and has caused blisters when
handled by some people.

ROBERT TATINA

Hairy Sweet Cicely

HAIRY SWEET CICELY
Osmorhiza claytonii
Carrot Family (Apiaceae)

Description: Softly hairy plant to 2½' tall, with large, alternate, fernlike leaves. The main leaves are long-stalked on the lower stem and become smaller and shorter-stalked upward. The base of the stalk sheaths the stem. Each leaf is divided into a branched and lobed array of bluntly toothed segments, each up to 3" long and usually broadest below the middle. The small white flowers are in branched clusters at the top of the stem branches. A cluster has up to 10 flowers and a series of small narrow bracts at the base. Each flower is ⅛" wide and has 5 white petals and 5 upright stamens. The stiff, bristly, club-shaped fruits are tipped with 2 sharply pointed styles and cling to clothing.

Bloom Season: Midspring–midsummer.

Habitat/Range: Common in moist to dry woods, sometimes increasing after disturbance; throughout the region.

Comments: Two related species occur in the region. Mountain Sweet Cicely (*O. chilensis*) lacks bracts under the flower clusters and is uncommon in the northern part of the region. Smooth Sweet Cicely (*O. longistylis*) is a larger, less hairy plant with longer styles, more than 10 flowers per cluster, and a strong licorice fragrance. It occurs in similar habitats throughout the region.

BLACK SNAKEROOT
Sanicula marilandica
Carrot Family (Apiaceae)

Description: Spindly plant to 3' tall and branched in the upper half. The leaf stalks are up to 8" long near the base of the plant and become progressively smaller upward. The upper leaves typically are stalkless. The lower leaf stalks have expanded papery bases that clasp the stem. Each leaf is divided into 3–7 irregularly sharp-toothed, elongate segments up to 3½" long, with narrow whitish edges and tiny bristle tips on each tooth. Flowers are in round heads up to ⅝" wide at the tips of short branches near the top of the plant. Each flower is ⅛" wide and has 5 narrow sepals; 5 narrow, pointed, white petals; and 5 protruding stamens. The fruits are covered with stout green bristles and cling to clothing.

Bloom Season: Late spring–summer.

Habitat/Range: Common in a variety of open woods, along woodland edges, and in thickets; throughout the region.

Comments: Clustered Black Snakeroot (*S. gregaria*) is a related but smaller plant with smaller heads of greenish yellow flowers. It occurs in moist woods throughout much of the region.

Black Snakeroot

WATER PARSNIP
Sium suave
Carrot Family (Apiaceae)

Description: Smooth plant to 6' tall, with stout stems that are hollow near the base. The large, stalked, alternate leaves are divided into as many as 17 narrow leaflets, each up to 4" long. The leaflets are usually widest just above the rounded bases and taper to pointed tips. Their edges are finely toothed and their veins form a network, rather than a clear set of parallel side veins. The base of the leaf stalk is broad and papery and clasps the stem. Finely divided, feathery submerged leaves may also be present in sites with standing water. At the top of the plant are abundant small flowers grouped in umbrella-like clusters up to 3" wide. Narrow, pale-edged bracts grow at the base of each cluster. Each flower is ⅛" wide and has 5 white petals and 5 protruding stamens.

Bloom Season: Summer.

Habitat/Range: Common in marshes, swamps, wooded depressions, shallow ponds, and along quiet shores, often in shallow standing water; throughout the region.

Comments: North American Indians are reported to have used the underground parts as food. However, several closely related plants are deadly poisonous.

Water Parsnip

Dogbane

DOGBANE
Apocynum cannabinum
Dogbane Family (Apocynaceae)

Description: Plant to 4' tall and usually branched near the top, with milky sap, reddish stems, and widely separated, stalkless or short-stalked opposite leaves. The leaves are up to 6" long, with tapering, rounded, or clasping bases and bluntly pointed tips. Individually stalked flowers are in branched clusters at the tops of the stems. Each white to greenish white flower is ⅛" wide and has a small calyx with 5 pointed lobes and a small, broadly tubular corolla with 5 small triangular lobes. The fruits are dangling paired pods up to 7" long but less than ¼" wide.

Bloom Season: Late spring–summer.

Habitat/Range: Occasional to common in moist to dry, open to lightly shaded sites in fields and open thickets, and along woodland edges, riverbanks, roadsides, and railroads; throughout the region.

Comments: North American Indians used the tough, fibrous stems to make cordage, and the plant is also called Indian Hemp. The plant is poisonous to livestock but has been used medicinally. This species is sometimes divided into 2 species based on leaf characteristics, but intermediate forms occur.

Water Arum

WATER ARUM
Calla palustris
Arum Family (Araceae)

Description: Low, fleshy-stemmed plant to 10" tall from thick, creeping and rooting underground stems. The leaves are all basal, with glossy, rounded, heart-shaped blades less than 4" long that have many curving, parallel veins. The leaf stalks are thick, spongy, and flattened on top, with papery bases that clasp the stems. The tiny flowers are crowded on a cylinder up to 1" long, which is surrounded by a clasping, pointed, hoodlike, bright white bract up to 2" long. These flowers are cream colored, have no sepals or petals, and develop into red berries.

Bloom Season: Late spring–midsummer.

Habitat/Range: Frequent in open or shaded sites in bogs, quiet ponds and lakes, and acidic woodland pools, often growing in thick sphagnum mats; throughout the region.

Comments: The stems and leaf stalks may be buried in thick, saturated moss mats, with only the leaves and flowers showing. North American Indians used the roots medicinally. In northern Europe, the acrid roots have been used to make bread, but the raw plants contain calcium oxalate and cause a painful, potentially dangerous swelling when eaten.

Bristly Sarsaparilla

BRISTLY SARSAPARILLA
Aralia hispida
Ginseng Family (Araliaceae)

Description: Plant to 3' tall and usually un-branched below the middle, with densely bris-tly lower stems and large, stalked, alternate, compound leaves. Each main leaf is divided into 3 stalked divisions that are further divided into 3–5 narrowly oval, toothed leaflets usually about 2" long. The upper leaves are often stalkless and divided into 3 leaflets. At the top of the plant are a few long-stalked umbrella-like clusters of individually stalked flowers. Each flower is ⅛" wide and has 5 small, spreading white petals and 5 erect stamens. The fruits are round dark purple berries.

Bloom Season: Late spring–midsummer.

Habitat/Range: Common in open to lightly shaded, well-drained soils, especially in sandy or rocky clearings, burned areas, sand barrens, on rock outcrops, and along the edges of sandy woods; throughout the region.

WILD SARSAPARILLA
Aralia nudicaulis
Ginseng Family (Araliaceae)

Description: Greenish to bronze plant to 2' tall, with short, leafless, flowering stems under long-stalked, compound basal leaves. Each leaf is di-vided at the top of the main stalk into 3 stalked divisions, and each division is usually further divided into 3–7 toothed, narrowly oval leaflets, each up to 6" long. These leaflets have pointed tips and stalkless bases. The flowering stalk is typically topped by 2 or 3 stalked umbrella-like clusters of individually stalked flowers. Each flower is ³/₁₆" wide and has 5 spreading green-ish white petals and 5 longer spreading stamens. The fruits are small purplish black berries.

Bloom Season: Midspring–early summer.

Habitat/Range: Common in moist to dry woods, especially in lightly shaded open woods; throughout the region.

Comments: The aromatic roots have been used to make a sarsaparilla-like beverage and were formerly thought to cure a variety of ailments.

Wild Sarsaparilla

JESSIE M. HARRIS

Spikenard

SPIKENARD
Aralia racemosa
Ginseng Family (Araliaceae)

Description: Smooth-stemmed, bushy plant to 6' tall and often nearly as wide, with large, alternate, stalked compound leaves, each up to 2½' long. The leaves have 3 stalked divisions, each of which is divided into several wide leaflets up to 6" long. These leaflets have toothed edges, pointed tips, and usually broad indented bases. Individually stalked flowers are abundant in open, multiple-branched clusters. Each flower is ⅛" wide and has 5 greenish white petals and 5 protruding stamens.

Bloom Season: Early summer–midsummer.

Habitat/Range: Frequent in rich moist woods and wooded ravines, and on cool shaded slopes; throughout the region.

Comments: The roots have a pungent spicy aroma and have been used for flavoring and medicine.

Dwarf Ginseng

KEITH BOARD

DWARF GINSENG
Panax trifolium
Ginseng Family (Araliaceae)

Description: Delicate, unbranched plant, usually less than 7" tall, with a single whorl of 3 compound leaves on the upper stem. Each stalked leaf is divided into 3–5 stalkless, toothed leaflets arising from the same point, like fingers on a hand. The 3 middle leaflets are larger than any others that may be present. At the top of the stem, usually well above the leaves, is a single umbrella-like cluster of many small individually stalked flowers. Each flower is ⅛" wide and has 5 small white (rarely pinkish) petals and 5 spreading stamens. The fruits are yellow berries less than ¼" wide.

Bloom Season: Midspring–late spring.

Habitat/Range: Frequent in moist to swampy woods, typically in open mossy areas under conifers, also on floodplains and in hardwood forests; throughout the region.

Comments: A related species, Ginseng (*P. quinquefolium*), occurs in rich woods throughout most of the region. It is a larger plant with stalked leaflets that are typically taller than the short-stalked cluster of green flowers, which develop into bright red berries. Ginseng has been collected for centuries for its reputed medicinal properties and is now rare.

Yarrow

YARROW
Achillea millefolium
Aster Family (Asteraceae)

Description: Fragrant, hairy plant to 3' tall, with well-spaced alternate leaves up to 5" long and finely divided into feathery, fernlike segments. These segments do not lie in a flat plane but tend to radiate at different angles. The basal leaves are usually larger and long stalked. Flower heads are in a flattish cluster at the top of the plant. Each head is ¼" wide and has small sepal-like bracts under 4–6 white (sometimes pink) petal-like rays, with a central cluster of creamy yellowish, tubular disk flowers.

Bloom Season: Late spring–fall.

Habitat/Range: Abundant, especially in previously disturbed areas, in open woods, clearings, old fields, and pastures, and along shores; throughout the region.

Comments: Yarrow occurs in both North America and Europe. Some scientists think that most North Woods populations are introduced European weeds, while others believe most local Yarrow plants are native to the region. North American Indians had more than 350 documented medicinal uses for the plant, and settlers later used it for a variety of purposes, including treatment of wounds, earaches, and toothaches. The plant has antiseptic properties and is reported to help stop bleeding when packed in wounds.

Pearly Everlasting

PEARLY EVERLASTING
Anaphalis margaritacea
Aster Family (Asteraceae)

Description: Sweet-smelling, unbranched or sparsely branched plant, which arises from shallow, creeping underground stems and seldom gets more than 2½' tall. The stems and leaves are covered with long, white cobwebby hairs. The stalkless alternate leaves are up to 5" long and ½" wide and slightly clasp the stem at their bases. The leaves have smooth downturned edges and are densely hairy on the lower surface, giving them a pale yellowish green color below. Flower heads are in a compact, nearly flat cluster at the top of the plant. Each head is ¼–⅜" wide and has many bright white, papery, blunt bracts surrounding a disk of dense, tiny, pale yellow, mostly female flowers with 5-lobed tubular corollas and protruding yellow styles.

Bloom Season: Midsummer–late summer.

Habitat/Range: Common in well-drained open sites, especially in dry sandy or gravelly soils in old fields, upland pastures, open woods, along roads, and more rarely in moist open areas; throughout the region.

Comments: North American Indians used this plant for a variety of ceremonial and medicinal purposes. The white sepal-like bracts become loose and spreading after flowering and are attractive in dried flower arrangements. A similar species that is less common in the region, Old-Field Balsam (*Gnaphalium obtusifolium*), has a strong maple fragrance, leaves that taper to narrow nonclasping bases, and small compact heads with off-white bracts.

ROBERT TATINA

Pussy Toes

PUSSY TOES
Antennaria howellii
Aster Family (Asteraceae)

Description: Low plant, usually less than 1' tall, with white woolly hairs on the stems and leaves. The smooth-edged main leaves have tapered bases and short pointed tips and occur in basal clusters. These leaves are up to 2" long and less than ¾" wide, widest above the middle, and strongly whitened on the lower surface. Each has a single, prominent central vein. There are usually some additional creeping shoots with smaller leaves. The flowering stems have narrow alternate leaves, and the flowers cluster in heads at the top of the stems. Each head is up to ¼" wide and has numerous papery, sepal-like bracts surrounding a dense cluster of tiny flowers. The male (pictured) and female flowers are on separate plants; the female flowers are in more slender heads on taller stems.

Bloom Season: Spring.

Habitat/Range: Frequent in well-drained open or lightly shaded sites, often in acidic soils, including rocky ledges, bluffs, sandy slopes, sterile fields, open sandy or rocky woods, and even sandy cemeteries; throughout the region.

Comments: This is one of several closely related species of Pussy Toes in the region, and the relationships among the species are poorly understood. Other species in similar habitats include *A. neglecta*, whose young leaves are densely hairy on their upper surfaces, and *A. parlinii* and a smaller-headed relative, *A. plantaginifolia*, both of which have at least 3 prominent veins along the length of their main leaves. A rare species of the extreme northern part of the region, *A. rosea*, has flower heads with pinkish-tipped bracts.

White Wood Aster

PANICLED ASTER
Aster lanceolatus
Aster Family (Asteraceae)

Description: Stout, usually narrow, leafy plant to 5' tall, with stalkless alternate leaves up to 6" long and 1½" wide, but often much narrower. These leaves taper from the middle to narrow bases and pointed tips, sometimes with scattered low teeth along the edges. Flower heads are usually abundant near the top of the plant, growing on individual stalks with small leaves. Each head is ¾" wide and has a series of small, pointed, overlapping, sepal-like bracts and more than 18 petal-like white rays surrounding a cluster of tiny, yellowish, 5-lobed tubular flowers.

Bloom Season: Midsummer–fall.

Habitat/Range: Common in a variety of moist open areas and along shores; throughout the region.

Comments: Two similar species occur in the region. Mountain Aster (*A. acuminatus*) has clustered upper leaves that are larger than the other leaves. The leaf edges are coarsely toothed, and the flower heads are up to 1½" wide. It occurs on wooded slopes, particularly in mountainous areas, from eastern Canada through New York and New England. Shore Aster (*A. tradescantii*) is a low plant usually less than 1½' tall. It occurs in most sites at scattered locations east of the Great Lakes.

WHITE WOOD ASTER
Aster divaricatus
Aster Family (Asteraceae)

Description: Plant to 3' tall, with broad, alternate, heart-shaped leaves on slender stalks. Each leaf is up to 6" long and 3½" wide, with sharply toothed edges and long-pointed tips. The largest leaves are near the middle of the stem, and the upper leaves are often stalkless or nearly so, with more tapering bases. Flower heads are in branched, open clusters on the upper stems. Each head is ¾" wide and has a series of pale green-tipped, sepal-like bracts and 5–12 petal-like white rays surrounding a cluster of tiny yellow, 5-lobed tubular flowers.

Bloom Season: Midsummer–fall.

Habitat/Range: Occasional in dry to moist, usually rich soils in woods from Maine and Quebec to New York and Ontario and southward.

Comments: Arrow-leaved Aster (*A. sagittifolius*) has flower heads in a more elongate cluster, along with broad, slightly winged stalks on the shiny lower leaves. It occurs in moist woods in the southern part of the region from southwestern Vermont to central Minnesota.

Panicled Aster

SIDE-FLOWERING ASTER

Aster lateriflorus
Aster Family (Asteraceae)

Description: Plant typically 2–3' tall, usually with many spreading branches on the upper stems. The leaves are up to 5" long and 1" wide but usually narrower; they are alternate and stalkless, gradually tapering to pointed tips and bases that slightly clasp the stem. There are usually some widely spaced, sharp teeth along the leaf edges, especially toward the leaf tip. The lower surface of the leaf is smooth and shiny except for a line of hairs along the central vein. Flower heads are mostly on one side of short branches at the base of the upper leaves, with small leafy bracts along these branches. Each head is ½" wide and has many narrow, overlapping, dark-green-tipped, pointed bracts and 10–16 white or pale bluish, petal-like rays surrounding a cluster of tiny, 5-lobed, yellow tubular flowers.

Bloom Season: Midsummer–fall.

Habitat/Range: Common in moist open or shaded areas in woods and wet thickets, on floodplains, and along stream banks and shores; throughout the region.

Comments: Ontario Aster (*A. ontarionis*) is a nearly identical species with leaves that are evenly hairy on their lower surface. It occurs in the southern half of the region from New York to Minnesota.

Side-flowering Aster

FLAT-TOP ASTER

Aster umbellatus
Aster Family (Asteraceae)

Description: Plant typically grows to 3' tall but occasionally to 7', with numerous toothless leaves up to 5" long and 1½" wide. Although the leaves are alternate along the stems, they are sometimes so close together that they appear opposite. The leaves are widest near the middle and taper evenly to pointed tips and narrow or short-stalked bases. Flower heads are usually abundant in a branched, nearly flat cluster at the top of the plant. Each head is ¾" wide and has a series of sepal-like bracts and 7–15 white, petal-like rays surrounding a cluster of 16–40 tiny, 5-lobed, yellow tubular flowers.

Bloom Season: Midsummer–early fall.

Habitat/Range: Abundant in open moist areas in marshes, openings in swamps, and wet thickets, and along streams and shores; throughout the region.

Comments: A western variant with 4–7 petal-like rays and 8–15 disk flowers occurs in similar habitats from northern Michigan northward and westward. It is sometimes considered a separate species, Northern Flat-top Aster (*A. pubentior*).

Flat-top Aster

KEITH BOARD

Fireweed

DAISY FLEABANE

Erigeron strigosus
Aster Family (Asteraceae)

Description: This slender plant may be annual or biennial. It grows up to 2½' tall, with small hairs pressed against the stem. The basal leaves are up to 4" long and less than 1" wide. They have long stalks and smooth or slightly toothed edges. The stem leaves are smaller, alternate, and mostly stalkless. Individually stalked flower heads are in branched clusters on the upper part of the plant. Each head is ½–1" wide and has narrow sepal-like bracts and up to 100 white, bristle-shaped, petal-like rays surrounding a disk of tiny, 5-lobed, tubular yellow flowers.

Bloom Season: Late spring–midsummer.

Habitat/Range: Common in well-drained open areas in pastures, fields, meadows, waste ground, and in thickets and open aspen woods; throughout the region.

Comments: A related plant of similar habitats throughout most of the region, Annual Fleabane (*E. annuus*), has broader, more coarsely toothed leaves and spreading hairs on its stem.

FIREWEED

Erechtites hieracifolia
Aster Family (Asteraceae)

Description: Stout, unbranched or alternate-branched annual 3"–100" tall, with alternate, irregularly sharp-toothed leaves that wilt easily and have pointed tips. The lower leaves have broad stalks, while the upper leaves are stalkless and often extend slightly past or clasp the stems at their bases. The drab flower heads are usually numerous and upright, in branched clusters on the upper part of the plant. Threadlike green bracts form on the flower branches. Each narrow cylindrical head is up to ¾" long and has a swollen base and narrow pointed sepal-like bracts surrounding many tiny, white to creamy, 5-lobed tubular flowers. The white-plumed seeds have a cottony appearance.

Bloom Season: Midsummer–fall.

Habitat/Range: Common in open or shaded disturbed sites, particularly moist areas, in woods, burned areas, open thickets, waste ground, and along marshes and shores; throughout the region.

Comments: The seeds germinate quickly after fire, water level changes, or soil disruption, and Fireweed often dominates an area for the first year after disturbance.

JESSIE M. HARRIS

Daisy Fleabane

COMMON BONESET
Eupatorium perfoliatum
Aster Family (Asteraceae)

Description: Hairy plant to 4' tall, with pairs of opposite, long-tapering, toothed leaves. These leaves are up to 8" long and united around the stem at their bases, so that the stem appears to pierce the leaves. At the top of the plant are numerous branched clusters of flower heads forming a broad, shallow dome. Each head is ¼" tall and has small sepal-like bracts and 9–23 small, tubular, dull white, 5-lobed flowers with protruding threadlike styles. Occasionally the leaves will be in whorls of 3 rather than opposite.

BloomSeason: Midsummer–early fall.

Habitat/Range: Abundant in open wet areas in marshes, beaver meadows, boggy areas, open swamps, and along shores; throughout the region.

Comments: Because of this plant's fused pairs of leaves, people once thought that a potion made from it would heal fractured bones; hence the common name. A bitter, vile-tasting tea made from the plant was once used as a tonic and folk medicine for a variety of ailments.

Common Boneset

CLAMMY CUDWEED
Gnaphalium macounii
Aster Family (Asteraceae)

Description: Single-stemmed annual seldom over 2' tall, with a coating of woolly white hairs pressed against the upper stems and lower surfaces of the leaves, creating a whitened appearance. The leaves are alternate, and their edges are wavy but untoothed. They are widest near the base and taper to pointed tips. These leaves are up to 3½" long and ⅜" wide, and they extend downward along the stem on each side of the clasping base. Flower heads are abundant at the tip of the branches. Each head is ¼" tall and has overlapping white, papery, sepal-like bracts surrounding several 5-lobed, tubular, yellowish white flowers. The plants smell somewhat like maple syrup.

Bloom Season: Midsummer–fall.

Habitat/Range: Frequent and somewhat weedy in well-drained fields and pastures, woodland clearings, open sandy woods, and along riverbanks and roadsides; throughout the region.

Comments: Old-field Balsam (*G. obtusifolium*) is a similar species with narrow nonclasping leaves. It is common in similar habitats throughout the region. Both species have been used in folk medicines for people and livestock.

Clammy Cudweed

White Snakeroot

DON KURZ

WHITE SNAKEROOT
Eupatorium rugosum
Aster Family (Asteraceae)

Description: Plant typically 2–3' tall, with opposite branches at the base of the main stem leaves. The dark green, stalked leaves are opposite and usually finely hairy. Each leaf is up to 6" long and 5" wide, pointed at the tip, and broadest near the rounded to tapering or indented base. There are sawlike teeth along the leaf edges. Abundant flower heads typically grow in spreading, opposite-branched clusters near the tops of the branches, usually with some bracts on each branch. Flower heads are about ¼" wide and have a series of narrow sepal-like bracts surrounding about 8–15 small, bright white, tubular flowers with 5 pointed lobes and 2 protruding threadlike style branches.

Bloom Season: Midsummer–fall.

Habitat/Range: Common in moist to dry woods, particularly along edges and in disturbed areas, usually under hardwoods; throughout most of the region.

Comments: The plant contains a poisonous alcohol-like substance that, when eaten by livestock, can be transmitted through the milk to humans, causing a potentially fatal illness called milk sickness. Abraham Lincoln's mother, Nancy Hanks Lincoln, died from this. The plants are bitter and avoided by grazing animals unless food is scarce.

Northern Sweet Coltsfoot

JESSIE M. HARRIS

NORTHERN SWEET COLTSFOOT

Petasites frigidus
Aster Family (Asteraceae)

Description: This plant often forms extensive colonies of large, stalked, basal leaves that are up to 10" wide. The leaves usually have 5–7 lobes that radiate from a common point, like fingers on a hand. These lobes have coarse teeth and smaller lobes along the edges, as well as woolly hairs on their lower surfaces. Flowers develop before the leaves expand, on a thick stalk up to 3' tall, with small, alternate, narrow, clasping, pointed bracts up to 2½" long. Flower heads form in dense clusters at the tops of the stems, with male and female flowers typically on separate stems. Each head is ½" wide and has a series of pointed sepal-like bracts and small, tubular, creamy white, 5-lobed flowers. Several of the flowers in a head typically have petal-like rays.

basal leaves

Bloom Season: Midspring–late spring.

Habitat/Range: Local in moist swampy woods, springy places, and low thickets; throughout the region.

Comments: A more northern species with larger, unlobed, arrowhead-shaped leaves, Arrowhead Sweet Coltsfoot (*P. sagittatus*) ranges southward into the region from Minnesota to Michigan.

White Lettuce

WHITE LETTUCE
Prenanthes alba
Aster Family (Asteraceae)

Description: Unbranched plant to 4' tall, with stout smooth stems and milky sap. The leaves are alternate, whitened underneath, widely spaced along the stem, and mostly smooth except for some hairs on the veins beneath. The leaf stalks are up to 6" long, and the upper stalks are often bordered with leafy strips. The lower leaves are often arrowhead-shaped, with broad lobes at the base; sometimes the rest of the leaf is further divided. The upper leaves are smaller and more rounded, often with no lobes. Flower heads are nodding in small stalked clusters. Each head has 7–10 narrow, smooth, pointed, purplish to green, sepal-like bracts about ½" long surrounding 8–11 tubular white or pinkish flowers, each with a single petal-like ray with 5 tiny teeth at the tip. A slender forked style protrudes from the flower.

Bloom Season: Midsummer–fall.

Habitat/Range: Frequent in rich or moist woods under both hardwoods and conifers, especially in openings and thickets, and along streams; throughout the region, but less common eastward.

Comments: Glaucous White Lettuce (*P. racemosa*) also occurs in the region, usually in more open or wetter sites. It has hairy sepal-like bracts and unlobed leaves. Tall White Lettuce (*P. altissima*) has 6 or fewer smooth sepal-like bracts and only 5 or 6 flowers per head. It occurs in woods in the eastern half of the region. Tall Rattlesnake Root (*P. trifoliolata*) is common in New England and northward; the undersides of its leaves are green, and its fruiting heads have pale bristles, as opposed to the cinnamon-colored bristles of White Lettuce.

STIFF ASTER

Solidago ptarmicoides
Aster Family (Asteraceae)

Description: Slender plant to 2' tall and un-branched below the middle, with narrow alternate leaves, each up to 7" long but less than ½" wide. Flower heads are in an open flat cluster at the top of the plant, on individual stalks with tiny alternate bracts. Each head is ¾" wide and has a series of narrow, pointed, sepal-like bracts and up to 25 petal-like white rays surrounding a disk of tiny, tubular, creamy flowers.

Bloom Season: Early summer–midsummer.

Habitat/Range: Local in open dry sites, usually in calcium-rich areas, in fens, open woods, and on sandy inland beaches and limestone exposures; throughout most of the region eastward to New Hampshire.

Comments: This species looks like an aster but hybridizes with goldenrods and is considered a goldenrod.

Stiff Aster

TOWER MUSTARD

Arabis glabra
Mustard Family (Brassicaceae)

Description: Plant to 4' tall and usually un-branched below the middle, with hairy lower stems and smooth upper stems covered with a pale waxy coating. There is usually a cluster of thick basal leaves, each up to 8" long, with tapering, stalkless bases and irregular to bluntly toothed edges. These leaves usually have tiny Y-shaped hairs. The stem leaves are smaller, smooth, and well separated, with slightly wavy, toothless edges and bases that strongly clasp the stem. Flowers are on short individual stalks along the tops of the upright branches, occurring in clusters that elongate as the fruits develop. Each flower is ³/₁₆" wide and has 4 small sepals and 4 spreading, creamy white petals. The fruits are slender erect pods up to 4" long.

Bloom Season: Late spring–summer.

Habitat/Range: Occasional in dry open to lightly shaded soil in woods, sand barrens, disturbed areas, and on rocky ledges; in most of the region eastward through Maine and Quebec.

Comments: Both raw and cooked leaves of Tower Mustard have been used for food.

Tower Mustard

May Apple

MAY APPLE
Podophyllum peltatum
Barberry Family (Berberidaceae)

Description: Plant to 1½' tall, often forming extensive colonies. Its large, shiny, umbrella-like leaves are attached at their centers to upright stalks. Each leaf is up to 15" wide and divided into as many as 9 lobes; these lobes are toothed and sometimes lobed along the edges. Sterile plants have an erect stalk with a single leaf at the top. The stems of fertile plants fork into 2 leaf stalks. Under the leaves, in the fork of the stem, nods a single stalked flower up to 2½" wide. The flower has 6 or 9 broadly rounded, white, waxy petals and 12 or 18 pale yellow stamens surrounding a large, rounded, greenish ovary. The greenish yellow, slightly oval fruits are about 2" long and ripen in summer. The 6 sepals fall off before the flower is fully open.

Bloom Season: Midspring–late spring.

Habitat/Range: Common in woods, especially in moist sites; in the southern half of the region from southern Quebec to southeastern Minnesota, and sometimes escaped from cultivation elsewhere.

Comments: When fully ripe, the soft yellowish fruits are edible and have a sweet, mildly acidic taste, although most parts of the plant, including the seeds, are somewhat poisonous. The resin has been used medicinally as a purgative and wart treatment.

Crinkleroot

CRINKLEROOT
Cardamine diphylla
Mustard Family (Brassicaceae)

Description: Smooth, unbranched plant to 1' tall, with long-stalked basal leaves and a single pair of similar, almost opposite, stalked, compound leaves near the middle of the stem. Each leaf is divided at the tip of the stalk into 3 broad toothed leaflets up to 3" long and 1½" wide; these have rounded bases. At the top of the stem is a small cluster of stalked flowers, each about ⅝" wide. Each flower has 4 sepals, 4 spreading white petals with narrow bases, and 6 erect stamens.

Bloom Season: Midspring–late spring.

Habitat/Range: Frequent in moist woods, particularly in springy depressions and on raised hummocks in conifer swamps; throughout most of the region westward through Wisconsin.

Comments: This plant is also called Broad-leaved Toothwort. A relative, Cutleaf Toothwort (*C. concatenata*), has fine hairs on its upper stems and a whorl of 3 compound leaves near the middle of the stem. The leaves are lobed and divided into narrow, coarsely toothed segments, mostly less than ⅝" wide. Cutleaf Toothwort occurs in moist to dry, typically deciduous, woods, mostly in the southern half of the region from Quebec to Minnesota. The crisp roots of both species are said to taste like watercress; hence another common name, Pepperroot.

CAROL GRACIE

Common Bitter Cress

COMMON BITTER CRESS
Cardamine pensylvanica
Mustard Family (Brassicaceae)

Description: Mostly smooth plant to 15" tall, with well-separated, alternate stem leaves and usually a cluster of basal leaves. Each leaf is up to 3½" long and divided along its length into several pairs of narrow lobes up to ¼" wide; these are arranged featherlike along the leaf axis. The end lobe of the leaf is usually more broadly rounded and sometimes has blunt teeth or lobes. Flowers are alternate on delicate individual stalks on the upper stem. Each flower is ³/₁₆" wide and has 4 tiny sepals and 4 white petals. The fruits are slender pods up to 1½" long.

Bloom Season: Midspring–fall.

Habitat/Range: Common in wet shaded areas in swamps, wet woods, springy places, shaded wet depressions, and along shores; throughout the region.

Comments: Three other closely related species occur in the region. Cuckoo Flower (*C. pratensis*) has similar leaves, but its flowers are ½" or more wide. Two varieties of Cuckoo Flower occur in the region. One, a cultivated European plant, has pink flowers and escapes into moist disturbed areas. The native variety, with white flowers, occurs in bogs, marshes, and swamps. Small-flowered Bitter Cress (*C. parviflora*) is usually a smaller plant with leaf lobes only ¹/₁₆" wide; it occurs in dry, often rocky sites throughout the region. Spring Cress (*C. rhomboidea*) has large white flowers like those of Cuckoo Flower, but the leaves are simple and undivided. It occurs in wet springy areas mostly in the southern half of the region, but it ranges northward to Quebec. The greens of all these plants have been used in salads and have a somewhat bitter, peppery taste.

STIFF SANDWORT
Arenaria stricta
Carnation Family (Caryophyllaceae)

Description: Thin, wiry plant, mostly less than 10" tall and usually arising from a base with spreading leafy shoots. The stems have pairs of stiff, needlelike, opposite leaves that are seldom more than ¾" long. Smaller leaves usually cluster at the bases of the main leaves, creating an appearance of whorled leaves. Flowers are in an open-branched cluster at the leafless top of the plant, with pairs of small bracts on the branches. Each flower is ⅜" wide and has 5 pointed pale-edged sepals, 5 white petals, and 10 stamens.

Bloom Season: Late spring–early fall.

Habitat/Range: Infrequent but sometimes locally abundant, in dry exposed sites near limestone or in calcium-rich sands, including exposed cliffs and ledges, gravelly slopes, sand barrens, and sandy or rocky woods; scattered throughout most of the region.

Comments: Mountain Sandwort (*A. groenlandica*) occurs in exposed rocky sites from Nova Scotia and Quebec northward and on a few exposed mountain summits in New England

Stiff Sandwort

and New York. It is a dwarf compact plant with notched petals and flowers nearly ½" wide; the leaves are not stiff.

WOOD SANDWORT
Arenaria lateriflora
Carnation Family (Caryophyllaceae)

Description: Plant to 8" tall, with finely hairy stems that usually have a few short side branches. The smooth-sided opposite leaves are stalkless, or nearly so, and up to 1" long and ½" wide. They have round to slightly pointed tips. Smaller leaves sometimes occur at the bases of the main leaves. Flowers are single on delicate stalks in groups of 1–5 at the branch tips. Each flower is ⅜" wide and has 5 blunt pale-edged sepals, 5 white (rarely pinkish) petals, and 10 stamens.

Bloom Season: Midspring–midsummer.

Habitat/Range: Occasional in dry to moist open woods, often in sandy soils or on rocky ledges and bluffs; throughout the region. This plant is also called Grove Sandwort.

Wood Sandwort

Field Chickweed

FIELD CHICKWEED
Cerastium arvense
Carnation Family (Caryophyllaceae)

Description: Slender, sprawling, round-stemmed plant to 15" tall. The smooth-edged, narrow, opposite leaves are typically 1" long and ⅛" wide, with narrowed bases. Tufts of small leaves usually arise at the bases of the main stem leaves. Flowers are in branched clusters on slender stalks at the top of the plant. Each flower is ½" wide and has 5 pointed sepals and 5 white petals that are cleft about half their length into 2 lobes. There are 5 styles.

Bloom Season: Midspring–early summer.

Habitat/Range: Locally common in low grassy areas, on rock outcrops, and in dry open sandy woods; throughout the region.

Comments: This species is sometimes planted as an ornamental and can escape to become a weak weed. See also Stitchwort (facing page).

HEDGE BINDWEED
Calystegia sepium
Morning Glory Family (Convolvulaceae)

Description: Smooth, twining vine to 10' long, with widely spaced, stalked, alternate, arrowhead-shaped leaves up to 4" long and 2½" wide. Each leaf has a pointed tip and a base with 2 prominent angular lobes flanking an indented notch where the stalk is attached. Stalked flowers occur singly at the bases of the leaf stalks, with 2 broad green bracts at the base of each flower. The funnel-shaped flower is up to 2½" wide and has 5 small, nearly transparent sepals and a shallowly 5-lobed corolla that is usually white but sometimes pink or striped.

Bloom Season: Late spring–early fall.

Habitat/Range: Common in moist open areas in thickets, beaver marshes, disturbed clearings, burned areas, and on riverbanks; throughout the region.

Hedge Bindweed

Stitchwort

STITCHWORT

Stellaria longifolia
Carnation Family (Caryophyllaceae)

Description: Weak, usually sprawling plant with somewhat ridged and angular stems up to 18" long. The narrow, pointed, opposite leaves are up to 2" long and ⅛" wide and are widest near the middle. Flowers are on delicate stalks in open, few-flowered clusters near the top of the plant, with tiny papery bracts in the clusters. Each flower is up to ¼" wide and has 5 pale-edged, pointed sepals and 5 white petals deeply cleft for more than half their length. There are usually 3 styles.

Bloom Season: Midspring–summer.

Habitat/Range: Occasional in moist, often shaded areas in woods, old bogs, shrubby areas, and along shores; throughout the region.

Comments: Starwort (*S. graminea*) is a well-established European weed in grassy areas in the region. It has slightly larger, more abundant flowers, and its leaves are only 1" long and widest below the middle. Northern Stitchwort (*S. borealis*) occurs in moist conifer forests at a few spots in the region. It either has no petals or its petals are shorter than the sepals. It also has tiny leaflike bracts on the flowering branches. Field Chickweed (facing page) has larger, less deeply cleft petals, round stems, and 5 styles inside the flower.

Low Bindweed

LOW BINDWEED
Calystegia spithamea
Morning Glory Family (Convolvulaceae)

Description: Unbranched, finely hairy plant to 1' tall, with stalked alternate leaves. Most of the plant is upright, but the upper stem above the flowers is weak and trailing. The leaves are smooth edged, up to 3½" long and 2" wide, and bluntly arrowhead shaped, with broad, notched bases. Each plant has 1–3 flowers that are single on stalks arising at the base of the main leaf stalks. Each bell-shaped flower is 1½" wide when fully open and has 2 large green bracts at the base, 5 small sepals, and a 5-lobed white corolla.

Bloom Season: Late spring–midsummer.

Habitat/Range: Occasional in dry sand, clay, or rocky soil, in open woods, especially under pine and aspen, and on rocky slopes; mostly in the western part of the region, eastward to Maine and Quebec.

BUNCHBERRY
Cornus canadensis
Dogwood Family (Cornaceae)

Description: Dwarf shrub to 8" tall, with a whorl-like cluster of veiny leaves under the single stalked flower head at the top of the plant. Non-flowering plants typically have 4 main leaves, while flowering plants usually have 6 leaves. The leaves are up to 3" long and taper to pointed tips and narrow, short-stalked bases. Pairs of tiny leaves or green scales usually form on the stems below the main leaves. The flower head is 1–1½" wide and has what appear to be 4 large, rounded, white petals. These "petals" are actually bracts surrounding a dense head of tiny, 4-petaled, yellowish green flowers. The fruits are clusters of bright scarlet berries, each about ¼" wide.

Bloom Season: Late spring–early summer.

Habitat/Range: A characteristic North Woods wildflower; abundant in moist woods, often under conifers, and in wooded swamps, shaded bogs, and peaty areas; throughout the region.

Comments: North American Indians used this plant to treat pain and colds.

Bunchberry

Wild Cucumber

WILD CUCUMBER
Echinocystis lobata
Gourd Family (Cucurbitaceae)

Description: Soft, high-climbing annual with green angular stems and widely spaced, short-stalked, alternate leaves. The leaves are typically about 3" long and are lobed into 3–7 pointed segments arranged like fingers on a hand. There are sparse fine teeth along the leaf edges and coiling, often branched tendrils at the bases of the leaf stalks. Male and female flowers are separate on the same plant; sometimes both types of flowers are at the base of the same leaf. Both flower types are about ⅜" wide and have 6 twisted, narrow, pointed, hairy, whitish-translucent petals. Male flowers occur in upright clusters, with each star-shaped flower on a stalk about ¼" long. Female flowers are similar but have shorter stalks; they grow singly or in small few-flowered clusters. The dangling, inflated, 4-seeded fruit is up to 2½" long and covered with soft prickles.

Bloom Season: Midsummer–late summer.

Habitat/Range: Locally abundant in moist ground, thickets, open swamps, moist disturbed areas, and on riverbanks; throughout the region.

Comments: This plant, also called Balsam Apple, is sometimes cultivated as a curiosity. A similar species, Bur Cucumber (*Sicyos angulatus*), has 5-petaled flowers, more broadly angular leaves, and smaller, single-seeded fruits with stiffer barbed prickles. It is uncommon in low woods in the southern three-fourths of the region.

ROBERT TATINA

KENNETH DRITZ

Common Dodder

COMMON DODDER

Cuscuta gronovii
Dodder Family (Cuscutaceae)

Description: The orange, stringlike, twining stems of this plant grow on other plants and produce scattered dense clusters of small white flowers. Unlike green plants, which need sunlight to produce their food, dodders are parasites that feed on other flowering plants by attaching to their stems with tiny sucker-like disks. Common Dodder has no apparent leaves. The flowers are about ⅛" wide and have 5 small, blunt, white sepals and 5 spreading white petals surrounding 5 stamens and a round ovary topped with 2 tiny styles.

Bloom Season: Midsummer–fall.

Habitat/Range: Common in moist open areas, marshes, wet thickets, and along shores, growing on a variety of woody plants and wildflowers—especially common on jewelweed and plants in the Aster Family; throughout the region, but sporadic west of Lake Superior.

Comments: Several other species of dodder occur in the region, often in wetlands. All appear similar and are difficult to differentiate.

TALL COTTON GRASS

Eriophorum viridicarinatum
Sedge Family (Cyperaceae)

Description: Slender grasslike plant to 3' tall, with 1 to several stems in a clump. The leaves are erect, flat, alternate, and clustered near the base of the plant. They range up to 5" long but are less than ¼" wide and have tapering, pointed tips. At the tops of the stems are clusters of stalked flower heads, with 2–4 leaflike bracts at the base of each cluster. The flower heads have many inconspicuous flowers, each covered by a small pointed scale. The tiny flowers have no regular petals or sepals but only bristlelike parts that elongate in fruit, forming conspicuous heads of bright white, cottony tufts.

Bloom Season: Midspring–early summer.

Habitat/Range: Common in bogs, open conifer swamps, and marshy or peaty areas; throughout the region.

Comments: Several other species of cotton grass occur in the region. One, Rusty Cotton Grass (*E. virginicum*), has cinnamon-brown bristles.

LEE A. CASEBERE

Tall Cotton Grass

Round-leaved Sundew

ROBERT TATINA

ROUND-LEAVED SUNDEW
Drosera rotundifolia
Sundew Family (Droseraceae)

Description: This delicate plant is usually less than 6" tall, with a basal cluster of long-stalked, round leaves less than ½" wide. The leaves are covered with spreading reddish hairs with sticky droplets at their tips; these trap and digest insects. The leafless stems have up to 15 tiny flowers in branched or unbranched clusters along the upper part, often on one side of the stem. Each flower is ³/₁₆" wide and has 5 tiny sepals and 5 (rarely 6) spreading, white to pinkish petals.

Bloom Season: Summer.

Habitat/Range: Common in acidic wetlands, usually in full sun, in bogs, swamps, peaty marshes, sandy seeps, and along shores; throughout the region.

Comments: Two other sundews occur in similar habitats in the region. Spoon-leaved Sundew (*D. intermedia*) has somewhat upright basal leaves less than ¼" wide and more than twice as long. Narrow-leaved Sundew (*D. linearis*) has leaves up to 2" long but less than ⅛" wide, with up to 4 flowers on the stem; it is rare in the northern part of the region, westward to Wisconsin. Because they contain protein-digesting enzymes, extracts of the leaves have been used to treat warts.

Leatherleaf

JESSIE M. HARRIS

LEATHERLEAF
Chamaedaphne calyculata
Heath Family (Ericaceae)

Description: Evergreen shrub to 4' tall, with grayish brown, fuzzy branches. The short-stalked alternate leaves are thick, waxy, pointed, and typically 1" long and ⅜" wide, with tiny teeth along the edges. The leaves usually are covered with tiny scales, giving them a granular appearance. At the top of the stem is a row of individually stalked flowers, each with a leafy bract at its base. Each flower is ¼" long and has 2 tiny, pointed, cuplike bracts; 5 small pointed sepals; and a tubular white corolla with 5 tiny, curved, triangular lobes at its narrow mouth.

Bloom Season: Midspring–late spring.

Habitat/Range: Common in saturated acidic sites and shallow water in bogs and along shrubby shores, where it often forms extensive stands bordering open water; throughout the region.

Comments: The Ojibway people prepared a tea from the leaves.

Creeping Snowberry

JESSIE M. HARRIS

CREEPING SNOWBERRY
Gaultheria hispidula
Heath Family (Ericaceae)

Description: This dwarf creeping shrub has small, thick, alternate leaves and is usually unbranched. The stems and leaves usually lie flat along the ground, with a row of leaves on either side of each brown-haired stem. The leaves are oval and less than ½" long, with pointed tips, downturned edges, and often brownish hairs on the lower side. The few individually stalked flowers mostly grow singly along the stem and are often hidden under the leaves. The tiny, bell-shaped, white flowers are less than ⅛" long and have 2 small bracts, 4 sepals, and a 4-lobed corolla. The fruits are bright white, elongate berries up to ⅜" long.

Bloom Season: Midspring–late spring.

Habitat/Range: Frequent in moist shaded sites, typically in moss mats or on rotting stumps and logs in wooded bogs and conifer swamps, also in open sandy woods under conifers; throughout the region.

Comments: The edible berries have a wintergreen flavor. The green bristly underside of the leaves distinguishes this plant from cranberries (p. 78), whose leaves have pale smooth undersides.

KEITH BOARD

Wintergreen

WINTERGREEN
Gaultheria procumbens
Heath Family (Ericaceae)

Description: Dwarf, creeping, evergreen shrub to 15" long, with alternate leaves clustered toward the tips of short upright branches. The leaves are oval and up to 4" long, with pointed tips, short stalks, and sparse irregular teeth and brown hairs along the edges. Flowers are mostly single on stalks dangling at the bases of the main leaves. Each white flower is ¼–⅜" long and has 2 small bracts, 5 slightly larger pointed sepals, and an urnlike tubular corolla with 5 small spreading lobes at its narrowed mouth. The fruits are round red berries about ⅜" wide.

Bloom Season: Early summer–midsummer.

Habitat/Range: Frequent in dry to moist, lightly shaded acidic soils, on sandy wooded slopes, in open mixed or conifer woods, and occasionally in wet mossy conifer forests; throughout the region.

Comments: The leaves have a strong wintergreen fragrance and have been used to make tea; the edible berries also have a wintergreen flavor. The wintergreen oil is toxic in quantity. North American Indians prepared a cold medicine from this plant, which may have anticancer properties.

Labrador Tea

ROBERT TATINA

LABRADOR TEA
Ledum groenlandicum
Heath Family (Ericaceae)

Description: Branching shrub, usually less than 2' tall, with hairy twigs and very short-stalked, thick, evergreen, alternate, narrowly oval leaves clustered on the upper parts of the branches. The fragrant leaves are shiny above and typically 1¼" long and less than ¼" wide. Their smooth edges turn downward, creating a raised rim around the lower surface, which is covered by a dense mat of tangled woolly hairs. These hairs are white on young leaves and turn rusty on older leaves. Flowers are on long, finely hairy stalks in dense rounded clusters at the tips of the branches, although new growth often makes the flowers appear to be in the middle of the branch. Each flower is just under ½" wide and has a tiny 5-lobed calyx; 5 spreading, rounded, white petals; and 5–7 slender upright stamens surrounding a finely hairy ovary with a thin upright style.

Bloom Season: Late spring–midsummer.

Habitat/Range: Locally common in bogs, tamarack and black spruce swamps, and northward also on sandy or rocky slopes, exposed heaths, and in conifer woods; throughout the region.

Comments: The leaves have been used to make tea and folk medicines.

Trailing Arbutus

TRAILING ARBUTUS
Epigaea repens
Heath Family (Ericaceae)

Description: Dwarf, creeping, hairy evergreen shrub to 15" long, with stalked, thick, leathery alternate leaves up to 3½" long and 2" wide. The leaves have round or pointed tips and round to heart-shaped bases. Individually stalked flowers form compact clusters at the ends of the branches. The fragrant pinkish to white flowers are about ½" long and have small bracts at the base. Each flower has 5 pointed sepals and a tubular corolla with 5 long, broadly rounded lobes.

Bloom Season: Early spring–midspring.

Habitat/Range: Common in lightly shaded, well-drained, acidic soil in rocky woods, on shaded sandy slopes, and on shaded outcrops and ledges, and sometimes in wet acidic woods; throughout the region.

Comments: North American Indians used this plant to treat a variety of internal problems. Trailing Arbutus is the provincial flower of Nova Scotia and the state flower of Massachusetts. It is sometimes called Mayflower.

PIPEWORT
Eriocaulon aquaticum
Pipewort Family (Eriocaulaceae)

Description: Soft plant to 6" tall, with a basal cluster of grasslike, translucent leaves up to 3½" long and less than ¼" wide. The angular flower stem is bare except for a thin pale sheath surrounding the lower part and a single buttonlike, ⅛–⅜" wide, ashy white flower head at the top. This head has several small, smooth, rounded bracts at its base and contains many tiny, closely packed flowers. Each flower has a small papery bract below 2 minute sepals, as well as 2 petals or a 2-lobed corolla, but the flowers are so tiny that a magnifying lens is needed to see this. Each head has separate male and female flowers.

Bloom Season: Midsummer–early fall.

Habitat/Range: Occasional in open wet sites, especially on lakeshores, and in sandy, peaty, or mucky soil under shallow water; throughout the region.

Comments: The plant often grows in shallow standing water and sometimes forms carpets in deeper clear water, where it does not flower. The pale stringy roots are patterned with narrow cross bars.

Pipewort

CANADA MILK VETCH
Astragalus canadensis
Bean Family (Fabaceae)

Description: Stout plant to 5' tall, with stalked, alternate, compound leaves. At the base of each leaf stalk is a pair of small, connected, triangular, bractlike stipules. There are also 11–31 short-stalked, smooth-edged, narrowly oval leaflets, each about 1–1½" long and ⅜–½" wide; these have some hairs on their undersides. Flowers are in dense spikelike clusters on long stalks at the bases of the main upper leaves. Each creamy whitish flower is ½" long and has a small cup-like calyx with 5 needlelike teeth and a hooded upper petal over 2 smaller side petals flanking a keel-like lower lip. The fruits are smooth, fat, pointed pods up to ¾" long.

Bloom Season: Summer.

Habitat/Range: Infrequent in moist open or lightly shaded sites in open woods and moist thickets and along shores and marshes; scattered from Vermont and Quebec westward.

Comments: Cooper's Milk Vetch (*A. neglectus*) is a rare plant in open, often limey sites at scattered spots from New York and Ontario westward. It is smaller, usually no more than 2' tall, and it has a pair of separate stipules at the base of each leaf stalk.

Canada Milk Vetch

ROBERT TATINA

Pale Vetchling

PALE VETCHLING

Lathyrus ochroleucus
Bean Family (Fabaceae)

Description: Smooth, sprawling vine to 3' long, with stalked, alternate, compound leaves, each with a pair of broad, pointed, bractlike stipules at the base of its stalk. Each leaf has 3–5 pairs of smooth-edged, stalkless leaflets up to 2½" long and 1½" wide. The end of each leaf forms a slender coiled tendril that is sometimes branched. Short branches with clusters of 4–10 individually stalked flowers arise at the base of the main upper leaf stalks. Each creamy white flower is up to ¾" long and has a cuplike green calyx with 5 unequal teeth; a round, spreading upper petal; and 2 smaller side petals flanking a keel-like lower lip.

Bloom Season: Late spring–early summer.

Habitat/Range: In well-drained soils in woods and burned areas and on rocky sites; common in the western half of the region and occasional eastward to Vermont.

NORTHERN BUGLE WEED

Lycopus uniflorus
Mint Family (Lamiaceae)

Description: Plant anywhere from a few inches to 2' tall, with finely hairy, square stems and opposite horizontal leaves. The leaves are about 2½" long and ½" wide and taper to pointed tips and narrow elongate bases. There are usually some coarse low teeth along each edge toward the leaf tip. Tiny flowers occur in dense clusters surrounding the upper stem at the bases of small pairs of leaves. Each flower has a small calyx with 4–5 triangular lobes, as well as a tubular, 2-lipped, white corolla about ⅛" long with a protruding pair of purple-tipped stamens and a pale style.

KENNETH DRITZ

Northern Bugle Weed

Bloom Season: Midsummer–late summer.

Habitat/Range: Frequent in a variety of wetlands, in crevices in shoreside rocks, and along shores; throughout the region, especially northward.

Comments: North American Indians used the roots for food. Two related species occur in similar habitats in parts of the region. Common Water Horehound (*L. americanus*) has more elongate, sharply pointed calyx teeth and deeply toothed or lobed leaves. Rough Water Horehound (*L. asper*) has more broadly rounded and distinctly stalked leaves.

JESSIE M. HARRIS

Dutchman's Breeches

DUTCHMAN'S BREECHES
Dicentra cucullaria
Fumitory Family (Fumariaceae)

Description: Soft, smooth, unbranched plant usually less than 10" tall, with long-stalked, compound basal leaves. Each leaf is divided into a series of stalked, bluish green, feathery-lobed leaflets. The lobes are less than ⅛" wide. The unusual flowers, which resemble upside-down pairs of pants, nod on slender alternate stalks along the upper part of the otherwise bare flower stem. Each flower is ⅝" long and has 2 minute sepals and 2 inflated, spurred, white outer petals that form the "legs" and end in spreading yellow lobes. These outer petals enclose 2 smaller inner petals.

Bloom Season: Spring.

Habitat/Range: Common in rich moist woods, shaded ravines, and on lower slopes, typically under hardwoods; throughout the region, but rare and scattered northward and apparently absent north of Lake Superior.

Comments: Squirrel Corn (*D. canadensis*) is a similar species; its flowers have low, round, inflated spurs instead of "legs." It is rarer in similar habitats in the southern part of the region from New Hampshire and Quebec to southeastern Minnesota. The roots of both plants are poisonous to livestock but have been used medicinally.

JESSIE M. HARRIS

Common Mountain Mint

COMMON MOUNTAIN MINT
Pycnanthemum virginianum
Mint Family (Lamiaceae)

Description: Branching, slightly fragrant, leafy plant to 3' tall. The square stems have smooth faces and hairs on their angular edges. The stalkless, opposite leaves have smooth edges and are up to 2½" long and less than ½" wide. They are widest near the broadly tapering bases and have pointed tips. Flowers are abundant in multibranched clusters of stalked heads at the top of the plant. At the base of each head are small leafy bracts. Each flower is ⅛" wide and has a tiny calyx with 5 hairy lobes and a white 2-lipped corolla, often with purplish spots. The lower corolla lip is divided into 3 lobes.

Bloom Season: Early summer–midsummer.

Habitat/Range: Occasional in fields, moist woods, and low areas; in the southern two-thirds of the region, eastward to Maine.

Comments: The fragrant leaves of this and other mountain mints have been used to make tea. Slender Mountain Mint (*P. tenuifolium*) has smooth stems and nonfragrant leaves less than ¼" wide. It occurs in dry sites mostly in the southern part of the region from Maine to Wisconsin.

KEITH BOARD

DON KURZ

Wild Leek

WILD LEEK
Allium tricoccum
Lily Family (Liliaceae)

Description: Plant with a strong oniony odor and usually 2 erect, pointed basal leaves that are typically 6" long and 1½" wide. These leaves grow on sheathlike, often reddish stalks, appearing in spring and typically dying back before the flowers appear. Flowers are on individual stalks in dense rounded clusters at the tops of the bare stems, which are up to 1½' tall. Each flower is ½" wide and has 3 narrow, pointed, white petals; 3 similar petal-like sepals; and 6 protruding stamens.

Bloom Season: Late spring–midsummer.

Habitat/Range: Common in rich moist woods, typically in alkaline soils, often forming extensive carpets on shaded floodplains and ravine slopes; throughout all but the northern part of the region.

Comments: The bulbs and leaves are commonly eaten and have a long history and folklore in North American Indian and pioneer culture. The shiny black seeds bounce when dropped on a hard surface.

KEITH BOARD

Colic Root

COLIC ROOT
Aletris farinosa
Lily Family (Liliaceae)

Description: Smooth, single-stemmed plant to 2½' tall, with a dense cluster of pointed, straplike basal leaves, each up to 8" long. The stem is leafless except for a few scattered, alternate, narrow, pointed bracts, each less than 1" long. Along the upper part of the stem is a narrow cluster of alternate flowers. Each flower is on a short stalk and is accompanied by tiny narrow bracts. The tubular white flower is just over ¼" long, with 6 small, narrowly triangular lobes. The flower is covered with microscopic projections, giving it a rough appearance.

Bloom Season: Late spring–midsummer.

Habitat/Range: Occasional in wet to dry, sandy or peaty acidic sites, including shores, meadows, and woodland openings, usually growing where other vegetation is sparse; from southern Maine through southern Ontario to Wisconsin.

Comments: A bitter tonic made from the roots of this plant was once thought to have medicinal properties.

CANADA MAYFLOWER
Maianthemum canadense
Lily Family (Liliaceae)

Description: Delicate, slightly zigzagging stems to 6" tall, with 1–3 widely spaced, alternate, shiny, dark green leaves that may be smooth or hairy on the underside. The leaves are rounded and taper to sharply pointed tips. They are stalkless or short stalked and have heart-shaped or broadly rounded bases that tend to clasp the stem. The leaves range from narrowly rounded and less than 1" wide to up to 3" wide and nearly as long. Small white flowers are individually stalked and alternate in elongate clusters along the upper part of the stems. Each flower is ¼" wide and has 4 small, white, petal-like segments and 4 stamens surrounding a flask-shaped ovary. The fruits are red berries about ⅛" wide.

Bloom Season: Midspring–early summer.

Habitat/Range: Abundant in all types of dry to wet woods, even in dense shade under closed conifer stands, and also in bogs and swamps; throughout the region.

JESSIE M. HARRIS

Canada Mayflower

FEATHERY FALSE SOLOMON'S SEAL
Smilacina racemosa
Lily Family (Liliaceae)

Description: Arching, single-stemmed, unbranched plant to 3' tall, with fine hairs and alternate, horizontally spreading leaves that point in opposite directions. The stem typically zigzags slightly, and the leaves are at widely spaced intervals. The leaves are slightly pleated and up to 8" long and 5" wide, with rounded bases and many parallel veins along their length. The flowers grow abundantly in branched feathery clusters at the tops of the stems. Each short-stalked white flower is less than ¼" wide and has 6 narrow, spreading, petal-like segments; 6 larger erect stamens; and a flask-shaped ovary. The red berries are about ³/₁₆" wide and marked with purple.

Bloom Season: Midspring–early summer.

Habitat/Range: Common in a variety of moist to dry woods and thickets, but especially in beech and beech-maple forests; throughout the region.

Comments: The roots and shoots have been used for food, and the berries are reported to be edible but have purgative properties.

Feathery False Solomon's Seal

Starry False Solomon's Seal

STARRY FALSE SOLOMON'S SEAL
Smilacina stellata
Lily Family (Liliaceae)

Description: Single-stemmed, unbranched, usually smooth plant to 2½' tall, with narrow, somewhat stiff, bluish green, alternate leaves that point in opposite directions. The leaves are up to 6" long and seldom more than 1½" wide. They are flat or folded upward along the middle and have parallel veins along their length, pointed tips, and bases that clasp the slightly zigzagging stem. Bright white flowers are alternate on slender individual stalks along the upper part of the stems. Each flower is ⅜" wide and has 6 narrow, spreading, petal-like segments; 6 curving stamens; and a flask-shaped ovary. The fruits are dark red berries about ⁵/₁₆" wide; they are often marked with dark lines.

Bloom Season: Midspring–early summer.

Habitat/Range: Locally frequent in sandy woods, well-drained thickets, and along sandy shores, and occasional in loamy moist woods and swampy forests; throughout the region.

JESSIE M. HARRIS

White Mandarin

WHITE MANDARIN
Streptopus amplexifolius
Lily Family (Liliaceae)

Description: Plant to 3' tall and usually branched, with alternate, smooth-edged leaves that nearly surround the stem at their deeply heart-shaped bases. Each broadly rounded leaf is up to 5" long and 2½" wide, with a whitish underside, fine parallel veins along its length, and a narrow pointed tip. The dangling flowers are mostly single on twisted or bent stalks up to 2" long that arise from the bases of the upper leaves. Each flower is ⅜" long and has 6 long-pointed, greenish white, petal-like segments that curve sharply backward. The fruits are oval berries about ⅝" long.

Bloom Season: Late spring–early summer.

Habitat/Range: Occasional in moist shaded sites in ravines and seeps, on slopes, and along stream banks; throughout most of the region, westward to western Lake Superior.

Comments: See Rose Mandarin (p. 83).

FALSE ASPHODEL
Tofieldia glutinosa
Lily Family (Liliaceae)

Description: Single-stemmed, unbranched plant to 1½' tall, with narrow grasslike leaves clustered near the base and small, dark, sticky spots along the upper part of the stem. Each leaf is up to 7" long but less than ½" wide, with a pointed tip. Toward the middle of the stem is a single bractlike leaf. Small white flowers form dense clusters at the top of the plant, with up to 3 individually stalked flowers at each point. Each flower is ¼" wide and has 3 tiny bracts at its base and 6 narrow petal-like segments surrounding 6 stamens and a central ovary.

Bloom Season: Summer.

Habitat/Range: Local in mineral-rich or alkaline wetlands and sometimes in acidic areas, in bogs, fens, wet sands, marl flats, and moist rocky areas; throughout the region, especially near the Great Lakes, but rare eastward.

LEE A. CASEBERE

False Asphodel

False Mayflower

KENNETH DRITZ

FALSE MAYFLOWER
Smilacina trifolia
Lily Family (Liliaceae)

Description: Smooth, single-stemmed, un-branched plant usually less than 10" tall, typically with 3 stalkless alternate leaves along the zigzagging stem. The leaves are up to 6" long and 1½" wide. They have pointed tips, parallel veins along their lengths, and tapering bases that slightly clasp the stem. Up to 12 slender-stalked white flowers are alternate along the flattened, twisted upper stem. Each flower is ¹/₃" wide and has 6 narrow, spreading, petal-like segments; 6 slender curving stamens; and a flask-shaped ovary. The fruits are round red berries about ¼" wide.

Bloom Season: Late spring–early summer.

Habitat/Range: Locally common in moist sphagnum mats in bogs, wet conifer forests, and shaded wet peaty areas; throughout the region.

Comments: This species resembles the more common Canada Mayflower (p. 192), but the flowers of False Mayflower have 4 parts and its leaves taper to the base. The flowers of Canada Mayflower have 6 parts, and the leaves have broad, heart-shaped bases. Canada Mayflower may be smooth or finely hairy, while False Mayflower is always smooth.

Large-flowered Trillium

LARGE-FLOWERED TRILLIUM
Trillium grandiflorum
Lily Family (Liliaceae)

Description: Smooth, unbranched plant to 18" tall, with a single whorl of 3 broad stalkless leaves at the top of each stem and a single flower rising above the leaves on a 1–3"-long stalk. Each leaf is typically 3–6" long and nearly as wide and has a tapering base and an abruptly long-pointed tip. Each large shiny flower is 3" wide and has 3 leafy sepals; 3 larger, wavy-edged white petals that turn pinkish with age; and 6 stamens surrounding a central ovary with 3 narrow stigmas.

Bloom Season: Spring.

Habitat/Range: Occasional in rich woods, especially on moist shaded slopes; most common in the central part of the region, becoming rare in northern New England and Quebec, and absent from northeastern Minnesota.

Comments: Large-Flowered Trillium is the provincial flower of Ontario.

NODDING TRILLIUM
Trillium cernuum
Lily Family (Liliaceae)

Description: Smooth unbranched plant to 15" tall, with a single whorl of 3 broadly rounded, short-stalked leaves at the top of the stem. Each leaf is 2½–5" long and nearly as wide, and tapers to a sharply pointed tip and broadly rounded base. The single nodding flower is at the top of the stem on a stalk up to 1½" long that droops below the leaves. The flower is 1½–2" wide and has 3 pointed green sepals; 3 broad, pointed, white petals; and 6 large pinkish stamens surrounding a pale to pinkish central ovary with 3 narrow stigmas.

Bloom Season: Spring–early summer.

Habitat/Range: Frequent in moist to wet woods, moist thickets, and on rich, shaded slopes and stream banks; throughout the region.

Nodding Trillium

WHITE CAMASS
Zigadenus elegans var. *glaucus*
Lily Family (Liliaceae)

Description: Single-stemmed plant to 2' tall, with closely clustered, alternate, grasslike leaves near the base. These leaves are up to 15" long and usually less than ¼" wide. Several alternate bractlike leaves are usually scattered along the stem. Flowers grow in a branched cluster along the upper part of the stem. At the base of each branch is a small, pointed, often purplish bract. Each white to pale greenish flower is ¾" wide and has 6 broad-based, rounded, petal-like segments with pointed, often inrolled tips, and 6 erect stamens surrounding an ovary with 3 short styles. Each petal-like segment is greenish to bronze or purplish on the outside, and there is a greenish 2-lobed gland at the base on the inside.

Bloom Season: Early summer–midsummer.

Habitat/Range: Local in moist alkaline or mineral-rich areas in fens, swamps, and on beaches and cliffs; mostly in the western half of the region, especially near the Great Lakes, eastward to Quebec and formerly in Vermont.

Comments: The plant is poisonous, and its flowers have a foul scent.

White Camass

BOGBEAN
Menyanthes trifoliata
Bogbean Family (Menyanthaceae)

Description: Soft, smooth plant less than 10" tall, with creeping, rootlike, underground stems. The leaves are stalked and appear to be both solitary along the underground stems and alternate along the short, thick, basally flattened flowering stems. At the top of the leaf stalk are 3 smooth, shiny, round leaflets with irregular edges. Each is up to 2½" long. The base of the leaf stalk is broad and thin and encloses the stem. Flowers are short-stalked and mostly alternate along the upper part of the stems. Each flower is ½" long and has a small 5-lobed calyx; a white to pinkish corolla divided more than half its length into 5 curving, pointed lobes with crooked white bristles; 5 small dark-tipped stamens; and a protruding style. The threadlike style elongates and remains on the distinctive flattened fruits.

Bloom Season: Midspring–early summer.

Habitat/Range: Frequent in wet open or shaded sites, often in acidic or mineralized waters, in bogs, fens, marshes, alder thickets, and conifer swamps; throughout the region.

Comments: The leaves resemble those of plants in the Bean Family (Fabaceae).

Bogbean

INDIAN PIPE

Monotropa uniflora
Indian Pipe Family (Monotropaceae)

Description: Ghostly, translucent-white, un-branched, fleshy, waxy plant to 10" tall. Occasional plants may be pale pinkish. This species lacks the green chlorophyll that most plants use to produce food and instead derives nutrients from fungi that feed on decaying plants or roots. Numerous small, alternate scales form along the stem, which is topped by a single nodding flower. The tubular flower, ½–¾" long, typically lacks sepals but has 5 long petals enclosing 8 or 10 stamens. After flowering, the stem becomes upright and has a round fruit capsule at the top. The plant turns dull black when picked and dried.

Bloom Season: Midsummer–early fall.

Habitat/Range: Occasional but locally common in leaf litter or humus in a variety of acidic woods; throughout the region. Populations often fluctuate greatly from year to year.

Small Enchanter's Nightshade

SMALL ENCHANTER'S NIGHTSHADE

Circaea alpina
Evening Primrose Family (Onagraceae)

Description: Weak plant to 1' tall and mostly unbranched below the flowers. Stalked opposite leaves typically cluster near the middle of the stems. The leaves are up to 2½" long and sometimes nearly as wide. They have broadly rounded to heart-shaped bases, pointed tips, and widely spaced teeth along their edges. The leaf usually extends as a narrow wing along the leaf stalk. Small white flowers are alternate at the top of the plant on slender, horizontal, hairy stalks. Each flower is ⅛" wide and has 2 rounded, petal-like, white sepals; 2 notched petals; and 2 small stamens. The small, bristly, teardrop-shaped fruits cling persistently to clothing.

Bloom Season: Late spring–summer.

Habitat/Range: Common in moist shaded sites in woods, swamps, and along bog edges and shores; also on rotten logs and stumps in conifer swamps; throughout the region.

Comments: Common Enchanter's Nightshade (*C. lutetiana*) is a larger relative, usually more than 1' tall. It has ridged fruits, more widely spaced flowers, and leaves much longer than they are wide. It occurs throughout the region in a variety of woods and on floodplains.

Indian Pipe

Water Lily

DOUG LADD

WATER LILY
Nymphaea odorata
Water Lily Family (Nymphaeaceae)

Description: Aquatic plant with long-stalked, floating leaves and long-stalked, floating, solitary flowers. The leaves are nearly circular and up to 8" across, with a narrow V-shaped cleft where the stalk is attached. The underside of the leaf is often deep purplish. Flowers are up to 5" wide, usually open in the morning, and typically close by midafternoon on sunny days. Each fragrant flower has 4 rounded sepals, numerous upright to spreading white petals, and 40 or more yellow stamens surrounding a central ovary with a disk-shaped stigma. Some of the outer stamens are broad and petal-like.

Bloom Season: Summer.

Habitat/Range: Common in quiet waters up to 5' deep in ponds, placid backwaters, and on sheltered lakeshores; throughout the region.

Comments: Water Shield (*Brasenia schreberi*), a plant in the Water Shield Family (Cabombaceae), occurs in ponds throughout the region. It has small, nonshowy, purplish flowers and oval floating leaves up to 4" long and resembles a miniature water lily. The submerged parts of the plant are covered with slimy, mucouslike jelly, and the stems are attached to the middle of the unnotched leaves. Pygmy Water Lily (*N. tetragona*), rare in cold bogs and ponds at a few sites in the northern part of the region, also has small leaves, but they have a cleft notch where the stem is attached.

WILLIAM CHAPMAN

Checkered Rattlesnake Plantain

CHECKERED RATTLESNAKE PLANTAIN

Goodyera tesselata
Orchid Family (Orchidaceae)

Description: Plant usually less than 1' tall, with a slender, finely hairy stem and a cluster of small, somewhat fleshy, evergreen basal leaves. These leaves are bluish green and up to 3½" long and 1½" wide. They have short wide stalks and are strikingly marked with broad silvery white lines that create a checkered pattern. Usually, 2–6 small alternate bracts grow along the stem. Flowers form an alternate spikelike cluster along the upper part of the stem and often appear spirally arranged. Each flower is ⅜" long and has a stalklike tubular ovary with 3 white, petal-like sepals; 2 slightly smaller white petals; and a pointed, white, saclike lower lip.

Bloom Season: Summer.

Habitat/Range: Frequent in moist rich woods, especially under conifers, in pine forests, white cedar swamps, and wet spruce woods; throughout most of the region westward to Wisconsin and northeastern Minnesota.

Comments: Several other species of rattlesnake plantain occur in the region. Downy Rattlesnake Plantain (*G. pubescens*) usually has more than 6 bracts on the stem and occurs under conifers and hardwoods throughout all but the northern edge of the region.

WHITE FRINGED ORCHID
Platanthera blephariglottis
Orchid Family (Orchidaceae)

Description: Smooth unbranched plant to 1½' tall, with 1–3 long, pointed, alternate leaves along the lower half of the stem and smaller bractlike leaves along the upper stem. A prominent, raised, central vein runs along the length of the underside of each main leaf. Usually more than 20 flowers form a compact cluster at the top of the stem. At the base of each flower is a small, green, pointed bract. Each white flower is ½" wide and has a narrow tubular ovary topped by 3 broad petal-like sepals and 2 much smaller, usually ragged upper petals. The larger, dangling lower lip is less than ½" long, with a narrowed base and deeply fringed edges. A slender tubular spur up to 1" long curves below and behind the lip.

Bloom Season: Summer.

Habitat/Range: Uncommon but sometimes locally abundant in bogs, acidic swamps, and saturated moss mats in shaded depressions, usually in open to lightly shaded conditions; throughout the eastern part of the region westward to Lake Michigan, but not much north of the latitude of Lake Superior except in the Canadian Maritimes.

JESSIE M. HARRIS

White Fringed Orchid

BOG CANDLES
Platanthera dilatata
Orchid Family (Orchidaceae)

Description: Slender, smooth, unbranched plant to 3' tall, with several narrow alternate leaves along the stem. The leaves become smaller and more bractlike toward the top of the plant. Flowers grow in a narrow elongate spike at the top of the stem, with each flower just above a pointed green bract that is sometimes longer than the flower. Each bright white flower is ⅜" wide and has a tubular ovary topped by 3 bluntly pointed, petal-like sepals; 2 smaller, curving, upper petals; and a dangling lower lip with smooth edges, a broad base, and a straplike tip. A narrow tubular spur less than ¾" long curves below the lip.

Bloom Season: Late spring–early summer.

Habitat/Range: Frequent in bogs, fens, marshy meadows, open conifer forests, and on mossy, seepy stream banks; throughout all but the southwestern corner of the region.

Comments: The flowers smell like cloves.

LEE A. CASEBERE

Bog Candles

JESSIE M. HARRIS

Blunt-leaved Orchid

BLUNT-LEAVED ORCHID
Platanthera obtusata
Orchid Family (Orchidaceae)

Description: Smooth, slender, unbranched stem to 1' tall, with a single blunt basal leaf up to 6" long and 2" wide. The leaf clasps the stem at its stalkless, tapering base. Greenish white flowers are alternate in a loose spike along the upper stem. Each flower is ¼" wide and has a small, pointed, green bract at its base and a curved tubular ovary topped by 3 spreading, petal-like sepals. The middle sepal is short, hoodlike, and broad based. Under the sepals are 2 smaller spreading petals that narrow abruptly above the middle, and a narrow, evenly tapered lower lip with a tubular spur less than ½" long that dangles below the base of the lip.

Bloom Season: Summer.

Habitat/Range: Uncommon in wet shaded sites, often on mossy mounds in wooded bogs and conifer swamps; throughout most of the region southward to central parts of New York and Wisconsin.

SLENDER LADIES' TRESSES
Spiranthes lacera
Orchid Family (Orchidaceae)

Description: Delicate, single-stemmed plant, usually less than 1' tall, with scattered alternate bracts along the stem and, sometimes, pointed oval leaves up to 2" long at the base of the plant. Flowers are arranged spirally along the upper part of the stem, much like steps in a spiral staircase. Each flower has a small, pointed, green bract at its base. The bracts are mostly shorter than the flowers, which are almost tubular and about ¼" long. Each flower has a stout tubular ovary topped by 2 petals and a petal-like sepal above 2 sepals flanking a broad lip with a green center and irregular edges.

Bloom Season: Summer.

Habitat/Range: Common in open to lightly shaded areas of open pine and aspen woods, rocky or sandy slopes, pastures, and sometimes in moist sites; throughout the region.

Comments: A related species occurring in the region from Michigan and Wisconsin to Maine and Nova Scotia, *S. casei*, has a lip with a white to yellowish center.

ROBERT TATINA

Slender Ladies' Tresses

Round-leaved Orchid

ALLISON W. BELL

ROUND-LEAVED ORCHID
Platanthera orbiculata
Orchid Family (Orchidaceae)

Description: Smooth, unbranched, leafless stems usually less than 1' tall. A pair of flat, shiny, round, fleshy leaves up to 6" long and wide lies along the ground, each leaf clasping the stem at its broadly rounded base. Small alternate bracts are scattered along the stem. Greenish white flowers are alternate along the upper half of the stem. Each flower is ⅜" wide and has a small pointed bract at its base. The stalked tubular ovary is topped by a broad, hooded, petal-like sepal flanked by a pair of narrow, widely spreading petals and a pair of slightly larger, widely spreading, petal-like sepals. Under these petals and sepals is a narrow, dangling lower lip more than 3 times as long as it is wide. A slender tubular spur extends horizontally from the base of the lip.

Bloom Season: Late spring–midsummer.

Habitat/Range: Occasional in a variety of woods, bogs, and conifer swamps; throughout the region except parts of lower Michigan and central Wisconsin.

Comments: The leaves were used in folk medicines. A similar but less common orchid, Hooker's Orchid (*P. hookeri*), has smaller and duller leaves, no bracts on the stem, and flowers with stalkless ovaries and tapering, narrowly triangular lips. It occurs in similar habitats throughout the region.

LEE A. CASEBERE

Hooded Ladies' Tresses

HOODED LADIES' TRESSES
Spiranthes romanzoffiana
Orchid Family (Orchidaceae)

Description: Slender unbranched plant, occasionally more than 1' tall, with fine hairs on the upper stems. Several alternate, pointed, narrow leaves usually occur near the base of the stem; the upper leaves become small and bractlike. Flowers are in a dense spike at the top of the stem. Under each flower is a pointed green bract that is often longer than the flower. When viewed from above, there are usually 3 distinct vertical rows of flowers. Each fragrant flower is less than ½" long and has a small stout ovary topped by 3 pointed, white, petal-like sepals and 2 smaller petals forming a hood above a downward-pointing lower lip. This lower lip is narrower in the middle and has irregular edges. The 2 side sepals have curving tips.

Bloom Season: Midsummer–early fall.

Habitat/Range: Frequent in moist open or lightly shaded areas in bogs, marshy meadows, moist thickets, seepage areas, and along shores, usually in mineral-rich or alkaline groundwater; throughout the region.

Comments: Two similar species of ladies' tresses occur in parts of the region. Nodding Ladies' Tresses (*S. cernua*) is common in a variety of habitats in most of the southern half of the region. It has a more open flower cluster, and the lower lip of the flower is not as strongly narrowed in the middle. Early Ladies' Tresses (*S. lucida*) grows in fens and seepy areas and along shores from Michigan eastward. Its flowers have a bright yellow center.

BLOODROOT
Sanguinaria canadensis
Poppy Family (Papaveraceae)

Description: Pale green plant to 6" tall at flowering, with reddish orange sap. Each plant has a single-stalked basal leaf and a flower at the top of a separate upright stalk. The leaf is pale beneath and deeply notched where it attaches to the leaf stalk. It is round in general outline but deeply lobed into 3–9 sections, with irregular edges. The leaves are initially small and curled around the flower stalk, but they continue to expand after flowering, eventually growing up to 9" wide. The flower is up to 1½" wide and has 2 sepals that fall early, 8–16 narrow white petals, and many yellow stamens.

Bloom Season: Spring.

Habitat/Range: Common in moist woods, especially on lower slopes; throughout the region but less common northward.

Comments: The bitter sap is poisonous and has caused fatalities. Nonetheless, it was used by North American Indians for insect repellent,

Bloodroot

dye, ceremonial pigment, and a variety of medicines. Extracts of the plant are used in toothpaste.

CINNAMON WILLOW HERB
Epilobium coloratum
Evening Primrose Family (Onagraceae)

Description: Bushy-branched, often purplish plant to 3' tall, with finely hairy stems. The leaves are narrow, alternate, short-stalked, pointed, and up to 5" long. They have small teeth along the edges. Individually stalked flowers occur singly or in few-flowered clusters at the bases of the upper leaves. Each whitish to pinkish flower is ¼" wide and has 4 sepals and 4 notched petals. The fruits are slender spreading pods up to 2" long. The seeds are topped with tufts of cinnamon-colored hairs.

Bloom Season: Summer–early fall.

Habitat/Range: Common in all types of wetlands, typically in open to lightly shaded sites; throughout the region.

Comments: Northern Willow Herb (*E. ciliatum*, including *E. glandulosum*) is a similar but less bushy species found in wetlands throughout the region. It has seeds with white tufts of hairs, and usually some of the lower leaves are opposite.

Cinnamon Willow Herb

Seneca Snakeroot

SENECA SNAKEROOT
Polygala senega
Milkwort Family (Polygalaceae)

Description: Plant to 18" tall, with fine short hairs. Usually, several unbranched stems grow from a single base. The leaves are alternate and up to 3½" long and 1" wide but often much narrower. They taper to narrow bases and pointed tips and sometimes have teeth along the edges. The lowest leaves on the stem are usually very small. Flowers are in a narrow cluster at the top of each stem. Each flower is ⅛" wide and has 3 small greenish sepals and 2 larger, white, petal-like sepals flanking a tube of 3 small white petals, the lower of which is fringed at the tip.

Bloom Season: Midspring–early summer.

Habitat/Range: Occasional in open rocky or marshy woods, on terraces along streams and rivers, and in boggy sites, often in calcium-rich soils; scattered throughout most of the region eastward to New Brunswick.

Comments: Seneca Snakeroot contains medicinally active chemicals and was used by North American Indians to treat snakebite and other ailments. A tiny, white-flowered relative, Whorled Milkwort (*P. verticillata*), has thread-like leaves and narrowly conical flower clusters. Typically less than 6" tall, it occurs in sterile sand from New England westward.

FRINGED BINDWEED
Polygonum cilinode
Buckwheat Family (Polygonaceae)

Description: Climbing vine with minutely hairy, usually reddish stems and widely spaced, stalked leaves with rounded, heart-shaped bases, smooth edges, and pointed tips. A papery, bristle-fringed sheath surrounds the stem at the base of each leaf stalk. Flowers form loose elongate clusters on short branches and at the ends of the stems. Each flower is ⅛" wide and has 5 unequal, white, petal-like calyx lobes. The fruits are dark triangular seeds covered by the calyx.

Bloom Season: Late spring–summer.

Habitat/Range: Common in dry woods, thickets, recently burned areas, and along woodland edges; throughout the region.

Comments: A related species, Climbing False Buckwheat (*P. scandens*), has papery sheaths on its stems, but the sheaths are not fringed with bristles. The fruiting calyx has prominent crestlike wings. This plant occurs in similar, but often wetter, habitats throughout the region.

JESSIE M. HARRIS

Fringed Bindweed

CAROL GRACIE

Mountain Knotweed

MOUNTAIN KNOTWEED
Polygonum douglasii
Buckwheat Family (Polygonaceae)

Description: Slender annual to 2' tall, with mostly upright branches and narrow, pointed, stalkless, alternate leaves typically up to 1½" long and ¼" wide. At the base of each leaf, encircling the stem, is a conspicuous bristle-fringed papery sheath. Flowers are on short nodding stalks less than ⅛" long, with 1–3 individually stalked flowers emerging from many of the upper sheaths. Each white to greenish flower is ⅛" wide and has a deeply 5-lobed calyx.

Bloom Season: Midsummer–early fall.

Habitat/Range: Local in open to lightly shaded rocky or gravelly areas and on outcrops, ridges, and exposed dry soils; scattered throughout the northern half of the region.

ROBERT TATINA

Smartweed

SMARTWEED
Polygonum punctatum
Buckwheat Family (Polygonaceae)

Description: Slender plant to 3' tall but often smaller, with short-stalked alternate leaves. These leaves grow up to 7" long and 1" wide, with pointed tips. A papery, bristle-fringed sheath encircles the stem at the base of each leaf stalk. Flowers are in loose alternate clusters along the branch tips and on small side branches. Each flower is ⅛" wide and has a green calyx divided into 5 petal-like lobes. The calyx is covered with small pale spots that are visible under magnification.

Bloom Season: Midsummer–fall.

Habitat/Range: Common in wet open or shaded sites in marshes, wet depressions, beaver marshes, thickets, floodplains, and along shores; throughout the region.

Comments: Several other smartweeds, both native and introduced, occur in the region. Native species include Mild Water Pepper (*P. hydropiperoides*), whose calyx is often pinkish and lacks pale spots; Pinkweed (*P. pensylvanicum*), which has a thick dense cluster of pale pinkish flowers; and Heartsease (*P. lapathifolium*), which has nodding thin clusters of whitish flowers.

ARROW-LEAVED TEARTHUMB
Polygonum sagittatum
Buckwheat Family (Polygonaceae)

Description: Sprawling branched annual with 4 lines of tiny, flexible, backward-pointing prickles along the stems and leaf stalks. The leaves are widely spaced, alternate, and up to 4" long and 1" wide, with 2 broadly angular to rounded lobes at their bases. The leaves are thin and wilt quickly when picked. Dense clusters of a few stalked flowers grow at the ends of the branches and the bases of the leaf stalks. Each flower is ⅛" wide and has 5 blunt, whitish to pale pink, petal-like sepals.

Bloom Season: Midsummer–early fall.

Habitat/Range: Common and locally abundant in marshes, wet meadows, swamps, and along shores; throughout the region.

Comments: This plant can form dense mats that tear clothing and skin.

DOUG LADD

Arrow-leaved Tearthumb

STARFLOWER
Trientalis borealis
Primrose Family (Primulaceae)

Description: Smooth delicate plant to 8" tall, with a single whorl of 5–10 unequal, narrow, thin leaves at the top of the stem, which also has small bracts near the middle. Each smooth-edged leaf is up to 4" long and ¾" wide, is broadest near the middle, and tapers to a pointed tip and narrow base. From 1 to a few flowers grow on slender individual stalks at the top of the stem. Each flower is ½" wide and typically has 7 narrow pointed sepals; a starlike corolla with 7 spreading, sharply pointed petals; and 7 stamens with bright yellow tips. Occasionally there may be 5–9 sepals, petals, and stamens in a flower.

Bloom Season: Late spring–midsummer.

Habitat/Range: Common in a variety of woods, mossy bogs, and conifer swamps; throughout the region.

ROBERT TATINA

Starflower

One-flowered Pyrola

ROBERT TATINA

ONE-FLOWERED PYROLA

Moneses uniflora
Shinleaf Family (Pyrolaceae)

Description: Delicate unbranched plant to 5" tall, usually with 1–3 whorls of 2 or 3 stalked round leaves on the lower part of the stem. The leaves are less than 1" long and have small teeth along the edges. At the top of the stem is a single nodding flower that is ¾" wide. This flower has 5 tiny, slightly cupped sepals; 4 or 5 horizontally spreading, broadly triangular white petals with irregular edges; 10 stamens; and a straight protruding style with a crownlike 5-lobed stigma. The fruiting stem becomes upright, with a round, brown, 5-lobed capsule topped by the persistent style.

Bloom Season: Late spring–midsummer.

Habitat/Range: Frequent in cool shaded sites, usually in mossy or sparsely vegetated areas in wet conifer woods, mossy swamps, wooded bogs, and moist forests; throughout the region.

ONE-SIDED SHINLEAF

Pyrola secunda
Shinleaf Family (Pyrolaceae)

Description: The unbranched stems of this plant are typically 5–7" tall. Clustered toward the base of the plant along with some small bracts are stalked, broadly rounded, shiny and somewhat leathery leaves. These leaves are less than 2" long and more widely separated and more clearly alternate than those of other shinleafs. The stem usually has small bracts above the middle. Flowers dangle in a single row from the arching upper part of the stem, which becomes upright in fruit. At the base of each flower stalk is a small pointed bract. Each flower is $^5/_{16}$" wide and has 5 minutely fringed calyx lobes, 5 white to greenish white petals, 10 stamens, and a protruding straight style.

Bloom Season: Late spring–early summer.

Habitat/Range: Frequent in a variety of moist to dry woods, usually in loamy or sandy soils; throughout the region.

Comments: A rare species scattered in the northern part of the region, Lesser Shinleaf (*P. minor*) has similar leaves and a tiny straight style that does not protrude from the flower.

One-sided Shinleaf

KAY YATSKIEVYCH

Large-leaved Shinleaf

LARGE-LEAVED SHINLEAF
Pyrola elliptica
Shinleaf Family (Pyrolaceae)

Description: Unbranched stems to 1' tall, with several stalked, thin, broadly oval leaves clustered near the base. Each leaf is up to 3" long and usually longer than the leaf stalk. The leaves have slightly toothed edges, tapering bases, and blunt or rounded tips. There are sometimes small pointed bracts along the stem. Flowers are alternate along the upper part of the stem, with small bracts at the bases of the flower stalks. Each fragrant nodding flower is ½" wide and has a tiny calyx with 5 lobes that are about as wide as they are long; 5 white petals with green veins; 10 stamens; and a protruding, upward-curved style.

Bloom Season: Early summer–midsummer.

Habitat/Range: Frequent in sandy or loamy woods and on shaded stream banks, especially under hardwoods; throughout the region.

Comments: Shinleafs contain an aspirin-like substance, and the leaves have been applied to injuries to reduce pain. Another species with curved styles and calyx lobes that are as wide as they are long is Green Shinleaf (*P. virens*), which has leaves scarcely more than 1" long and shorter than their stalks. It occurs in similar habitats throughout the region, especially in dry, sandy conifer woods.

Red Baneberry

Red Baneberry

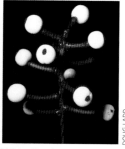

White Baneberry

RED BANEBERRY

Actaea rubra
Buttercup Family (Ranunculaceae)

Description: Bushy plant to 3' tall, with large, stalked, compound leaves. The leaflets are further divided, with segments sharply toothed or even lobed and up to 2½" long. There are usually some hairs on the veins of the lower leaf surface. The flowers are about ¼" wide and alternate on delicate individual stalks in dense clusters at the tops of the stems. The sepals fall off as the flower opens, so each flower has 4–10 tiny white petals surrounding many protruding white stamens and a flattened 2-lobed stigma. The plants are most conspicuous in fruit, when each flower develops into a shiny round berry about ¼" wide, with a dark "eye" spot.

Bloom Season: Midspring–late spring.

Habitat/Range: Occasional in moist or rich woods, often in full shade; throughout the region.

Comments: The fruits give rise to another common name for the plant: Doll's Eyes. Some forms of this plant have white fruits and resemble the related White Baneberry (*A. alba*), whose leaflets are often hairless and whose fruits are on stout thickened stalks. White Baneberry also occurs in rich woods throughout the region. To make matters more confusing, there is also a rare red-fruited form of White Baneberry. Both baneberries consistently have white flowers. The plants are mildly poisonous and were used medicinally by North American Indians.

Meadow Anemone

MEADOW ANEMONE
Anemone canadensis
Buttercup Family (Ranunculaceae)

Description: Hairy plant to 2' tall, with long-stalked basal leaves, each deeply divided into 3 narrow tapering segments that are toothed and sometimes lobed. On the main stem is a single whorl of similar but stalkless leaves. Above that are 1 or more long stalks, sometimes with a whorl of smaller leaves. Each of these stalks is topped by a single flower that nods in bud but becomes erect as it opens. The flowers vary in size but can be up to 2" wide. Each has 5 white petal-like sepals of slightly different sizes and numerous yellow stamens. The seed head is a burlike cluster of beaked flattened fruits.

Bloom Season: Midspring–summer.

Habitat/Range: Frequent, often in large patches, in moist open thickets, low woods, drier areas of marshes, open floodplains, and along streams and shores; throughout the region, but local and uncommon east of the Great Lakes.

Comments: North American Indians used a preparation of the roots and leaves to treat wounds. This plant is also called Canada Anemone.

Wood Anemone

VIRGIN'S BOWER

Clematis virginiana
Buttercup Family (Ranunculaceae)

Description: Clambering or sprawling vine that is often woody at the base, with angular stems up to 10' long. The leaves are stalked, alternate, compound, and spaced at least 2" apart along the main stems. Each leaf is divided into 3 leaflets on short stalks; the leaflets are up to 3" long and 1½" wide and have broadly rounded to indented bases. The leaf stalks are often twisted. The basal half of each leaflet is usually smooth, while the upper half is toothed or even sharply lobed. Flowers grow in stalked, leafy-bracted clusters at the bases of the main stem leaves. Each individually stalked flower is ¾" wide and usually has 4 pointed, finely hairy, white, petal-like sepals surrounding many pale stamens and a central mass of slightly curved, blunt-tipped styles. These styles become elongated, curved, and feathery in fruit, creating the appearance of a fuzzy ball.

Bloom Season: Midsummer–early fall.

Habitat/Range: Common in moist thickets, low woods, and along riverbanks, especially in calcium-rich soils; throughout the region.

Comments: The plant is toxic but was once used to make ointments for skin problems.

WOOD ANEMONE

Anemone quinquefolia
Buttercup Family (Ranunculaceae)

Description: Delicate plant to 8" tall, with a single whorl of 3 stalked compound leaves at the middle of the stem. Each leaf is divided into 3 leaflets with narrow tapering bases. The leaflets are up to 2" long, coarsely toothed, and sometimes lobed. At the base of the plant is a single similar but longer-stalked leaf. The stem above the leaves is finely hairy. At the top of each stem is a single flower that is ¾–1" wide and usually has 5 blunt petal-like sepals surrounding many pale stamens. The sepals are sometimes reddish on the outside.

Bloom Season: Spring–early summer.

Habitat/Range: Frequent in moist woods, clearings, thickets, and swampy forests and along stream banks; throughout the region.

Comments: A similar species with 4 or more leaves in the main whorl and a thimblelike fruiting head more than 1" long is Thimbleweed (*A. cylindrica*). It occurs in dry exposed places. Tall Anemone (*A. virginiana*) is a coarser, taller plant of dry meadows and woods. It is more than 1' tall and has stout hairy stems and usually several erect flower stalks. Its thimblelike fruiting heads are mostly less than 1" long.

Virgin's Bower

GOLDTHREAD
Coptis trifolia
Buttercup Family (Ranunculaceae)

Description: Delicate plant, usually less than 5" tall, with basal leaves and slender bare flower stalks that arise from stringlike, golden yellow, creeping roots. The leaves are stalked and divided into 3 shiny, dark green leaflets up to 1" long. These leaflets are toothed and occasionally lobed, with tapered bases. The flower stalk usually has small bracts scattered along its length and a single flower at its top. Each flower is ½" wide and has 5–7 white petal-like sepals that sometimes have purple stripes on the outside; some flattened, yellow, sterile stamens; and numerous pale, fertile stamens.

Bloom Season: Midspring–early summer.

Habitat/Range: Common in moist conifer forests, conifer swamps, shaded boggy areas, and mountain woods; throughout the region.

Comments: North American Indians produced a yellow dye from the roots. The roots also have antibacterial properties and have been used to flavor beer and relieve eye and mouth ailments.

ROBERT TATINA

Goldthread

JESSIE M. HARRIS

False Violet

FALSE VIOLET
Dalibarda repens
Rose Family (Rosaceae)

Description: Delicate, hairy plant less than 6" tall, with creeping stems that are often shallowly buried. Long-stalked leaves occur at widely spaced intervals along the stems, growing either singly or in clusters. The leaves are rounded, toothed, and up to 2" long and wide, with heart-shaped bases. Tiny, toothed, bractlike stipules form at the bases of the leaf stalks. Each leaf cluster has 1 to a few long-stalked flowers. Each flower is ½" wide and has 5 or 6 sepals, 3 of which are larger and sometimes toothed. Each also has numerous slender stamens and 5 white petals that often fall off soon after the flowers open. These flowers are usually sterile, but there are shorter-stalked fertile flowers with no petals.

Bloom Season: Early summer–midsummer.

Habitat/Range: Occasional in moist woods and conifer swamps in the eastern part of the region, westward to southern Ontario and a single site in Michigan.

White Avens

THREE-TOOTHED CINQUEFOIL

Potentilla tridentata
Rose Family (Rosaceae)

Description: Dwarf shrub usually less than 8" tall, with stalked, shiny, evergreen leaves that mostly cluster near the base of the plant, sometimes forming mats. Each leaf stalk has a pair of narrow bractlike stipules at the base and 3 leaflets near the tip. Each leaflet is ½–1" long, widest near the squarish 3-toothed tip, and otherwise toothless. The leaflets taper at the base. Individually stalked flowers are in a branched flattened cluster at the top of the plant, with small bracts on the branches. Each flower is up to ½" wide and has 5 pointed sepals alternating with 5 smaller bracts, 5 white petals, and about 20 slender stamens surrounding a conical center.

Bloom Season: Late spring–midsummer.

Habitat/Range: Local in exposed dry sites on cliffs, ledges, rocky shores, peaty areas, and dry open sandy or rocky woods; scattered throughout the region.

WHITE AVENS

Geum canadense
Rose Family (Rosaceae)

Description: Hairy, somewhat sprawling plant to 2½' tall, with stalked, widely spaced, alternate leaves. The lower leaves typically have 3 large toothed leaflets at the top of the stalk and a pair of leafy stipules at the base. Sometimes there are much smaller, toothed, bractlike leaflets along the lower leaf stalk. The leaf stalks become progressively shorter toward the top of the stem, and the upper leaves are sometimes unlobed and almost stalkless. Individually stalked flowers occur in open clusters near the tops of the stems. Each flower is ⅝" wide and has 5 pointed sepals about as long as the 5 white petals. Numerous stamens surround a rounded center, which develops into a bristly oval head.

Bloom Season: Summer.

Habitat/Range: Common in woods, especially along woodland edges, and in shady disturbed or grazed areas; throughout the region, but less common northward.

Comments: Rough Avens (*G. laciniatum*) also has white flowers, but its petals are shorter than the sepals, and the flower stalks are covered with long hairs. Rough Avens occurs in wet areas throughout the region but is uncommon west of Lake Michigan.

Three-toothed Cinquefoil

ROBERT TATINA

Wood Strawberry

WOOD STRAWBERRY
Fragaria vesca var. *americana*
Rose Family (Rosaceae)

Description: Low plant to 5" tall, spreading via runners. The stalked compound leaves have 3 sharply toothed leaflets that are widest near the middle and up to 1½" long. Individually stalked flowers are in a cluster above the leaves. Each flower is ½" wide and has what appear to be 10 pointed sepals (actually 5 sepals alternating with 5 narrower bracts). Each flower also has 5 rounded white petals and many yellow stamens surrounding the central receptacle, which develops into a small strawberry. Unlike the seeds of commercial strawberries, the small seeds of the Wood Strawberry are on the surface of the fruit, rather than embedded in small pits or dimples.

Bloom Season: Midspring–early summer.

Habitat/Range: Occasional in open rocky woods, on bluffs, ledges, rocky slopes, and some-times in swampy woods or on exposed shores; throughout the region.

Comments: Wood Strawberry also occurs in Europe, and some plants in the North Woods were introduced from there. The common Wild Strawberry (*F. virginiana*), whose fruits are miniature versions of the commercial fruit, is common throughout the region. When not in fruit, it is very difficult to tell Wood Strawberry from Wild Strawberry. The flowers of Wild Strawberry are usually slightly larger, ranging up to ¾" wide. The hairs on the flower stalks of Wild Strawberry are usually spreading, while in Wood Strawberry the hairs are usually pressed against the stem. In Wild Strawberry, the tooth at the leaf tip is shorter than its neighbors, while in Wood Strawberry it is longer than the neighboring teeth. The fruits of both species are delicious.

Thimbleberry

JESSIE M. HARRIS

THIMBLEBERRY
Rubus parviflorus
Rose Family (Rosaceae)

Description: Low bushy shrub to 4' tall, with tiny knob-tipped hairs on the young stems and the long leaf stalks. The leaves can be up to 1' long and nearly as wide. They are alternate and have deeply notched bases and typically 5 shallow, toothed lobes arranged like fingers on a hand. At the tips of the branches are clusters of several stalked flowers. Each showy white flower is 2" wide and has 5 rounded sepals ending in threadlike tips and 5 broad papery petals surrounding more than 100 tan to brownish stamens. The fruits resemble broad, tart raspberries.

Bloom Season: Late spring–early summer.

Habitat/Range: Locally common in open woods, clearings, and along woodland edges in the western Great Lakes area in Ontario, Michigan, Minnesota, and Wisconsin.

Comments: The fruits can be eaten raw or used to make jam. This species is widespread in western North America, and North Woods populations are isolated far east of the plant's main range.

ROBERT TATINA

Dwarf Raspberry

DWARF RASPBERRY
Rubus pubescens
Rose Family (Rosaceae)

Description: Wiry stems creep in or on the ground, with thornless upright branches that arise near the base and sometimes also along the stem. Each branch has up to 5 alternate, long-stalked leaves that are divided into 3 sharply and irregularly toothed and often asymmetrical leaflets. These are typically 1–2" long and have broadly tapering, usually toothless bases. At the base of each leaf stalk are 2 small bractlike stipules. Flowers grow singly or in stalked clusters of 2 or 3 at the bases of the upper leaf stalks. Each flower is ½" wide and has 5 widely spreading or backward-curving, pointed sepals, 5 narrow white (rarely pink) petals, and many upright stamens.

Bloom Season: Midspring–midsummer.

Habitat/Range: Occasional in bogs, tamarack and white cedar swamps, mossy wet woods, mucky thickets, and exposed moist rocky sites; throughout the region.

Comments: The fruits are small red raspberries with few segments. They are very tasty but difficult to remove from the plant. This is the only common member of the raspberry group in the region that is not woody.

Meadowsweet

ROUGH BEDSTRAW

Galium asprellum
Bedstraw Family (Rubiaceae)

Description: Scratchy, pale green plant that clings to clothing and sprawls onto other plants, with weak, squarish, branched stems to 7' long. The leaves grow in whorls of 6 and are up to ¾" long and ¼" wide. They are widest near the middle and have sharply pointed tips and rough edges. Flowers occur in short branched clusters at the branch tips. Each flower is ⅛" wide and has a white 4-lobed corolla that develops into a small, smooth, round fruit.

Bloom Season: Summer.

Habitat/Range: Locally abundant in swampy thickets, beaver meadows, white cedar swamps, and on shrubby shorelines and bog edges; throughout the region.

Comments: Several other bedstraws with whorls of 6 or 8 leaves occur in the region. Cleavers (*G. aparine*) is an annual with weak scratchy stems, bristly fruits, and leaves in whorls of 8. The main leaves are more than 1" long. Sweet-Scented Bedstraw (*G. triflorum*) is a woodland plant with weak, smoothish stems, bristly fruits, and leaves in whorls of 6. Marsh Bedstraw (*G. palustre*) is similar to Rough Bedstraw but much smaller and less harsh and clingy. It has rounded to bluntly pointed leaves. White Bedstraw (p. 255) is a stiff, erect plant with smooth fruits and thick shiny leaves in whorls of 6. It does not cling to clothing.

MEADOWSWEET

Spiraea alba
Rose Family (Rosaceae)

Description: Bushy shrub, typically 1½–7' tall, with brittle brown twigs and abundant, short-stalked, alternate leaves. The leaves taper from the middle to the base and have a pale, prominent, raised vein running along the length of the underside. They are green on both sides, about 2" long and ½" wide, and uniformly sized, except for some smaller leaves that appear just below the flowers. The edges of the leaves are sparsely toothed in the upper half and smooth or toothed in the lower half. Flowers grow in dense, branched, pyramid-shaped clusters at the branch tips. Each individually stalked flower is less than ¼" wide and has 5 tiny triangular sepals; 5 rounded, white, papery petals that narrow abruptly at their bases; and numerous pale stamens.

Bloom Season: Summer.

Habitat/Range: Abundant in sunny areas, in both moist and dry sandy or rocky soils; throughout the region.

Comments: North American Indians made a tea from the leaves of this plant.

Rough Bedstraw

ROBERT TATINA

Northern Bedstraw

NORTHERN BEDSTRAW

Galium boreale
Bedstraw Family (Rubiaceae)

Description: Plant to 3' tall, with squarish stems and often with short, leafy side branches at the bases of the main leaf whorls. The stalkless leaves are in well-separated whorls of 4. Each is up to 2" long but less than ¼" wide and widest near the base. Each leaf has smooth edges and 3 prominent veins along its evenly tapering length. Small stalkless flowers form much-branched clusters at the tops of the stem branches, with pairs of small leafy bracts at the branch points in the cluster. Each fragrant flower is ⅛" wide and has a white corolla with 4 pointed, spreading lobes. The small round fruits are bristly.

Bloom Season: Late spring–summer.

Habitat/Range: Common in open woods and on forest edges, especially under aspens and pines, as well as in moist meadows, fens, and tamarack swamps, on open slopes and rocky banks, and along shores; throughout the region.

Comments: Several other bedstraws in the region have leaves in whorls of 4. Two, both known as Wild Licorice, have greenish yellow to purplish flowers, leaves more than ¼" wide, and bristly fruits. The leaves of *G. lanceolatum* are broadest near the base, while those of *G. circaezans* are widest near the middle. Three weak-stemmed, more delicate species of open wet areas in the region have white flowers and smooth fruits. Wild Madder (*G. obtusum*) has 4-lobed corollas and leaves in whorls of 4, 5, or 6. Small Bedstraw (*G. trifidum*) has 3-lobed corollas and leaves in whorls of 4, and Stiff Bedstraw (*G. tinctorium*) has 3-lobed corollas and at least some whorls of 5 or 6 leaves.

KEITH BOARD

Partridge Berry

PARTRIDGE BERRY
Mitchella repens
Bedstraw Family (Rubiaceae)

Description: Creeping, dwarf evergreen shrub forming open mats. Stems are branched and often root along their length. At well-spaced intervals along the stem are pairs of small, thick, shiny, rounded, stalked opposite leaves up to ¾" long. These leaves often have a network of pale veins. Flowers usually occur at the tips of the branches, in pairs that are joined at the base. Each fragrant flower is ½" long and has a small 4-toothed calyx and a trumpet-like white corolla with 4 fuzzy spreading lobes. Some plants have flowers with a protruding style and small stamens, and some have flowers with 4 protruding stamens and a short style. The pair of flowers develops into a single ¼"-wide red berry marked with 2 spots.

Bloom Season: Late spring–midsummer.

Habitat/Range: Frequent in acidic woods, often in sandy soil or among mosses in sparse vegetation; throughout the region.

Comments: The berries are edible but nearly tasteless. North American Indians used the plant for a variety of medicines.

FALSE TOADFLAX
Comandra umbellata
Sandalwood Family (Santalaceae)

Description: Yellowish green plant to 15" tall and partially parasitic on the roots of other plants. The leaves are alternate, stalkless or short stalked, and up to 1½" long and ¾" wide. They have rounded or slightly pointed tips. Numerous flowers occur in flattened to rounded clusters at the tips of the main stems and sometimes at the ends of the upper branches. Each flower is ⅛" wide and has 5 (rarely 4) pointed, white, petal-like sepals that are united at their bases into a short tube. There are no petals. The round single-seeded fruits are about ¼" wide.

Bloom Season: Midspring–early summer.

Habitat/Range: Occasional in sandy, gravelly, or rocky areas in open oak or pine woods, wetlands, on rocky ridges and exposed headlands, and along rocky shores, usually in the open or under sparse timber; throughout the region.

Comments: The fruits were eaten by North American Indians and are said to taste sweet.

ROBERT TATINA

False Toadflax

MITREWORT
Mitella diphylla
Saxifrage Family (Saxifragaceae)

Description: Hairy plant to 1' tall, with several long-stalked basal leaves and a pair of opposite stalkless leaves on the upper part of the stem. The basal leaves usually have 3–5 sharp-pointed lobes, while the stem leaves are usually 3-lobed; the middle lobe is largest. Flowers are alternate and widely spaced along the upper part of the stem. Each cuplike flower is about ¼" wide and has 5 triangular calyx lobes and 5 small, fringed, white petals. The pale papery fruits are open, exposing the shiny dark seeds.

Bloom Season: Midspring–late spring.

Habitat/Range: Occasional in moist loamy soils in rich or rocky forests, often in calcium-rich sites; from New Hampshire and Quebec westward except along the northern edge of the region.

ALLISON W. BELL

Mitrewort

Grass of Parnassus

GRASS OF PARNASSUS
Parnassia glauca
Saxifrage Family (Saxifragaceae)

Description: Smooth plant to 20" tall, with clusters of long-stalked, somewhat rubbery, rounded basal leaves and a single, smaller clasping leaf on the lower part of the stem. The basal leaves are up to 2" long and have broadly rounded to heart-shaped bases and narrow leafy strips along their upper stalks. The single flower at the top of each stem is ¾–1¼" wide, with 5 small blunt sepals, 5 white petals marked with fine green lines, 5 spreading stamens, and 15 stamenlike filaments produced by sterile stamens (staminodia).

Bloom Season: Midsummer–fall.

Habitat/Range: Locally common in wetlands with limey or mineralized water in springy areas, fens, wet meadows, and marshes over limestone, on riverbanks, and along shores of mineral-rich lakes; throughout the region from New Brunswick to Wisconsin, and north and west of Lake Superior.

Comments: Two related species occur in similar habitats in the region. Both have thinner leaves and many more than 15 apparent false stamens. Small Flowered Grass of Parnassus (*P. parviflora*) has basal leaves with tapering bases and petals less than ¼" long; it occurs in the northern part of the region westward to Lake Michigan, as well as farther west and north. Arctic Grass of Parnassus (*P. palustris*) has basal leaves with heart-shaped bases and petals longer than ¼"; it occurs in northern North America, south to Minnesota and rarely eastward in Michigan, New York, and eastern Canada.

JESSIE M. HARRIS

DON KURZ

Early Saxifrage

EARLY SAXIFRAGE
Saxifraga virginiensis
Saxifrage Family (Saxifragaceae)

Description: Delicate, hairy plant with 1 or more leafless stems and a cluster of basal leaves. The plant is only a few inches tall at flowering but eventually elongates to as much as 18". The basal leaves are up to 2½" long, sometimes toothed along the edges, and taper to broad stalks. Flowers are in compact branched clusters at the tops of the stems. There are narrow leaflike bracts at the bases of the main branches of the flower clusters. These clusters open and expand as the season progresses. Each flower is ⅜" wide and has 5 triangular sepals; 5 spreading, narrow, white petals; and 10 small stamens.

Bloom Season: Midspring–early summer.

Habitat/Range: Occasional on cliffs, exposed ledges and outcrops, and in well-drained rocky woods, often growing over limestone or basic rocks such as serpentine; throughout most of the region eastward to Maine and New Brunswick.

Comments: Several other northern saxifrages rarely extend southward into the region, mostly on mountains or in unique areas such as Isle Royale. One species, White Alpine Saxifrage (*S. aizoon*), occurs on exposed rocks at scattered locations in Minnesota, Michigan, northern New England, and in Canada east to Nova Scotia. It has thick, sharply toothed, basal leaves with white crusty pores along the edges and scattered small alternate leaves on the flower stem.

ALLISON W. BELL

Foam Flower

FOAM FLOWER
Tiarella cordifolia
Saxifrage Family (Saxifragaceae)

Description: Hairy plant to 1' tall, with long-stalked basal leaves and leafless flowering stems. The basal leaves have notched bases and are up to 4" long and nearly as wide. They have coarse irregular teeth and angular lobes along their edges, with the end lobe usually the largest. Flowers are alternate along the upper stems on short, horizontally spreading, individual stalks. Each flower is ¼" wide and has 5 small blunt sepals, 5 delicate white petals that taper to pointed tips and narrow bases, and 10 slender spreading stamens that are longer than the petals. Some plants have creeping, alternate-leaved stems at the base.

Bloom Season: Midspring–early summer.

Habitat/Range: Common in rich or moist woods and shaded ravines, and sometimes in swampy areas; in the eastern part of the region westward to northeastern Wisconsin.

TURTLEHEAD
Chelone glabra
Snapdragon Family (Scrophulariaceae)

Description: Smooth, mostly unbranched plant to 3' tall, with angular stems and widely spaced pairs of opposite, short-stalked or stalkless leaves. These leaves are up to 6" long and 1½" wide, broadest near the middle, and evenly toothed along the edges. They taper to narrow bases and pointed tips. The flowers form dense elongate clusters at the tops of the stems. Each flower is 1" long and has a bluntly 5-lobed calyx hidden by 2 or 3 sepal-like bracts, as well as an inflated, tubular, 2-lipped, white corolla. The hooded upper lip of the corolla is shallowly 2-lobed and arches over the 3-lobed lower lip. The middle lip of the lower lobe is hairy inside and almost blocks the mouth.

Bloom Season: Midsummer–early fall.

Habitat/Range: Frequent in low wet areas in swampy openings, fens, marshes, wet woods, and along shores; throughout the region.

ROBERT TATINA

Turtlehead

CAROL GRACIE

Foxglove Beard Tongue

FOXGLOVE BEARD TONGUE
Penstemon digitalis
Snapdragon Family (Scrophulariaceae)

Description: Stout shiny plant to 4' tall, with widely spaced pairs of stalkless opposite leaves. These leaves are up to 6" long and 2½" wide, broadest near the base, and have smooth edges and long-pointed tips. At the tops of the stems are branched upright clusters of flowers, with pairs of small opposite bracts below each cluster. Each flower is about 1" long and has a small cuplike calyx with 5 pointed lobes and an often hairy, tubular, white corolla that abruptly enlarges near the middle and ends in 5 spreading, rounded lobes. The corolla tube is often faintly tinged with purple and marked inside with fine purple lines.

Bloom Season: Late spring–midsummer.

Habitat/Range: Occasional and somewhat weedy in dry open woods, along woodland edges, and in fields; mostly in the central part of the region and scattered elsewhere.

Comments: Some populations may be escapes from cultivation. Hairy Beard Tongue (*P. hirsutus*), a related plant in similar habitats from Quebec to Michigan, has hairy stems and a uniformly narrow corolla tube.

White-flowered Ground Cherry

EDWARD G. VOSS

WHITE-FLOWERED GROUND CHERRY
Leucophysalis grandiflora
Nightshade Family (Solanaceae)

Description: Bushy plant to 3' tall, with sticky hairs and stalked alternate leaves. These leaves have smooth edges and are up to 5" long and 2" wide, with broadly rounded bases and pointed tips. The leaf stalks are often bordered with narrow leafy strips. Individually stalked flowers occur in groups of 1–4 at the bases of the upper leaves and branch junctions. Each flower is typically 1–1½" wide and has a hairy, 5-toothed, cuplike calyx and a delicate, petunia-like, white to pale violet corolla with a yellow center, 5 stamens, and an erect style.

Bloom Season: Late spring–summer.

Habitat/Range: Rare but sometimes locally abundant in well-drained sandy or rocky areas with recent disturbance, including burned or cleared woods and graded land; throughout most of the region eastward to Quebec and Vermont. Most of this plant's total range lies within the North Woods region, although it also occurs westward to Saskatchewan.

CANADA VIOLET
Viola canadensis
Violet Family (Violaceae)

Description: Plant to 15" tall, usually with several leafy stems and basal leaves. The leaves are alternate, long-stalked, and up to 3½" long and nearly as wide. They have deeply heart-shaped bases, pointed tips, and small teeth along the edges. Along the stem, at the base of each leaf stalk, is a pair of papery, pointed, bractlike stipules. Single flowers grow on long hook-tipped stalks at the bases of the upper leaf stalks. Near the middle of the flower stalk is a pair of tiny bracts. Each flower is ⅝" wide and has 5 narrow pointed sepals and 5 white petals. The petals are often tinged with bluish purple on the outside and yellow at the base on the inside. The lowest petal is larger and prolonged at the bottom into a short spur. The inside of the flower is usually marked with fine purple lines.

Bloom Season: Midspring–midsummer.

Habitat/Range: Common in moist rich woods, often in limey soils; throughout the region.

Canada Violet

BOG VALERIAN
Valeriana uliginosa
Valerian Family (Valerianaceae)

Description: Plant to 3' tall, with long-stalked, coarsely toothed, mostly undivided basal leaves up to 5" long and 1½" wide. There are also 3–6 pairs of short-stalked, opposite stem leaves, each divided featherlike into 3–15 toothless veiny segments. The end segment is the largest (up to 2" long). Sometimes the lower stem leaves are alternate. The flowers form dense clusters at the tops of the stems and are associated with small narrow bracts. Each flower is ⅛" wide and has a tiny calyx, a small white to pinkish tubular corolla with usually 5 spreading lobes, and a protruding threadlike style. In fruit, the calyx lobes develop into several long feathery filaments.

Bloom Season: Late spring–early summer.

Habitat/Range: Uncommon in fens, limey bogs, and alkaline swamps under white cedars or tamaracks; from Maine and Quebec to the Lake Michigan area.

Comments: Garden Valerian (*V. officinalis*) is an Old World plant cultivated for its fragrant flowers; it regularly escapes in disturbed areas. All of its basal leaves are deeply divided. Valerian roots smell like dirty socks and have been used in a variety of folk medicines.

Bog Valerian

ROBERT TATINA

Smooth White Violet

SMOOTH WHITE VIOLET
Viola macloskeyi var. *pallens*
Violet Family (Violaceae)

Description: Plant typically to 3" tall, with clusters of basal leaves and a few leafless flower stalks arising from a shallow underground stem. The leaves are smooth, broadly rounded, and up to 1½" long. They have rounded, deeply heart-shaped bases, blunt tips, and low teeth along the edges. Each nodding flower stalk is as tall as or slightly taller than the leaves, with a pair of tiny bracts near the middle. Each flower is ½" wide and has 5 narrow pointed sepals and 5 white petals. The lower 3 petals are marked inside with fine dark purple lines near their bases, and the lowest petal is prolonged at the base into a short spur.

Bloom Season: Midspring–early summer.

Habitat/Range: Common in moist areas in boggy sites, conifer forests, swamps, thickets, and along shores; throughout the region.

Comments: Several other white-flowered violets with only basal leaves occur throughout the region. The leaves of Lance-leaved Violet (*V. lanceolata*) are much longer than they are broad and taper gradually at their bases. The plant occurs in wet exposed sites. Sweet White Violet (*V. blanda*) has leaves with pointed tips and usually reddish flower stalks, and its 2 upper petals are narrow and bent sharply backward. It is uncommon in moist woods. Kidney-leaved Violet (*V. renifolia*) has downy flower stalks and larger leaves that are blunt and wider than they are long. It occurs in white cedar swamps and wet conifer forests.

Green, Brown, and Inconspicuous Flowers

Jack-in-the-pulpit

This section includes plants with flowers that are green or greenish, brown, or tiny and easily overlooked. Some of these flowers are associated with unusual structures and do not appear flowerlike at first glance. Greenish flowers can also be variants of normally white- or yellow-flowered species, so you should check those sections of the guide, too.

Sweet Flag

SWEET FLAG

Acorus calamus
Sweet Flag Family (Acoraceae)

Description: Plant with a dense cluster of erect, narrow, strap-shaped leaves often more than 3' tall but usually less than ¾" wide. The tiny flowers are in a dense, 2–4"-long cylinder called a spadix, which projects upward from the side of a leaflike flowering stem. Each flower has 6 tiny, yellowish brown sepals, 6 stamens, and a single ovary.

Bloom Season: Spring–early summer.

Habitat/Range: Occasional in shallow water in marshes, ponds, seepy meadows, and along shores; throughout the region.

Comments: Sweet Flag typically grows in dense stands, sometimes without flowering for several years. The fragrant roots have been used in cosmetics and medicine, and the boiled, sugared roots can be made into candy, although care must be taken since some similar plants are poisonous. Some North Woods populations are introduced from Eurasia.

Marsh Pennywort

MARSH PENNYWORT
Hydrocotyle americana
Carrot Family (Apiaceae)

Description: Low smooth plant with slender, branched, creeping stems and widely spaced, long-stalked, round leaves up to 2" wide and long. The leaves have heart-shaped bases and unevenly blunt-toothed edges. At the bases of some leaf stalks are inconspicuous, mostly stalkless clusters of 2–7 tiny flowers. Each flower is 1/16" wide and has 5 spreading, pointed, greenish white petals; 5 dark-tipped stamens; and an inflated basal ovary.

Bloom Season: Summer.

Habitat/Range: Occasional in wet sites, usually where other vegetation is sparse, including along shores and in marshes, open swamps, and seepy areas; throughout most of the region, but rare west of Lake Superior.

Skunk Cabbage

ROBERT TATINA

SKUNK CABBAGE
Symplocarpus foetidus
Arum Family (Araceae)

Description: As its name implies, this is a low, foul-smelling plant. It has large basal leaves with broadly heart-shaped bases and a conspicuous network of connected veins. The leaves appear after the flowers and grow up to 20" long. The short flower stalk is topped by a hooded, pointed, bractlike structure that is green to purple or a mottled brownish color; it is 3–6" tall and encloses a dense fleshy cluster of flowers. The flowers are similar to those of the related Jack-in-the-pulpit (facing page).

Bloom Season: Late winter–early spring.

Habitat/Range: Locally common in swamps, wet woods, and seepy areas, especially in shaded sites with alkaline seepage, often forming large colonies; throughout the region.

Comments: Skunk Cabbage produces sufficient heat to melt snow, and the plant often emerges and flowers when snow is still on the ground. Young shoots are edible if cooked in several changes of water, although the raw plants are toxic. Several similar-looking shoots are poisonous.

ROBERT TATINA

Jack-in-the-pulpit

JACK-IN-THE-PULPIT
Arisaema triphyllum
Arum Family (Araceae)

Description: Smooth soft plant to 3' tall but often shorter, with 1 or 2 stalked, compound, basal leaves. Each leaf is divided into 3 tapering pointed leaflets that, at flowering, can be up to 10" long and 4" wide but are often less than half that size. The leaves enlarge after flowering. The outer leaflets are often unequal on either side of the central vein. The stout flower stalk arises at the base of the leaf stalk and is typically shorter than the leaf. At the top of the stalk is a hooded, rolled, often purplish or purple-striped sheath with a 2–3"-long clublike structure (spadix) inside. The spadix contains a dense cluster of tiny male flowers at the top and small, greenish yellow, female flowers below. There are no petals or sepals. The fruits are bright scarlet, angular berries about ⅜" thick.

Bloom Season: Midspring–early summer.

Habitat/Range: Common in moist or swampy woods and shaded springy areas; throughout the region.

Comments: A related species of similar habitats mostly in the southern part of the region, Green Dragon (*A. dracontium*), has 7–13 narrow leaflets per leaf and a narrow, rolled, flowering sheath that tapers to a point. If eaten, both plants have a dangerous stinging and swelling effect on the mouth, tongue, and throat, but the starchy roots have been used as a food source after soaking and drying. North American Indians prepared a variety of medicines from the roots of both plants.

ROBERT TATINA

KENNETH DRITZ

Blue Cohosh

BLUE COHOSH
Caulophyllum thalictroides
Barberry Family (Berberidaceae)

Description: An unusual and inconspicuous wildflower that is most often noticed when in fruit. The plant is smooth and typically has a waxy, bluish white coating. In early spring, an unbranched, often purplish stem grows 1–2' tall, with 1 or rarely 2 long-stalked clusters of individually stalked, yellowish green flowers. Each flower has 3 or 4 tiny green bracts at its base, as well as 6 yellow-green, petal-like sepals, 6 inconspicuous glandlike petals, and 6 stamens. Later, a large leaf develops below the flowers. This leaf is divided into several long-stalked leaflets that are each further divided, so there appears to be a whorl of 3 stalked, compound leaves. There is often a similar but smaller leaf just above the main leaf. The leaflets are up to 5" long, with rounded bases and 2–5 forward-pointing lobes at the tips. The round fleshy fruits are about ⁵/₁₆" wide and turn a beautiful, deep, iridescent blue.

Bloom Season: Early spring–midspring.

Habitat/Range: Frequent in moist or rich woods, under both conifers and hardwoods; throughout the region.

Comments: The sepals are sometimes purplish. Blue Cohosh is poisonous if eaten, and it also irritates the skin of some people. It was formerly used in a variety of folk medicines.

STRAWBERRY BLITE

Chenopodium capitatum
Goosefoot Family (Chenopodiaceae)

Description: Branching annual to 3' tall, with alternate, stalked, broadly triangular or arrowhead-shaped leaves that are 1–4" long and have coarse lobelike teeth along the edges. The tiny inconspicuous flowers occur in clumps along the upper stems or at the bases of the leaf stalks. These flowers develop into bright red, fleshy fruiting clusters that from a distance resemble strawberries.

Bloom Season: Late spring–midsummer.

Habitat/Range: Sporadic but sometimes locally abundant in open dry woods and clearings, especially after fire or other disturbance; throughout the region.

Comments: The fruiting heads are edible.

Strawberry Blite

MAPLE-LEAVED GOOSEFOOT

Chenopodium gigantospermum
Goosefoot Family (Chenopodiaceae)

Description: Bushy-branched annual to 5' tall, with thin, alternate, stalked, triangular to somewhat narrowed, pointed leaves. These leaves are up to 7" long and 4" wide and usually have 1–4 large, lobelike, triangular teeth along each edge. The inconspicuous flowers occur in clusters along the upper stems and small side branches. Each flower is $1/16$" wide and has tiny green sepals but no petals. Sometimes the flowering branches are a powdery white.

Bloom Season: Summer.

Habitat/Range: Frequent in disturbed, dry, shaded sites in open woods, at the base of bluffs and ledges, and along clearings and edges, rarely in moist areas; throughout the region.

Comments: Lamb's Quarters (*C. album*) is an abundant weed in open disturbed ground throughout the region. It has thicker, whitish-mealy leaves typically less than 3" long.

Maple-leaved Goosefoot

Plantain-leaved Sedge

KENNETH DRITZ

PLANTAIN-LEAVED SEDGE
Carex plantaginea
Sedge Family (Cyperaceae)

Description: Plant to 18" tall, with triangular stems, and broad grasslike leaves near the purplish-red base. The lower leaves are up to 10" long and 1" wide, while the leaves on the flowering stems are mostly tiny or reduced to sheaths. Tiny flowers occur in about 5 upright, stalked clusters along the upper part of the stem. Each cluster contains several flowers, and each flower has a small pointed scale at its base. The flowers have no sepals or petals and are usually not noticed. The top cluster, which has purplish black scales, is usually all male flowers with yellow stamens. The other clusters, often with paler scales, are female flowers; these have protruding white stigmas and produce hard triangular fruits about $^3/_{16}$" long.

Bloom Season: Spring.

Habitat/Range: Occasional in moist to dry woods, especially in beech-maple stands and on rich rocky slopes; throughout most of the region except northeastern Minnesota.

Comments: This is one of more than 200 different sedges that occur in woods, wetlands, and other habitats throughout the region. All are true wildflowers, although their tiny, wind-pollinated flowers are usually overlooked. Sedges play a critical role in the region, stabilizing soil and providing food and cover for wildlife.

INDIAN CUCUMBER ROOT
Medeola virginiana
Lily Family (Liliaceae)

Description: Unbranched plant to 2' tall with woolly hairs on the young stems. Some of these hairs usually persist near the leaf bases. The stalkless, narrow, pointed leaves are in 2 whorls: a whorl of 5 or more leaves near the middle of the stem and a whorl of typically 3 or 5 smaller leaves at the top of the stem. At the top of the plant are several flowers on arching individual stalks. Each greenish yellow flower is ½" wide and has 6 widely spreading to backward-curving, petal-like segments; 6 slender protruding stamens; and 3 thin spreading styles that are longer than the stamens. The fruits are dark purple berries about ⅜" wide on the now upright flower stalks.

Bloom Season: Late spring–early summer.

Habitat/Range: Common in rich, often acidic woods, particularly in moist areas and depressions; throughout the eastern part of the region, but not often found west of Lake Michigan.

Comments: The crisp root is pure white inside and said to taste like cucumber.

Indian Cucumber Root

White Hellebore

WHITE HELLEBORE
Veratrum viride
Lily Family (Liliaceae)

Description: Stout, hairy, unbranched plant to 5' tall, with many alternate, slightly pleated leaves that clasp the stems at their tapering, sheathlike bases. The leaves are up to 10" long and 6" wide. They are widest near the middle and have smooth edges and pointed tips. Flowers are in branched or unbranched clusters at the bases of the upper leaves. Each individually stalked, yellowish green flower is ⅞" wide and has 6 slender stamens and 6 petal-like, narrow-based segments with slightly ragged edges.

Bloom Season: Late spring–midsummer.

Habitat/Range: Common in swamps, wet woods, seepy thickets, and along stream banks; in the eastern half of the region from Ontario to Maine and New Brunswick.

Comments: This plant is very toxic, but it has been used in some folk medicines and to slow the heartbeat.

ROBERT TATINA

Downy Solomon's Seal

DOWNY SOLOMON'S SEAL
Polygonatum pubescens
Lily Family (Liliaceae)

Description: Arching, single-stemmed, un-branched plant typically to 2' tall, with alternate horizontal leaves arranged ladderlike along the stem. The leaves are up to 5" long and 2" wide and taper abruptly to pointed tips and short-stalked or somewhat clasping bases. Each leaf points in the opposite direction from the leaves above and below it, and each has up to 9 prominent parallel veins with fine hairs on the underside. Slender stalks dangle from the bases of the upper leaves, with 1–3 pale greenish flowers per stalk. Each tubular flower is ⅜" long and has 6 tiny, rounded, green-tipped lobes. The fruits are deep blue berries up to ⅜" wide.

Bloom Season: Midspring–early summer.

Habitat/Range: Common in moist woods, often in rich, loamy soils, and in thickets and on shaded sandy slopes; throughout the region.

Comments: The roots of this and other species of Solomon's seal have been used for food and medicine, and the shoots have been cooked like asparagus. Smooth Solomon's Seal (*P. biflorum*), found in a variety of habitats in the southern half of the region, is a larger plant with up to 19 hairless veins on the leaves and often more than 3 flowers per cluster.

LONG-BRACTED ORCHID
Coeloglossum viride
Orchid Family (Orchidaceae)

Description: Smooth, single-stemmed, un-branched plant to 1' tall or rarely taller, with several widely spaced, alternate, usually pointed leaves up to 6" long that clasp the stem at their tapering bases. The leaves are progressively smaller and more bractlike toward the top of the stem. Flowers are alternate in a narrow spike along the upper stem. Each greenish flower is ¼" wide and has a longer, pointed, green bract at its base and a stout tubular ovary topped by 3 hooded, petal-like sepals and 2 small narrow petals, under which is a straplike lip with a broadly notched tip. The lip is often purplish at the base and has a tiny pouchlike spur underneath.

Bloom Season: Midspring–midsummer.

Habitat/Range: Occasional in moist woods, usually under hardwoods or mixed stands; throughout the region.

Comments: This plant is also called Frog Orchid. See the comments under Northern Rein Orchid (p. 244).

JESSIE M. HARRIS

Long-bracted Orchid

HEART-LEAVED TWAYBLADE
Listera cordata
Orchid Family (Orchidaceae)

Description: Delicate single-stemmed plant, usually less than 8" tall, with 1 pair of small, broadly rounded, opposite, stalkless leaves just below the middle of the stem. Each shiny leaf is 1" long. Several small purple to greenish flowers alternate in a close cluster along the finely hairy upper stem. Each flower is ¼" long and has a small thickened ovary topped by a ⅛"-wide display of 2 small petals and 3 similar petal-like sepals above a downward-arching lower lip that is about twice as long as the other petals and deeply cleft. The lip resembles a snake's tongue.

Bloom Season: Late spring–early summer.

Habitat/Range: Occasional in deep wet forests, bogs, and conifer swamps; in all but the southwestern part of the region.

Comments: Another green to purple-flowered species, Southern Twayblade (*L. australis*), has a larger lip that is usually more than 3 times as long as the other petals. It occurs in New York, Vermont, and adjacent Canada.

ROBERT TATINA

Heart-leaved Twayblade

BROAD-LEAVED TWAYBLADE
Listera convallarioides
Orchid Family (Orchidaceae)

Description: Single-stemmed plant to 9" tall, with a single pair of broadly rounded, opposite leaves near the middle of the stem. These leaves are up to 2" long and 1½" wide and clasp the stem at their bases. There are fine hairs on the upper half of the stem. Flowers grow on short individual stalks along the upper part of the stem, and at the base of each flower stalk is a tiny bract. Each pale greenish flower has a short tubular ovary covered with fine hairs and topped by 3 small narrow sepals and 2 similar petals. The latter are bent away from a dangling, fan-like lower lip. This lip is up to ⅜" long and has a notched tip and narrowed base.

Bloom Season: Early summer–midsummer.

Habitat/Range: Rare in wet mossy areas and springy seeps in boreal forests and conifer swamps; throughout the northern half of the region and northward.

Comments: A related species, Auricled Twayblade (*L. auriculata*), occurs in sandy woods throughout the northern half of the region. Its flowers have a smooth ovary and a lip with a broad clasping base.

WELBY SMITH

Broad-leaved Twayblade

LEE A. CASEBERE

Green Twayblade

GREEN TWAYBLADE
Liparis loeselii
Orchid Family (Orchidaceae)

Description: Unbranched plant usually less than 8" tall, with a pair of upright, smooth, shiny leaves near the base. Each leaf is up to 4" long and tapers to a rolled sheathing base that surrounds the stem. Up to 15 flowers are alternate along the top of the stem, and at the base of each flower is a tiny papery bract. Each greenish flower is ½" wide and has a slender tubular ovary topped by 3 narrow petal-like sepals and 2 threadlike side petals that usually spread below the flower and flank a broadly spreading, pointed lower lip.

Bloom Season: Midspring–early summer.

Habitat/Range: Occasional in wet open or shaded places in bogs, fens, seeps, swampy woods, and along sandy shores; throughout the region.

GREEN ADDER'S MOUTH
Malaxis unifolia
Orchid Family (Orchidaceae)

Description: Delicate plant typically 3–8" tall, with a single broadly rounded leaf up to 1½" long near the middle of the stem. The base of the leaf wraps around the stem. Usually more than 20 small green flowers form a compact cluster at the top of the stem, with a small bract at the base of each flower. Each flower is ⅛" wide and has a slender stalklike ovary topped by 3 tiny sepals, 2 curving threadlike petals, and a broader lower lip that is cleft at the tip. At the base of the cleft is a tiny triangular lobe.

Bloom Season: Late spring–midsummer.

Habitat/Range: Occasional but often overlooked in bogs, conifer swamps, wet thickets, and sandy or rocky woods; throughout the region.

Comments: A similar species occurring throughout the region, White Adder's Mouth (*M. monophyllos*), has a lower lip with a pointed, undivided tip.

JESSIE M. HARRIS

Green Adder's Mouth

CLUB-SPUR ORCHID

Platanthera clavellata
Orchid Family (Orchidaceae)

Description: Slender, single-stemmed, un-branched orchid to 1' tall but often much smaller. On the lower part of the stem is a single leaf that tapers to a narrowed base that clasps the stem. Above this leaf are usually several much smaller, alternate, bractlike leaves. Flow-ers are arranged alternately on a short spike on the upper part of the stem; they often twist slightly sideways. Each flower is ¼" wide and has a small pointed bract at its base and a tubu-lar ovary topped by 3 greenish petal-like sepals, 2 paler petals, and a dangling lower lip with a blunt, minutely 3-lobed tip and a curving club-shaped spur below.

Bloom Season: Early summer–midsummer.

Habitat/Range: Occasional but locally abun-dant in bogs, wet conifer swamps and forests, wet sandy seeps, and along shaded peaty shores, often growing in moss mats or on rotted logs; throughout the region.

Comments: This tiny inconspicuous orchid is easily overlooked.

KEITH BOARD

Club-spur Orchid

LEE A. CASEBERE

Northern Bog Orchid

NORTHERN BOG ORCHID

Platanthera hyperborea
Orchid Family (Orchidaceae)

Description: Smooth, unbranched, single-stemmed plant less than 1½' tall, with several stalkless alternate leaves that clasp the stem at their bases. The lowest leaf is short and rounded, while the other leaves are more elongate; the largest is typically 6–10" long. The leaves be-come progressively smaller toward the top of the stem. Flowers are alternate in a narrow spike along the upper stem, and under each flower is a small, pointed, leafy bract. Each flower is less than ¼" wide and has a tubular ovary topped by a hoodlike green cluster of 2 petals and a sepal. Under these is a small, narrow, spurred, green lip flanked by 2 spreading green sepals.

Bloom Season: Late spring–midsummer.

Habitat/Range: Locally frequent in moist areas, especially in acidic or mineralized waters, in bogs, fens, conifer swamps, moist woods, and along seepy stream banks; throughout the region.

JESSIE M. HARRIS

Northern Rein Orchid

RAGGED FRINGED ORCHID

Platanthera lacera
Orchid Family (Orchidaceae)

Description: Unbranched plant usually less than 2' tall, with long alternate leaves. The lower leaves are up to 1¾" wide, while the upper leaves are progressively smaller and more bractlike. Yellowish green to whitish flowers are alternate along the upper stem, and at the base of each flower is a prominent leaflike bract. Each flower is up to ½" wide and has a slender tubular ovary topped by 3 bluntly pointed, petal-like sepals; 2 narrower petals; and a large lip that is divided nearly to the base into 3 parts. Each part is deeply fringed and divided into threadlike segments. A tubular spur up to 1" long extends below the flower from the base of the lower lip.

Bloom Season: Late spring–midsummer.

Habitat/Range: Occasional in a variety of open wet sites, including wet meadows, bogs, wet thickets, moist open sand, sedge meadows, and on grassy stream banks; throughout all but the northern edge of the region.

Comments: Eastern Prairie Fringed Orchid (*P. leucophaea*) is very rare and local in bogs and grassy marshes at a few sites in the region. It has white flowers and broader lip segments.

NORTHERN REIN ORCHID

Platanthera flava var. herbiola
Orchid Family (Orchidaceae)

Description: Smooth, unbranched, angular stems to 1½' tall, with widely spaced, stalkless, alternate leaves that clasp the stems at their tapering bases. The leaves are progressively smaller toward the top of the stem. Flowers are alternate in a narrow spike along the upper stem, and under each flower is a narrow pointed bract. Most of the bracts are longer than the flowers. Each flower is less than ¼" wide and has a stout tubular ovary topped by 3 hoodlike sepals above 2 yellowish green petals and a dangling, curved, blunt lower lip. This lip has a round tip, a short tubular spur underneath, and a wartlike tubercle inside.

Bloom Season: Summer.

Habitat/Range: Uncommon in swampy woods, often in wet depressions covered with fallen leaves, and in hardwood swamps, sandy seeps, and springy places; throughout the region northward to central New Brunswick and the southern Lake Superior area.

Comments: This species resembles Long-bracted Orchid (p. 240), which has a short sac-like spur and a notched lip that is distinctly greenish and marked with purple at its base. Northern Bog Orchid (p. 243) has a pointed lower lip with no tubercle inside.

ROBERT TATINA

Ragged Fringed Orchid

JESSIE M. HARRIS

Northern Toadflax

Northern Toadflax

JESSIE M. HARRIS

NORTHERN TOADFLAX

Geocaulon lividum
Sandalwood Family (Santalaceae)

Description: Inconspicuous plant to 10" tall, often with a reddish or purplish cast. The leaves are alternate, stalkless, and up to 1" long. They have smooth edges, blunt tips, and tapering bases. There are a few clusters of 3 (rarely 2 or 4) flowers on slender stalks at the bases of some stem leaves. The 2 side flowers in each cluster are male and fall early, while the central flower is ⅛" wide and has 5 small, greenish bronze sepals and no petals. This flower produces a round, orange-to-scarlet fruit about ¼" wide. Northern Toadflax is partially parasitic on the roots of other plants.

Bloom Season: Late spring–midsummer.

Habitat/Range: Uncommon and local in exposed boggy sites such as mountain bogs, moist heaths, seepy headlands, and exposed damp acidic sands; scattered throughout most of the region, especially northward.

Golden Saxifrage

GOLDEN SAXIFRAGE
Chrysosplenium americanum
Saxifrage Family (Saxifragaceae)

Description: Small plant with branched, creeping, angular stems usually less than 8" long; these sometimes root along their length. The short-stalked leaves are mostly less than ½" long and nearly as wide, with broad bases and irregularly scalloped edges. The leaves are mostly opposite, although some of the upper leaves can be alternate. The inconspicuous flowers grow singly at the end of the branches. Each flower is less than ¼" wide and usually has 4 bluntly pointed, broadly triangular, green to reddish green sepals and no petals. There are usually 8 tiny, reddish tipped stamens on a central disk and 2 squat pointed styles.

Bloom Season: Midspring–late spring.

Habitat/Range: Common in saturated, shaded, muddy sites in woods, seepy areas, and quiet spring discharges; throughout the region.

SMALL BISHOP'S CAP
Mitella nuda
Saxifrage Family (Saxifragaceae)

Description: Delicate, hairy plant to 6" tall, with several long-stalked, round, basal leaves and a flowering stem that may have small stalkless leaves. The basal leaves are up to 2" wide, with toothed edges and heart-shaped bases. Flowers are alternate on short individual stalks along the upper part of the stem. Each flower is ⅜" wide and has 5 broadly triangular calyx lobes and 5 yellowish green petals that are divided into feathery, fringed segments. The pale papery fruit opens to form a platterlike disk with 2 clusters of tiny, shiny, dark seeds.

Bloom Season: Late spring–midsummer.

Habitat/Range: Frequent in wet shaded sites in bogs, swampy woods, and conifer forests; throughout the region.

ROBERT TATINA

Small Bishop's Cap

DITCH STONECROP
Penthorum sedoides
Saxifrage Family (Saxifragaceae)

Description: Plant to 2' tall and unbranched or branching in the upper half. There are small gland-tipped hairs along the upper flowering stems. The alternate, sharply toothed leaves are up to 5" long and 1½" wide and taper evenly from the middle to pointed tips and stalkless bases. Flowers are alternate on short stalks in branched clusters at the tops of the stems. Each flower is ³/₁₆" wide and has 5 narrow, spreading, pale greenish sepals; no petals; and 10 stamens surrounding 5 pistils that develop into a disklike fruit.

Bloom Season: Summer–early fall.

Habitat/Range: Common in open muddy places, including marshes, shores, and ditches; throughout most of the region eastward to Maine.

JESSIE M. HARRIS

Ditch Stonecrop

Swamp Saxifrage

POD GRASS
Scheuchzeria palustris
Pod Grass Family (Scheuchzeriaceae)

Description: Fleshy plant usually less than 1' tall, with alternate, narrow, grasslike leaves that mostly point upward and give the plant a zig-zag appearance. Each somewhat tubular leaf has a small round hole at the tip and a broad, pale greenish, papery base that clasps the stem. Long hairs are hidden inside the bases of the sheaths. The few flowers typically occur in threes on short stalks at the tops of the unbranched stems. At the base of the lowest flower in each cluster is a small papery bract. Each flower is ¼" wide and has 3 inconspicuous yellow-green sepals, 3 similar petals, and 6 stamens. Each flower develops into 3 spreading, round fruits.

Bloom Season: Late spring.

Habitat/Range: Locally common in saturated sphagnum mats in open to lightly shaded bogs throughout the region. Populations at an individual site vary greatly from year to year.

Comments: The tiny open pore at the tip of the leaf is distinctive. Bog Arrow Grass (*Triglochin maritimum*) is a related slender,

SWAMP SAXIFRAGE
Saxifraga pensylvanica
Saxifrage Family (Saxifragaceae)

Description: Hairy leafless stems to 3' tall, with a cluster of thick basal leaves. Each leaf is up to 1' long and with a prominent, raised, central rib on the underside. These leaves are widest near the middle and they taper abruptly to short pointed tips but have long tapering bases. The flowers initially form dense clusters at the tops of the stems. These clusters become more open and widely branched, with tiny bracts at the bases of the main branches. Each flower is ¼" wide and has 5 pointed sepals that fold back along the flower stalk; 5 very narrow, greenish or purple petals; 10 stamens; and 2 erect conical styles.

Bloom Season: Midspring–early summer.

Habitat/Range: Locally frequent in marshes, wet meadows, open swampy woods, springy areas, and moist sandy depressions; throughout most of the region eastward to Maine.

Pod Grass

grasslike plant that inhabits bogs and shores in the region. It has only basal leaves and small flowers in narrow elongate clusters on the upper stems.

DWARF MISTLETOE
Arceuthobium pusillum
Mistletoe Family (Viscaceae)

Dwarf Mistletoe

Description: Dwarf brown or greenish brown shrub, typically less than ½" tall, parasitic on the small branches of conifers, and often appearing to be part of the tree branch. Dwarf Mistletoe sometimes causes the host tree to form abnormally dense clusters of small twigs, called "witches-brooms." There are separate male and female plants, and usually a tree will host plants of only one sex. The small stems are stout and shiny, with tiny, opposite, rounded, scalelike leaves surrounding the stem. Flowers are produced from the bases of the scales on plants that are at least 4 years old. The flower buds resemble short side branches. Male plants have tiny 3- to 4-lobed flowers with a stalkless yellow stamen on each lobe. Female plants (pictured) have 2-lobed flowers with a small ovary. The fruits are tiny berries.

Bloom Season: Midspring–early summer.

Habitat/Range: Locally common on branches of black spruce in bogs and swamps, and also reported rarely on tamarack, white spruce, and red pine; throughout the region.

Comments: Although inconspicuous, this plant is a true wildflower and demonstrates the diversity and adaptations of North Woods plants. Sometimes a heavy infestation of Dwarf Mistletoe may kill the host tree.

EARLY FIGWORT
Scrophularia lanceolata
Snapdragon Family (Scrophulariaceae)

Description: Spindly square-stemmed plant to 6' tall, with stalked, widely spaced, opposite leaves that sometimes have branches or tufts of smaller leaves at their bases. The main leaves are up to 8" long and 3½" wide. They have broad bases, pointed tips, and coarsely toothed edges. Individually stalked flowers are abundant in a branched elongate cluster at the top of the plant. Each flower is ¹⁄₃" long and has a shallow 5-lobed calyx and a short, shiny, brownish, tubular, 2-lipped corolla with a 2-lobed upper lip and a shorter 3-lobed lower lip.

Bloom Season: Late spring–midsummer.

Habitat/Range: Common in open woods, thickets, and at the edges of wet places; throughout the region.

Comments: Late Figwort (*S. marilandica*) is uncommon in the southern part of the region. It blooms from midsummer on and has a dull corolla and finer teeth along the leaf edges.

Early Figwort

Wood Nettle

WOOD NETTLE

Laportea canadensis
Nettle Family (Urticaceae)

Description: Large single-stemmed plant with coarse stinging hairs and alternate, horizontally spreading, toothed leaves on stalks that are 3–4" long. Each leaf is up to 7" long and 5" wide and has a broadly rounded to tapering base. The flowers form pale, feathery-branched clusters at the bases of the main stem leaves. Leaflike bracts sometimes form at the base of the flower stalk. The flowers themselves are minute (about $^1/_{32}$" wide), stalkless, and scattered along the branches of the cluster. The flowers at the bases of the lower leaves are mostly male and consist of 5 stamens, while the flowers arising from the bases of the upper leaves are female. Each female flower produces a single, shiny, dark, flattened seed about ⅛" wide.

Bloom Season: Summer.

Habitat/Range: Common in moist woods and on shaded stream banks and floodplains; throughout the region.

Comments: When a person brushes against the plant, a small bulb at the tip of each hair breaks off, and the sharp hollow tip injects an irritating fluid into the skin. This species often forms extensive stands that effectively repel hikers. North American Indians used fibers from this plant to make cordage. Another species with inconspicuous flowers and stinging hairs, Stinging Nettle (*Urtica dioica*), has narrower, opposite leaves and often occurs in more open habitats. Despite its name, its sting is less painful than that of Wood Nettle.

WEEDS

JESSIE M. HARRIS

Moneywort

*European settlers introduced hundreds of species of
weeds to the North Woods. Several with
conspicuous and often attractive flowers occur in
wooded habitats, where they associate with a
variety of native wildflowers for which they are
sometimes mistaken. Weeds are especially common
in severely disturbed habitats such as graded
roadsides, cultivated fields, and waste ground. A
sampling of the most common and widely
distributed of these weeds is included in the
following section.*

COMMON MILKWEED
Asclepias syriaca
Milkweed Family (Asclepiadaceae)

Milky sap and rounded clusters of pinkish purple flowers; stout native weed of fields, pastures, open thickets, and roadsides.

BURDOCK
Arctium minus
Aster Family (Asteraceae)

Purple thistlelike flowers develop into clinging rounded burs; large "elephant ear" leaves form patches in disturbed shaded areas.

DEVIL'S PAINTBRUSH
Hieracium aurantiacum
Aster Family (Asteraceae)

Milky sap and orange, dandelion-like flowers; abundant in dry fields, on roadsides, along woodland edges, and in open disturbed woods.

TANSY
Tanacetum vulgare
Aster Family (Asteraceae)

Tall fragrant plant with alternate fernlike leaves and buttonlike yellow flower heads that look like daisies with the rays removed; common in waste ground, thickets, and on rocky shores. A close relative, *T. huronense,* is a rare native plant found on a few Great Lakes dunes and beaches in Michigan, Ontario, and Wisconsin, and along rivers in Maine and the Maritimes.

YELLOW ROCKET
Barbarea vulgaris
Mustard Family (Brassicaceae)

The four-petaled yellow flowers bloom in early spring. The plant is abundant in fields, on waste ground, and in disturbed open woods and thickets.

DAME'S ROCKET
Hesperis matronalis
Mustard Family (Brassicaceae)

Four-petaled flowers are purple or sometimes white; locally common along woodland edges and in open moist woods.

COMMON ST. JOHN'S WORT
Hypericum perforatum
St. John's Wort Family (Clusiaceae)

Abundant small, opposite leaves and 5-petaled yellow flowers with black spots; a common weed of pastures, roadsides, and open grassy woods, but similar native species also occur in the North Woods.

CREEPING CHARLIE
Glechoma hederacea
Mint Family (Lamiaceae)

Low, creeping, square-stemmed, aromatic plant with small, tubular, bluish purple flowers; often forms extensive mats in shaded lawns, degraded thickets, and moist degraded woodlands.

ORANGE DAY LILY
Hemerocallis fulva
Lily Family (Liliaceae)

Large, semi-succulent, narrow leaves and tall stalks with orange flowers; forms dense patches along woodland edges and roadsides and is also commonly cultivated.

PURPLE LOOSESTRIFE
Lythrum salicaria
Loosestrife Family (Lythraceae)

Beautiful spikes of purple flowers seem pleasant but soon choke out native plants and destroy habitat; an aggressive and destructive wetland weed.

HELLEBORINE ORCHID
Epipactis helleborine
Orchid Family (Orchidaceae)

Greenish purple flowers and large alternate leaves; a locally common and spreading introduced orchid in woodlands from Wisconsin eastward to New Brunswick.

MONEYWORT
Lysimachia nummularia
Primrose Family (Primulaceae)

Creeping stems grow flat on the ground with round opposite leaves and 5-petaled yellow flowers; found in moist shaded woods and along shaded, muddy, stream banks.

TALL BUTTERCUP
Ranunculus acris
Buttercup Family (Ranunculaceae)

Alternate, lobed, shiny leaves and bright yellow, 5-petaled flowers; common throughout the region except in deep shade and wetlands; now the most common buttercup in the North Woods.

WHITE BEDSTRAW
Galium mollugo
Bedstraw Family (Rubiaceae)

Smooth plant with narrow leaves in whorls of 6 and dense clusters of tiny, white, 4-lobed corollas; common in fields, grassy areas, and along roadsides. See also Rough Bedstraw (p. 220).

COMMON SPEEDWELL
Veronica officinalis
Snapdragon Family (Scrophulariaceae)

Low creeping plant with opposite leaves and tiny, pale bluish, 4-petaled flowers; common in disturbed open woods and grazed shaded areas.

BITTERSWEET NIGHTSHADE
Solanum dulcamara
Nightshade Family (Solanaceae)

Coarse, poisonous, semiwoody vine with bad-smelling foliage, purple flowers with yellow centers, and clusters of bright red berries; common in weedy thickets, waste areas, and degraded fens.

GLOSSARY

acidic. Nutrient-poor conditions with low pH, characterized by sour or sterile soils.

alkaline. Mineral-rich conditions with high pH, characterized by sweet or rich soils.

alternate. Placed singly along a stem or axis, one after another, usually each successive item on a different side from the previous; often used in reference to the arrangement of leaves on a stem (see **opposite**).

angular. Having angles or sharp corners; generally used in reference to stems, as contrasted with round stems.

annual. A plant completing its life cycle, from seed germination to production of new seeds, within a year and then dying.

basal. At the base or bottom of; basal leaves often appear to be independent from the main stems of a plant.

biennial. A plant that completes its life cycle in two years, and normally not producing flowers during the first year.

bog. Poorly drained permanent wetland fed by surface runoff, typically with acidic, nutrient-poor conditions.

bract. A reduced or modified leaf, often associated with flowers.

bristle. A stiff hair, usually erect or curving away from its attachment point.

bulb. An underground plant part derived from a short, usually rounded shoot that is covered with scales or leaves.

bulblet. A small bulblike structure typically nestled at the junction of a leaf base and the stem, and capable of producing a new plant.

capsule. A dry fruit that releases seeds through splits or holes.

calyx. The outer set of flower parts, composed of the sepals, which may be separate or joined together; usually green.

clasping. Surrounding or partially wrapping around a stem or branch.

cluster. In this book, any grouping or close arrangement of individual flowers that is not dense and continuous.

compound leaf. A leaf that is divided into two or more leaflets, each of which may look like a complete leaf but which lacks buds. Compound leaves may have the leaflets arranged along an axis like the rays of a feather, or radiating from a common point, like fingers on a hand.

conifer. A nonflowering tree or shrub that produces seed-bearing cones and typically narrow, flattened or needlelike leaves that are usually evergreen; examples include pines, spruces, and junipers.

corolla. The set of flower parts interior to the calyx and surrounding the stamens, composed of the petals, which may be free or united into a single part; often brightly colored.

deciduous. Falling off, usually in the same year produced, such as the leaves of most broad-leaved trees and shrubs.

disk flower. A small tubular flower in the central portion of the flower head of many plants in the Aster Family (Asteraceae).

disturbed. As used here, referring to habitats that have been impacted by actions or processes not associated with the pre-European settlement environment, such as ditching, grading, or large-scale clearing.

erect. Upright, standing vertically or directly perpendicular from a surface.

escape. As used here, referring to a plant that has been cultivated in an area and has spread from there into the wild.

evergreen. Having green foliage persisting through the winter.

family. A group of plants having biologically similar features, such as flower anatomy, fruit type, etc.

fen. A wetland permanently supplied with groundwater flowage, often resulting in highly mineralized conditions.

fertile. In flowers, referring to ability to produce seeds and/or pollen; in habitats, referring to sites with a rich supply of nutrients and minerals.

floodplain. An area, usually flat, that borders a stream or river and has formed through water-based processes and that is typically influenced by periodic flooding.

flower head. As used in this guide, a dense and continuous group of flowers, without obvious branches or space between them; used especially in reference to the Aster Family (Asteraceae).

genus. A group of closely related species, such as the genus *Viola*, encompassing the violets. The genus forms the first part of a scientific name (see **specific epithet**).

gland. A bump, projection, or rounded protuberance, usually colored differently than the object on which it occurs, and often sticky or producing sticky or oily secretions.

hardwood. A broad-leaved tree that produces flowers, such as an oak or maple; in the North Woods region, all hardwoods are deciduous.

hooded. Arching over and partially concealing or shielding.

host. As used here, the plant from which a parasitic plant derives nourishment.

introduced. Refers to plants that were not a component of the pre-European settlement landscape, but that have been accidentally or deliberately brought to the region and subsequently become established as weeds.

keel. A sharp lengthwise fold or ridge, referring particularly to the two fused petals forming the lower lip in many flowers of the Bean Family (Fabaceae).

leaflet. A distinct, leaflike segment of a compound leaf.

lobe. A segment of an incompletely divided plant part, typically rounded; often used in reference to leaves.

marl. Calcium-rich, clayey soil usually formed in mineral-rich wetlands.

native. Refers to plants that were present as a component of some aspect of the pre-European settlement landscape.

node. The point on a stem where leaves or branches arise; often distinguished by a swelling.

opposite. Paired directly across from one another along a stem or axis (see **alternate**).

ovary. The portion of the flower where the seeds develop, usually a swollen area below the style (if present) and stigma.

parallel. Side by side approximately the same distance apart for the entire length; often used in reference to veins or edges of leaves.

parasitic. Growing on or attached to and deriving nutrients from another plant.

peat. Soil composed of partially decomposed plants, often associated with acidic or oxygen-poor wetlands.

perennial. A plant that normally lives for 3 or more years.

petal. An individual segment of the corolla, often brightly colored and the most visible part of the flower.

pistil. The seed-producing, or female, unit of a flower, consisting of the ovary, style (if present), and stigma; a flower may have one to several separate pistils.

pod. A dry fruit that splits open along the edges.

pollen. Tiny, often powdery male reproductive cells formed in the stamens and typically necessary for seed production.

prickle. A small, sharp, spinelike outgrowth from the outer surface.

ray flower. A type of flower in the Aster Family (Asteraceae) with a single strap-shaped corolla that resembles one flower petal; ray flowers may surround the disk flowers in a flower head, or in some species such as Dandelions, the flower heads may be composed entirely of ray flowers.

runner. A creeping stem that roots at the tip and/or nodes.

sap. The juice within a plant.

seep. Referring to an area with small volumes of subsurface water supply.

sepal. An individual segment of the calyx; typically green but sometimes enlarged and brightly colored.

simple leaf. A leaf that has a single leaflike blade, although this may be lobed or divided.

spadix. A dense cluster of small flowers on a thickened, fleshy axis.

specific epithet. The second word of a plant's scientific name, identifying the particular species (see **genus**).

spike. An elongate, unbranched cluster of stalkless or nearly stalkless flowers.

spine. A thin, stiff, sharp-pointed projection.

spreading. Extending outward from; at right angles to; widely radiating.

stalk. As used here, the stem supporting the leaf, flower, or flower cluster.

stalkless. Lacking a stalk; a stalkless leaf is at-tached directly to the stem at the leaf base.

stamen. The male unit of a flower, which produces the pollen; typically consisting of a long filament with a pollen-producing tip.

staminodia. Modified stamens that produce no pollen and sometimes appear petal-like.

sterile. In flowers, refers to the inability to produce seeds and/or pollen; in habitats, refers to poor nutrient and mineral availability in the soil.

stigma. The portion of the pistil receptive to pollination; usually at the top of the style, and often appearing fuzzy or sticky.

stipule. A bract or leafy structure occurring in pairs at the base of the leaf stalk.

style. The portion of the pistil between the ovary and the stigma; typically a slender stalk.

succulent. Thickened and fleshy or juicy.

swamp. A wooded wetland with abundant standing water for all or much of the growing season.

talus. A sloping mass of rock fragments, typically fractured over time from an overtopping cliff or escarpment.

tendril. A slender, coiled or twisted filament with which climbing plants attach to their support.

toothed. Bearing teeth, or sharply angled projections, along the edge.

tuber. A thick, creeping, underground stem; sometimes also used to denote thickened portions of roots, which are sometimes described as tuberous.

tubercle. A small rounded bump or swelling.

tubular. Narrow, cylindrical, and tubelike.

underside. The side of a leaf or other part that normally faces the ground or away from the upper stem.

upper surface. The side of a leaf or other plant

part that normally faces away from the ground, or toward the upper stem.

variety. A group of plants within a species that has a distinct range, habitat, or structural characteristics.

vein. In plants, referring to a bundle of small tubes that carries water, minerals, and nutrients.

vine. A trailing or climbing, long-stemmed plant incapable of supporting itself, frequently twining or with tendrils.

weed. A disturbance-adapted plant capable of colonizing new ground; most weeds in the North Woods region are introduced species.

whorled. Having three or more parts attached at the same point along a stem or axis; often surrounding the stem.

winged. Having thin bands of leaflike tissue attached lengthwise along the edges of a stem, leaf stalk, or other plant part.

# FURTHER READING

Listed below are additional readings that provide information about the North Woods and its natural heritage. A visit to a local or university library will reveal additional works about plants in your state or province.

Couplon, Francois. *The Encyclopaedia of Edible Plants of North America.* New Canaan, Conn.: Keats Publishing, 1998. [Discussion of food uses for most edible species in the North Woods region.]

Daniel, Glenda, and Jerry Sullivan. *The North Woods of Michigan, Wisconsin, Minnesota, and Southern Ontario.* San Francisco: Sierra Club, 1981. [General natural history of the western half of the North Woods region.]

Foster, Steven, and James Duke. *A Field Guide to Medicinal Plants.* Boston: Houghton Mifflin Co., 1990. [Detailed account of historical and modern medicinal uses of eastern North American plants, including many North Woods species.]

Gleason, Henry, and Arthur Cronquist. *Manual of Vascular Plants of the Northeastern United States and Adjacent Canada.* Bronx: New York Botanical Garden, 1991. [Technical manual with complete coverage of the flowering plants, conifers, ferns, and fern relatives of the North Woods; forms the basis for most of the scientific names used in this guide.]

Marchand, Peter. *North Woods: An Inside Look at the Nature of Forests in the Northeast.* Boston: Appalachian Mountain Club, 1987. [Insightful, readable discussion of North Woods systems; focused on New England, but of interest throughout the region.]

Moerman, Daniel. *North American Indian Ethnobotany.* Portland, Ore.: Timber Press, 1998. [Exhaustive cross-referenced catalog of North American Indian uses for plants.]

Pielou, E. *After the Ice Age: The Return of Life to Glaciated North America.* Chicago: University of Chicago Press, 1991. [Excellent in-depth, popular-level summary of how glacial patterns and plant and animal characteristics shaped modern North America, including the North Woods region.]

Roland, Albert, and Marian Zinck. *Roland's Flora of Nova Scotia.* Halifax: Nimbus Publishing, 1998. [Technical treatment of the Nova Scotia flora, with good habitat and distribution information; useful for much of the northeastern part of the North Woods.]

Slack, Nancy, and Allison Bell. *Field Guide to New England Alpine Summits.* Boston: Appalachian Mountain Club, 1995. [Includes alpine plants and animals not included in this guide.]

Smith, Welby. *Orchids of Minnesota.* Minneapolis: University of Minnesota Press, 1993. [Excellent, detailed accounts of almost all of the orchids of the North Woods region.]

Sutton, Ann and Myron. *National Audubon Society Nature Guide to Eastern Forests.* New York: Alfred Knopf, 1997. [General guide to eastern woodlands and some of their plants and animals; good discussion of woodland types.]

Voss, Edward. *Flora of Michigan* (3 volumes). Bloomfield Hills, Mich.: Cranbrook Institute of Science, 1972, 1985, 1996. [The most detailed, usable, and insightful scientific treatment of the flora of a state or province in the North Woods; valuable throughout the region.]

*J*NDEX

ABOUT THE AUTHOR

Doug Ladd has been interested in the flora of the North Woods since his early childhood in Barre, Vermont, when his mother taught him to identify the common local wildflowers. After majoring in botany and chemistry in college, he conducted his master's research under Robert Mohlenbrock on the flora of Washington County, Vermont. Since that time, he has conducted botanical fieldwork in every state and province in the North Woods region, to which he continues to make annual summer pilgrimages.

For the past 20 years he has been involved with natural areas research and management in the Midwest. He has spent the last 15 years with The Nature Conservancy, where he is currently director of conservation science for the Missouri Field Office. In addition to numerous scientific articles and reports, he is the author of the Falcon field guide *Tallgrass Prairie Wildflowers* and the coauthor of *Distribution of Illinois Vascular Plants* and *Discover Natural Missouri*. He lives in Webster Groves, Missouri, with his wife, Deborah, and his 15-year-old daughter, Melica.

FALCONGUIDES ® Leading the Way™

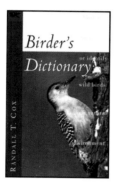
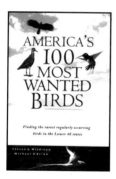

FALCON GUIDES ® Leading the Way™

www.Falcon.com

Since 1979, Falcon® has brought you the best in outdoor recreational guidebooks. Now you can access that same reliable and accurate information online.

❏ <u>Browse our online catalog</u> for the latest Falcon releases on hiking, climbing, biking, scenic driving, and wildlife viewing as well as our Insiders' travel and relocation guides. Our online catalog is updated weekly.

❏ A <u>Tip of the Week</u> from one of our guidebooks or how-to guides. Each Monday we post a new tip that covers anything from how to cross a rushing stream to reading contour lines on a topo map.

❏ A chance to <u>Meet our Staff</u> with photos and short biographies of Falcon staff.

❏ <u>Outdoor forums</u> where you can exchange ideas and tips with other outdoor enthusiasts.

❏ Also <u>Falcon screensavers and panoramic photos</u> of spectacular destinations.

And much more!

Plan your next outdoor adventure at our web site. Point your browser to www.Falcon.com and get FalconGuided!

FALCON®

FALCON GUIDES ®Leading the Way™

FALCON GUIDES ® are available for where-to-go hiking, mountain biking, rock climbing, walking, scenic driving, fishing, rockhounding, paddling, birding, wildlife viewing, and camping. We also have FalconGuides® on essential outdoor skills and subjects and field identification. The following titles are currently available, but this list grows every year. For a free catalog with a complete list of titles, call FALCON® toll-free at 1-800-582-2665.

SCENIC DRIVING GUIDES

Scenic Driving Alaska and the Yukon
Scenic Driving Arizona
Scenic Driving the Beartooth Highway
Scenic Driving California
Scenic Driving Colorado
Scenic Driving Florida
Scenic Driving Georgia
Scenic Driving Hawaii
Scenic Driving Idaho
Scenic Driving Indiana
Scenic Driving Kentucky
Scenic Driving Michigan
Scenic Driving Minnesota
Scenic Driving Montana
Scenic Driving New England
Scenic Driving New Mexico
Scenic Driving North Carolina
Scenic Driving Oregon
Scenic Driving the Ozarks
Scenic Driving Pennsylvania
Scenic Driving Texas
Scenic Driving Utah
Scenic Driving Virginia
Scenic Driving Washington
Scenic Driving Wisconsin
Scenic Driving Wyoming*
Scenic Driving Yellowstone and
    the Grand Teton National Parks
Scenic Byways East & South
Scenic Byways Far West
Scenic Byways Rocky Mountains
Back Country Byways

HISTORIC TRAIL GUIDES

Traveling California's Gold Rush Country
Traveling the Lewis & Clark Trail
Traveling the Oregon Trail
Traveler's Guide to the Pony Express Trail

WILDLIFE VIEWING GUIDES

Alaska Wildlife Viewing Guide
Arizona Wildlife Viewing Guide
California Wildlife Viewing Guide
Colorado Wildlife Viewing Guide
Florida Wildlife Viewing Guide
Indiana Wildlife Vewing Guide
Iowa Wildlife Viewing Guide
Kentucky Wildlife Viewing Guide
Massachusetts Wildlife Viewing Guide
Montana Wildlife Viewing Guide
Nebraska Wildlife Viewing Guide
Nevada Wildlife Viewing Guide
New Hampshire Wildlife Viewing Guide
New Jersey Wildlife Viewing Guide
New Mexico Wildlife Viewing Guide
New York Wildlife Viewing Guide
North Carolina Wildlife Viewing Guide
North Dakota Wildlife Viewing Guide
Ohio Wildlife Viewing Guide
Oregon Wildlife Viewing Guide
Puerto Rico & the Virgin Islands
    Wildlife Viewing Guide
Tennessee Wildlife Viewing Guide
Texas Wildlife Viewing Guide
Utah Wildlife Viewing Guide
Vermont Wildlife Viewing Guide
Virginia Wildlife Viewing Guide
Washington Wildlife Viewing Guide
West Virginia Wildlife Viewing Guide
Wisconsin Wildlife Viewing Guide

 *To order any of these books, check with your local bookseller or call FALCON ® at **1-800-582-2665**.
Visit us on the world wide web at:*
www.falcon.com